Splintered Accountability

SUNY series in Public Policy

Anne L. Schneider and Helen M. Ingram, editors

Splintered Accountability

State Governance and Education Reform

ARNOLD F. SHOBER

Published by State University of New York Press, Albany

© 2010 State University of New York

For information, contact State University of New York Press, Albany, NY
www.sunypress.edu

Production by Diane Ganeles
Marketing by Michael Campochiaro

Library of Congress Cataloging-in-Publication Data

Shober, Arnold F., 1976–
    Splintered accountability : state governance and education reform / Arnold F. Shober.
        p. cm. — (Suny series in public policy)
    Includes bibliographical references and index.
    ISBN 978-1-4384-3075-1 (hardcover : alk. paper)
    1. State departments of education—United States—States. 2. Educational accountability—United States—States. 3. Education—Standards—United States—States. 4. School improvement programs—United States—States. I. Title.

    LB2809.A2S43 2010
    379.1'520973—dc22   2009024753

10 9 8 7 6 5 4 3 2 1

For Clara

Contents

PART 1

PART 2

PART 3

Tables

Figures

Acknowledgments

This book could not have been completed without the indulgence of the politicians, bureaucrats, and opinion leaders who all loved kids. Many still work in education and, by their request, they shall remain nameless. They could, of course, never agree on *how* to help children, but their contribution to this project was invaluable.

The librarians and archivists in Ohio, Georgia, and Wisconsin were exceedingly helpful in winnowing out the reams of records that previous superintendents and governors left in their care. The state archivists in Georgia deserve special mention for their insightful conversations with me on that state's educational history.

David Canon, John Coleman, Meghan Condon, Matthew Dull, Mark Frazier, Bill Hixon, Paul Manna, Julie Mead, David Parker and David Weimer helped push me on in this adventure, both by offering encouragement at the start and scholarly support at various stages of its composition. The predoctoral Interdisciplinary Training Program at the University of Wisconsin, funded by the U.S. Department of Education's Institute for Education Sciences, provided time and finances for a portion of the research. Lawrence University provided resources to finish it.

John Witte deserves more credit for pushing me through this project than I can express here. His optimism was limitless. His encouragement was persistent but always practical. I only wish that I could somehow absorb even half of his energy and creativity.

Abbreviations

AFT	American Federation of Teachers
APA	(Georgia) Administrative Procedures Act
CAT	California Achievement Test
CCSSO	Council of Chief State School Officers
CESA	(Wisconsin) Cooperative Educational Service Agency
DOA	(Wisconsin) Department of Administration
DPI	(Wisconsin) Department of Public Instruction
ESEA	Elementary and Secondary Education Act
GADOE	Georgia Department of Education
GEM	(Ohio) Governor's Education Management Council
GKAP	Georgia Kindergarten Assessment Program
NAEYC	National Association for the Education of Young Children
NASDTEC	National Association of State Directors of Teacher Education and Certification
NCLB	No Child Left Behind Act
NEA	National Education Association
NGA	National Governors' Association
OBE	Outcomes-Based Education
ODE	Ohio Department of Education
OEA	(Georgia) Office of Educational Accountability
OFT	Ohio Federation of Teachers

Abbreviations

QBE	(Georgia) Quality Basic Education
QEO	(Wisconsin) Qualified Economic Offer
WASB	Wisconsin Association of School Boards
WEAC	Wisconsin Education Association Council

Part 1

1

Introduction

The most important duty of the state should not be overseen by an unwieldy department with splintered accountability.

—Ohio Governor Ted Strickland,
State of the State, February 6, 2008

"You can't do anything! The governor thinks he's God," bluntly stated Mike Ellis, the Wisconsin senate majority leader. State Superintendent John Benson was on his knees pleading to stay budget cuts that would nearly eliminate the Department of Public Instruction (DPI)—or so remembers one veteran Wisconsin lobbyist. Benson was unsuccessful, but within a year, the Supreme Court had rebuked the governor and restored the DPI.

"We had it just about right. It's amazing in how many ways we anticipated No Child Left Behind. At the beginning, we had everyone behind us, the governor, everyone," said one employee of Georgia's Department of Education (GADOE). Even though the state's Quality Basic Education program quickly lost the support of key interest groups and "just about killed everyone," GADOE maintained the program through sometimes vicious political opposition.[1]

"They have a bunker mentality over there," said a lobbyist for the Ohio Department of Education (ODE). "They're too tight with the governor." But even if ODE allegedly had its head in the sand, it was able to implement a regimented student assessment system and fend off the state supreme court's challenge to the school finance system.

In each of these cases, the state's department of education was able to prevail in setting the direction of state education policy. Yet at other times, departments failed miserably, and ambitious governors and legislators reined in their scope, as if they were afraid of competition. This book explores why.

From the outside, American education governance is a quagmire. Responsibilities for setting standards, distributing funding, and hiring personnel overlap in a crazy-quilt of jurisdictions. School districts raise money; interest groups crowd the hallways of legislatures; and teachers' unions stuff the mailboxes of members. In the middle of this confused environment lies a state agency—sometimes sleepy and sometimes volcanic—charged with the oversight of state schools. In the fifty states, its name varies from an "Office of the Superintendent" to the "Department of Public Instruction." It employs from dozens to thousands. American education agencies provide fertile ground to understand the bureaucratic policy process.

State education agencies are caught in the American federal system between penurious school districts and an increasingly demanding federal government. Their policy areas may be as restricted as discharging federal monies or as expansive as drafting budgets for financially delinquent school districts. Administrators with seemingly less capable agencies lamented too-great local control: "You could replace 'America's Dairyland' with the 'Home of Local Control' " said one state education official in Wisconsin, referring to the state's license-plate motto. The Iowa department's mission is to *strengthen* local control. In other states, department personnel could make no such complaint. State departments in Georgia and Texas, for example, control or heavily influence textbook selection and distribution, materials at the very heart of day-to-day teaching and learning.

Yet over the last twenty years, the federal government has repeatedly signified its willingness to enter the fray. Although presidents as early as Dwight D. Eisenhower sought to increase federal involvement in public education, and Lyndon B. Johnson and others tried to ensure equal access to education for various disadvantaged groups, the 1983 report *Nation at Risk* heralded the entry of Washington into the grit of daily education politics. Secretary of Education William Bennett could only use the U.S. Department of Education as a bully pulpit (including his famous "Wall Chart" of educational statistics), but talk of national standards was not far behind. In 1990, George H. W. Bush convened an education summit to discuss standards, and many governors who attended appeared energized by the meeting. Although hints of these standards appeared in the 1994 reauthorization of the 1965 Elementary and Secondary Education Act (ESEA), nothing with "teeth" troubled state departments of education. The 2001 reauthorization of ESEA, called the No Child Left Behind Act (NCLB), removed all doubt that the federal government intended to be involved at the classroom level. The act declared not only that all students had to be tested annually for a range of grades, but that all students had to become proficient; that teachers have to be "highly qualified," and that some form of school choice must be offered when schools do not meet the law's standards. The law permits states to decide what "proficient" means and allows states to design or purchase their own tests. NCLB announced that the federal government was watching the front line of instruction, even if from afar.

Policy conundrums make education policy a minefield. State departments of education are uniquely suited to sort these out. The difficulties surrounding these policies attract—and deserve—serious study, but these puzzles are temporary, shaped by the current political and sociodemographic climate. Over time, the forms of public education and the demands the public places on it will change, but the federal structure of American education remains. This structure, combined with the murky policy waters, makes state education agencies (SEAs) ideal subjects to study bureaucratic policy making. Instead of seeking to unravel the difficulties of student assessment, teacher licensure, and school finance—subjects highlighted in this book—I hope to improve understanding of the process by which an education agency can use its unique powers to address policy problems fruitfully.

Specifically, this book asks two theoretical questions: When can government agencies shape and change the policy preferences of their overseers? When do legislators and governors step aside for an agency chief to pursue her or his own policy vision for state education? Said another way, when can agencies act autonomously by demanding accountability of others while limiting outsiders' access to their own decision-making process?

The answers are important, for three concrete reasons. First, they are pertinent to any policy area with many "street-level bureaucrats" such as education (Lipsky 1980). In these fields, street-level bureaucrats, such as police officers, teachers, or social workers, have ample opportunity to skew the implementation of programs that their agency administers. Much ink has been spilled on the difficulties of "going to scale" with education reform, and teachers have substantial control of education as soon as the starting bell rings (Hoff 2002; Elmore 1996; Smith and O'Day 1991).

Reforms are often difficult to maintain because they overlap or because a new "reform" comes along before the previous one is implemented. An agency that can effectively change the preferences of governors and legislators may well be able to sustain reforms longer—perhaps long enough to reduce local push-back—than an agency that follows the political winds.[2]

Second, the answers will help illuminate the multilevel relationship between the federal government and state agencies. For many "federal" programs, state agencies do the lion's share of the administration. If an agency is able to resist the advances of governors and legislators (thus resisting micro-accountability for its decisions), then it should be able to implement federal mandates more easily—if the agency buys into the federal program. One scholar has suggested that federal requirements allow state bureaucracies to resist new legislation and oversight from *state* legislatures and governors (Hills 1999). The federal government frequently expects that state agencies have the appropriate freedom of action to be able to adapt the federal program (or, more likely, to reshape a state program) to the local context.[3] Scholars have asked how the federal government can be effective in policy areas where the states have had long dominance, and one answer is that the federal government "borrows strength" from state agencies, to use Manna's (2006) phrase. Yet for a number of reasons, including political jealousy, compliance-centric state policy, and a rapid expansion of demands, state agencies have been playing catch-up with federal expectations in this area (Manna 2006, chapter 5). An autonomous agency should have less spread between its actual capabilities and expectations. That is, an autonomous agency should be a more effective federal partner.

Beyond their role as administrators, states have a special position in federal politics that makes them a valuable site for the study of American public policy and bureaucracy generally. Not only do they share substantial governing characteristics with the federal government, but they have unique informational and political advantages over both school districts and the federal government. Further, federalism endows state-level bureaucracies (as opposed to state government generally) with leverage over local governments and perhaps over state legislatures as well. These will be detailed in turn.

State governments share two major characteristics with the federal government. First, both levels of government enjoy a system of separated powers. Like the federal government, each state has competing branches filled with governors and legislators with different term lengths. That is, there are no parliamentary systems. In this arrangement, state agencies have to compete with other state agencies for money and personnel through an open budget process, just as federal agencies must. Second, state governments can expect push-back from semi-independent lower governments. In education, this includes schools and their employees who are the knowledgeable street-level bureaucrats that can make or break policy implementation (Lipsky 1980). Many state departments of education have to work with school districts that have independent revenue authority through the property tax, allowing districts to set absolute financial parameters on state mandates (Wong 1999). Further, some schools also may have independent authority, as with site-based management (McDermott 1999) or charter schools (Nathan 1996; Mintrom 2000; Shober, Manna and Witte 2006).

Yet officials in state governments have a distinct difference from their federal counterparts: they have peers who share information. Should an assistant state superintendent in Wisconsin wonder how to respond to a provision of NCLB, she or he can call up her or his counterpart in Minnesota or Pennsylvania. This not only gives state workers a "national" perspective on federal requirements but also provides them with evidence of other states' practices for responding to federal queries. (This situation is close to Axelrod's (1984) "prisoner's dilemma," where both parties cooperate to receive the greatest global benefit.)

State government agencies also have the political advantage of national extra-governmental representation through the Council of Chief State School Officers (CCSSO), the Education Leaders Council, the National Governors' Association (NGA), the National Association of State Budget Officers, and others. In education, the NGA's influence on the 1994 reauthorization of ESEA is well known (Vinovskis 1999). In the 1990s, Georgia state superintendent Linda Schrenko, among others, felt that the CCSSO was sufficiently influential (but wrongheaded) and thus dropped her membership in that organization and joined the Education Leaders Council instead (Jacobson 1999).

A third difference that state bureaucracies may use to their advantage is that they have federal oversight agencies. They have a "boss." Federalism may enable state bureaucracies to use federal legislation to trump local and even state legislative concerns (see Hills 1999). The logic is that a state legislature may balk at, say, annual assessment of students' academic progress, even though the state education agency has been advocating such a move. The state agency has plans for the program that it cannot implement. If the federal government then enacts a law to encourage or require such testing, then the state agency can move quickly to enact its program, despite the objections.

In this light, the arrival of No Child Left Behind serves as the ultimate test of state agency autonomy. Many state legislatures and state bureaucracies saw the law as an untoward intrusion of federal activity into state policy making. A number of districts as well as Utah and Vermont threatened a court battle; Connecticut did so (Connecticut Attorney General 2005; Keller 2005). This book studies the twenty years before the act. If education agencies are able to do what the act expects them to do—that is, designing and adopting state standards, promoting teaching reform, rating schools and districts, and otherwise enforcing test-based accountability—then state departments should have made strides toward these *independently* and *prior* to the act. State departments should have a record of autonomy and scope, and it should appear in this time frame.[4] The fruits of the departments' past autonomy will become apparent as the debate reopens at the act's reauthorization in Congress.

The third reason this book's answers are important is that state agencies do, in practice, shape many of the functions of government. ODE successfully implemented grade-by-grade exams in the 1990s, despite considerable uproar throughout the decade. GADOE had similar test success on a smaller scale in the late 1980s, and in the 1990s it issued test contracts without legislative or even state board approval. Other states, such as Colorado or Iowa, have education departments with small budgets and appear to be less successful at shaping their scope. These departments have to corral a large number of interests to keep limited budgets. Indeed, the introduction to the Colorado Department of Education's fiscal year 2000 budget lists fourteen interest groups consulted in drafting the department's budget to demonstrate the broad support it had. Such state departments are not likely to be able partners in implementing state programs, new federal regulations, or in creating new state policy—whether standards-based reform, teacher licensure, or school finance. It is much more likely that the legislature, governor, or even school districts themselves will take the lead.[5]

What are the benefits of autonomy for an agency? An autonomous agency should be able to make politically difficult decisions that could be stalled indefinitely in the legislature. Because high-level state employees are subject to scrutiny by legislators, the press, and the governor, decisions that agency leaders make are likely to be carefully considered. If the agency steps too far or too quickly from the preferences of the governor or legislators (as discussed in chapter 6), then it will be at risk of official sanction. Therefore, agencies are able to circumvent some veto points that typically block legislation but only after careful groundwork. Similarly, a policy that may be supported by a legislative majority might be blocked by interest group opposition; an autonomous agency may be able to break the logjam (as discussed in chapter 5). (Chapter 10 will consider the risks and benefits of such freedom.)

Agency autonomy bolsters the general public's ability to connect an effect of public policy with a cause. Agency activity provides a much better sense of government activity than do legislators' voting records, despite the fact that the public can only directly influence officials standing for election, and not bureaucrats. Legislators tend to be keen on avoiding traceability (Arnold 1990; Pierson 1994). On the other hand, government agencies have no way to avoid the glare: if the Department of Education sends a memorandum that all kindergarteners must take an "exit exam" from kindergarten, then there is no secret as to who sent the memo. The Department of Education is to blame or praise. Thus watching agency activity gives voters a direct window on state government that is unavailable through the normal legislative process.

The following section presents a brief overview of my theoretical argument. Then I offer a historical sketch of the general development of state oversight of education. Next I explain how Ohio, Georgia, and Wisconsin offer relevant examples of different modes of state control. Finally, I outline the rest of the book.

A Brief Theoretical Overview

In the previous discussion, I used the words "autonomy" and "scope." Both are central to my argument. "Autonomy" is the exercise of independent choice by an agency, regardless of the initial preferences of the governor or legislature. "Scope" is an agency's set of tasks formally specified by law and accompanied by a budget sufficient to do them. Scope is derived from the mutual preferences of the legislature and the governor. A highly autonomous agency will be able to move the preferences of the governor and legislators toward its own preferred policy and thereby gain broader scope to fulfill that policy preference without having to act autonomously in the future.

I propose that an agency's success at building autonomy and scope is drawn from three sets of factors: institutional, active, and passive. The first, *institutional*, is essentially constitutional structure. All three of the state cases have educational administration outlined broadly in their constitutions. Although constitutions are not static (for example, Ohio's clauses changed several times between 1900 and 1954, see chapter 4), the changes are rare relative to legislative changes. Thus constitutional effects occur largely in the background—but governors and others have been frustrated often by the intentionally splintered accountability found in state constitutions.

A second set of factors, *active* or endogenous factors, includes leadership and the pursuit of interest group support and allows an agency to actively expand its autonomy and scope. An agency leader may engage in any number of techniques to encourage his or her agency to pursue a program autonomously or to implore the public, governors, and legislators that his or her agency needs broader scope. High-profile, public leaders may bring short-term public pressure on other branches of government. In the long term, however, those same governors and legislators remember the highly visible conflicts that these agency leaders sometimes prompt and are likely to try to restrict the autonomy of the agency. Leaders may also use behind-the-scenes, insider approaches to build support, one legislator at a time; or, they may use political leadership, making political appeals to legislators and the governor. (For example, two of the state superintendents I interviewed were frequent visitors to the governor's office; they made good use of that image to garner support for their agency.) Both of these will be more successful in the long term because they are generally cooperative approaches.

Agency personnel may also manipulate interest groups to their own benefit, another active factor. Agencies can support their position by sending out trial balloons to interest groups. This can alert an agency to policies that will generate opposition. Although the department may still push ahead, it will be prepared to handle complaints. For example, Georgia's landmark reform, Quality Basic Education (QBE), had significant backing from every major interest group at its implementation, but as some of its more stringent accountability standards came on line, strong resistance coalesced in the field. GADOE fended off criticism by saying that its QBE team had worked with all of the groups and had their support. Second, membership interest groups may serve to help ease policy implementation. In Wisconsin, the DPI has used the state teachers' union to hold seminars to prepare teachers for the state testing regimen (and later, Wisconsin's implementation of the No Child Left Behind Act). The value of interest groups will vary based on the dominance of those groups: if the teachers' unions are the big player, then agencies would do well to include them in their implementation plans. But if there are multiple, competing groups, then an agency may find that using a single-interest group for implementation hampers its activities in other areas. Finally, if an agency actively consults interest groups, then it may be able to avert legislative suspicion about its activities. Congress uses interest groups to alert them of agencies gone amiss; state legislatures have fewer resources for oversight and are therefore likely to do the same (Balla and Wright 2001). (The increasing frequency of "fire alarms" over time from interest groups may actually weaken this function; if so, then agencies are doubly insulated against legislative encroachments on their scope or autonomy; see Gray and Lowery 2004; Lowery and Gray 1995; McCubbins and Schwartz 1984).

The final group contains *passive*, or exogenous, factors. I expect that electoral changes, legislative salience, and legal actions in the courts will impact autonomy and scope. None of these can be controlled by an agency; indeed, they may cause shifts in government that no one expects. Electoral changes may bring new legislators to state assemblies with whom agencies must learn to work; old friends may lose office. Nevertheless, frequent turnover is in an agency's interest for building autonomy and scope, because legislators will not have the time to develop expertise to counter an agency's natural informational advantage.

Legislative salience is not necessarily related to turnover. What I mean by this term is simply how attentive legislators are to some policy area. In Ohio, state agency officials lamented to me that they had lost some longtime friends in the early 1990s. Voters selected several new legislators with strong opinions about education in the mid-1990s, though they had opinions distinctly different than what some top ODE administrators preferred. Salience can be imperfectly measured by the number of education-related bills and the relative desirability that legislators place on education committees.

Last I consider court rulings. Legal challenges may shift an agency's environment significantly in or away from its favor. In education, legal challenges often dispute a state agency's abuse of autonomy or shirking of some scope. Yet frequently even the plaintiff must rely on data provided by the state agency, particularly in cases about school finance. Thus although legal challenges may appear to constrict agencies, they may simply reconfigure their distribution of autonomy and scope. It is difficult to theorize further the effect of legal challenges, because court rulings are multifaceted, and state courts themselves often have few resources to understand technical problems. They, too, must rely on agency information. This was aptly demonstrated by a long school finance case in Ohio where the state's supreme court ruled based on a faulty cost estimate provided by the plaintiff (see chapter 5). When the court ruled, apparently inadvertently, that the state had to spend $1.2 billion more on schools than it currently did—a budgetary impossibility—the court was forced to recant and effectively surrender the case specifics to ODE's school finance staff.

These factors work in a circular fashion: an autonomous agency will have greater ability to widen scope, and an agency with greater scope will find it easier to argue that it needs more freedom of action to coordinate that scope effectively. The aforementioned factors only mediate between the two.

This presents some problems needing explanation. If these are recursive, then how can the factors I just identified be causal? Büthe (2002) argues that this problem is particularly acute in historical studies (such as this one) where new ideas and social constructs can change over time in ways that are interrelated but possibly unrelated to the question at hand. For example, in my cases, the rapid increase in the availability of fast and cheap computer technology weakened the information monopoly that state education departments once had. Easy computer access also changed ideas about student assessment as it became easier to analyze and report scores. This change (and others, such as partisan alignments) was unrelated to the state education agency per se but reordered the effects of other factors. Legislative salience may have been less important when information was scarce, but when technology reduced that barrier, salience became more important—though neither the agency nor the legislators had otherwise changed.

Büthe acknowledges that allowing explanatory variables to have different effects at different times introduces a problem of endogeneity into the analysis. His solution is to construct work to explicitly analyze the *sequence* of changes. "Time itself thus becomes an element of the causal explanation . . . [and] operates in the background to affect other variables in a variety of ways" (486). As such, in the chapters that follow, I seek to explore the temporal nature of autonomy and scope and note how the same set of factors may not interact in the same way in, say, 1995, as they did in 1980.

The Development of State Oversight

No state education agency operates in a vacuum. Most agencies have had to fight an uphill battle for scope and autonomy against not only legislators and governors but also local school systems. Local control has, after all, been the defining ideology in American education since European colonists first opened schools. In this section, I show how state government became involved in this quintessentially local issue, and I highlight groups whose cooperation and co-optation were necessary in building the general autonomy and scope of state education agencies.

In the colonial era, the New England school was scarcely separate from either home or church.[6] In this environment, there was little need—and little tolerance—of colonial or state oversight of education. Later, Thomas Jefferson unsuccessfully tried to convince Virginia to establish publicly funded schools to make education available to more than the privately tutored plantation class. Even Horace Mann, often credited as the founding father of tax-supported education, met setbacks in Massachusetts' House Committee on Education. The committee found in 1840 that state influence was unnecessary: "District schools in a republican government need no police regulations, no systems of state censorship, no checks of moral, religious, or political conservatism, to preserve either the morals, the religion, or the politics of the state" (Timar 1997, 239).

Only when educational reformers became concerned about the inequities between districts did the state gain a foothold for oversight and control. By the 1830s, the perceived poor quality of teachers, particularly in frontier towns, helped lead to the creation of minimum teacher requirements. Although localities often set the requirements, state government would withhold its share of funding from districts without local certification, particularly in northern states (Beadie 2000, 56). At this time, a number of states created state superintendencies for the purpose of inspecting district practices and withholding state funds, if necessary. In many states, this state agent—the "education department" was usually but one person—frequently made strenuous pleas for increasing state aid to education or for establishing state-controlled teacher colleges. The minuscule breadth of scope assigned to these officers, however, severely limited their autonomy, and state legislatures had little need to take them seriously. Many state education offices were abolished soon after they had been established (including Georgia's and Ohio's).

In the 1850s, state legislatures began requiring local governments to levy taxes for education to correct for disparities. (Previously, state governments had allowed such collection, but the funds were often permanently "borrowed" for other purposes [Beadie 2000, 59].) By 1900, some states even imposed state-wide taxes or maintained state school funds disbursed by state superintendents. By the end of the nineteenth century, legislatures were celebrating a "centennial" of public education (Ohio General Assembly 1876). Thus even at this early stage states were creating a domain inside of which agencies could later pursue autonomy and wider scope.

Although state government succeeded in rooting out opposition to the idea of tax-funded education, by no means were state powers strong. Wisconsin's superintendent of public instruction had only one secretary in the 1890s. Many states' education departments existed to collect data and to deliver an annual report to the legislature. State power relied heavily on local compliance, which was often spotty and weakest in rural areas (where the majority of America still lived). Nevertheless, "the real struggle entailed establishing in law that education was a matter of public, not private, interest. And this was the real victory" (Timar 1997, 240).[7]

In the late nineteenth and early twentieth centuries, state departments of education began to corral interest groups to bolster their autonomy and scope. In Wisconsin, for example, the DPI often hosted the state education association's annual meeting, and the state superintendent was frequently a serious candidate for president of the group. Without fail, state education groups sought increased state powers to ensure more equal benefits for teachers and administrators and to compel increased funding from recalcitrant school boards. The association with elite interest groups reached its zenith in the Progressive era. Teachers' organizations, such as the National Education Association (NEA), were organs of Progressive reform.[8] At this time, agencies gained a new language of autonomy: "Experts" should settle how best to resolve teacher issues, civil rights remedies, and school funding.

State superintendents, using their position as a leader with statewide visibility, pushed for more efficient, technical control, often urging the legislature to grant them power to regulate teacher licensure, force district consolidation, and select textbooks. Some state departments championed the equalization of school funding. State superintendents had advocated for many of these ideas for sixty years, but a combination of the ascendancy of Progressive reformers in the 1910s, a rural depression in the 1920s, and the Great Depression in the 1930s squelched local opponents. School districts could no longer argue convincingly that education was a local prerogative—they could no longer fund educational programs. For example, the state of Michigan provided 20 percent of education funds in 1930 but 45 percent in 1939 (Beadie 2000, 75).[9] State education agencies appeared to win the day's battle with their NEA allies, but their supremacy was to be short-lived.

Portents of federal involvement had appeared on the horizon by the 1950s. If educational equality and excellence could be a state issue, then there was little that could logically prevent it from being a national issue. The math and science scare in the 1950s—prompted by the Soviet atomic experiments and *Sputnik*—led the National Science Foundation and Congress to demand better curriculum. But federal monies were small (about 2 percent of all education funds compared to about 7 percent at present) and did not significantly challenge the organization of state departments. Still, most departments did hire math and science specialists by the end of the 1950s (although five states initially rejected federal money) (Timar 1997, 247).

The first sustained entrance of the federal government into local public education came with the 1965 Elementary and Secondary Education Act, which was meant primarily as a way to alleviate the effects of poverty on education.[10] Despite the limitations on the money provided by the ESEA, the act did include funds to enhance the administrative ability of state education departments in Title V.[11]

The introduction of federal monies also provided the wedge to separate state education departments from the interest groups they had fostered and, some might argue, to which they had become captive. By the 1960s, improving teachers' economic situation had become a primary tenet of unions, displacing equity between districts (Kerchner and

Mitchell 1988, chapter 3). As the political climate and state departments of education further shifted from an equity focus to an "excellence" focus in the '70s and beyond, unions again had to adjust to include more excellence-focused verbiage in their lobbying repertoire in order to maintain clout with governors, legislators, and state departments of education (for example, see Beilke 2001, 89). Interest groups again became a tool of state education agencies.

As had been the case when states sought to wrest control from districts, the federal intrusion into local education was premised on the existence of inequity. Reformers concerned about disparities between districts in the 1920s and 1930s saw equity between students explode onto the national stage in the 1960s. States had not done enough, according to activists, and what served administrators and bureaucrats did not appear to serve all children. The concern for equity began to trump a concern for local democracy.

Paradoxically, the federal "intrusion" created a space for agencies to expand their own autonomy and scope. With the ESEA and subsequent federal monies (nominally voluntary), education departments became the guardians of "equal opportunity" for special-needs children, ethnic minorities, and others. This led directly into state involvement in setting curriculum standards (and naturally continuing financial involvement). Like finance, educational quality would not be left up to the vagaries of local politics, so state education departments—and some interested legislators (some of whom would later work in the same departments)—began to push for a more uniform curriculum. Although basic requirements were not new, by the 1970s states were adding courses and course-taking requirements, especially in high school. In the 1980s, this only intensified as governors and legislators rhetorically tied education to economic development.

At the same time, the federal government grew to expect more of them (Manna 2006). Some observers, and certainly some of my interviewees, wondered whether "Washington" was out to make fifty branch offices of the U.S. Department of Education. This view is too simplistic: even in the heady days of the 1960s and the ESEA, characteristics of the American federal system left state agencies with substantial room to maneuver (Anton 1989; Posner 1998; Gormley 2006).

First, the federal government has never provided sufficient money to fully implement any educational program. Federal funding frequently comes with a "supplement-not-supplant" clause to *prevent* federal dollars from actually paying for an entire program: state effort, and thus state decision making, is required. Even if some federal program came with enough funding to pay for every paper clip used to fulfill a federal education mandate, the state and local districts would still be left with filling in the rest of the constellation of education: the school building, paying other teachers, funding health insurance costs for teachers, keeping track of district lines, and selecting curriculum. That is, the federal government sponsors *individual* programs and not comprehensive ones (although the ESEA now provides some circumstances for school-wide Title I funding, somewhat weakening this claim). This leaves states freedom to "frame" how effective programs are.

Second, the federal government has rarely used "teeth" when states miss deadlines or even ignore mandates. Instead, Congress or the federal bureaucracy is likely to modify the mandate or overlook the misstep. For example, the 1994 ESEA reauthorization required states to develop content standards and a method to assess student performance. By 2001, only eleven states had fulfilled this legal requirement—the U.S. Department of Education had waived the deadlines (Manna 2006, 113). The authors of No Child Left Behind of 2001 did not want a repeat of this lax enforcement, so they required the testing of all students as a condition of federal money. Yet after states complained that some of the neediest schools (and some of the least needy) would not make adequate yearly progress, Education Secretary Margaret Spellings granted greater leeway for meeting the law's requirements (Dillon 2005). Even in specific instances, the federal bureaucracy has proven remarkably pliable: Gormley (2006, 532) reports that the U.S. Department of Education granted three quarters of the waivers that states submitted between 1995 and 2004 (669 of 882).

Third, the federal government has repeatedly taken ideas from the states to expand them at the national level. There is a large literature that asks whether federalism is cooperative or combative. If it were cooperative, then the states and the federal government would act in concert to design and implement the most agreeable policies. If it were combative, then states and localities would drag their feet and use administrative and legal recourse to hamper implementation (see Gormley 2006; Agranoff and McGuire 2001). In either case, the federal government must be responsive to state preferences. In education, an "equality of outcomes" requirement, similar to Outcomes-Based Education that nearly appeared in Ohio (see chapter 6), was taken out of the 1994 ESEA reauthorization when state departments of education complained (Jennings 1998). And throughout the life of the ESEA, the *state* has been responsible for designing standards and creating (or buying) the tests. Testing may be a major federal requirement with NCLB, but allowing the state to dictate what is actually on that test is a major concession. Thus state departments retained considerable freedom, despite federal demands.

To conclude, state education departments had credible claims on significant policies with concrete local effects throughout the 1980s and 1990s. State superintendents (and any department official) could point to three major areas to argue for wider scope and the need to increase their autonomy: the technical responsibility for developing and maintaining an adequate state education funding formula, the maintenance of financial equality between districts, and the creation of a basic, state-wide curriculum. Education leaders in Ohio, Georgia, and Wisconsin would find each of these elements of scope useful to emphasize when under scrutiny by governors, legislators, courts, and the general public.

Three Paths Taken: Georgia, Ohio, and Wisconsin

To explore the relationship of autonomy and scope ultimately leading to policy outcomes, I use in-depth case studies of the Wisconsin Department of Public Instruction, the Ohio Department of Education, and the Georgia Department of Education across the twenty years before the No Child Left Behind Act, roughly 1981 to 2001. This section explains why these three states were selected. Broadly, these three cases represent three traditions in state educational responsibilities, and each has a distinct approach to state educational governance. Case studies are particularly important for understanding the causal mechanism driving the growth or decay of agency autonomy and scope. Further, using the same cases over time holds constant unobserved state influences that would weaken a cross-sectional analysis. Using the same time period for all three also controls for the national educational currents of the time.[12]

Each of these state departments had a different starting point in its attempt to gain autonomy and scope. (I recount more of the departments' histories in chapter 4.) Before Reconstruction in Georgia, legislators universally considered education a private matter and provided financial support to private academies and poor schools. After the Civil War, the Reconstruction government was highly suspicious of local intentions (particularly regarding African Americans), so some education was centralized. The suspicion of local control, as well as strong state centralization, continues today.

Ohio was the first state carved out of the Northwest Territories, in 1803, and it was the first to implement the Northwest Ordinance's provision that "schools and the means of education shall forever be encouraged."[13] Many of the school lands designated by the ordinance for this purpose were lost in political deals through the nineteenth century, and Progressives were deeply concerned that state-level education efforts had taken a partisan tinge. They succeeded in replacing the elected post with one appointed by the governor. Proponents of a state school board made the same argument in the 1950s—that the top education post was too political—to remove the superintendent one step farther from the electorate. The state board of education was to appoint the state superintendent.

Partisanship was much less of a concern in Wisconsin, where the state officer has always been officially nonpartisan. "Local control" is Wisconsin's watchword. By law, the state had no practical regulatory authority over the state's numerous one-room schools (extant until 1970), and the state department was only one of many competing state education boards and commissions, a maze at best, although the DPI has clearly become the chief agency.

Aside from their different histories, each state represents a different way to govern schools. Table 1.1 shows the selection mechanism for each state's school chief and state board, if any. Georgia and Wisconsin have independently elected chiefs, though Georgia's is partisan; Georgia has an appointed state board; and Ohio's chief serves at the pleasure of a part-appointed, part-elected state board. Because I expect that the leadership of an agency plays a major part in how effectively an agency can seek new autonomy and scope, the appointment process can limit the persuasive powers of the chief. Further, the table shows that most states control education with a board. Because of this, it is important to understand how education departments work *without* one: Wisconsin

Table 1.1. State Educational Governance Structures

| Schools Chief | State Board | | None |
	Elected	Appointed	
Elected	WA	AZ, CA, *GA,* ID, IN, ME, MT, NC, ND, OK, OR, SC, WY (13)	*WI*
Appointed	AL, CO, HI, KS, MI, NE, NV, <u>TX</u>, UT (9)	AK, AR, CT, <u>DE</u>, FL, <u>IA</u>, IL, KY, LA, MD, MA, MS, MO, NH, <u>NJ</u>, NM, NY, *OH,* <u>PA</u>, RI, <u>SD</u>, <u>TN</u>, VT, <u>VA</u>, WV (25)	<u>MN</u>

Note: Governor-appointed state schools chiefs are <u>underlined</u> (9). All other appointed chiefs are board appointed. (26). Cases in this study are *italicized.* Most appointed boards are appointed by the governor, although many states' boards include a combination of appointed and elected members.

Source: National Association of State Boards of Education (2007).

serves as this foil. Such a contrast should highlight the importance, if any, of a state board of education.

Further, the payrolls of Georgia's, Ohio's, and Wisconsin's departments suggest that they *should* exhibit different levels of autonomy and scope. Figure 1.1 shows a scatter plot of the payroll for state-level education (adjusted to account for varying state median family income levels) versus the size of state-level education offices (in terms of students per full-time-equivalent employee) in 1991, the middle of the time span. The dashed lines indicate the national means for both variables. Note that most Southern states have well-paying, large state departments. Local control is far weaker in these states due to historical circumstances, thereby leading to more power being placed in the hands of state government. For the three cases at hand, Georgia pays its employees the national average, but it employs far more people per student than one might expect (notice the location of California, Florida, and Texas). This should give Georgia extra leverage in terms of scope and autonomy, because it has deep personnel resources. Wisconsin, on the other hand, is in the lower right-hand quadrant. Not only does it pay less than the national average, but there are fewer state employees

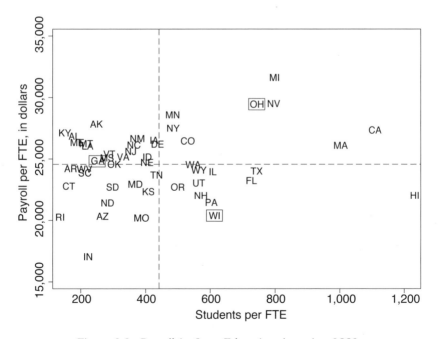

Figure 1.1. Payroll in State Education Agencies, 1991.

per student. Wisconsin should have more trouble. Finally, Ohio is above the mean for both pay and size. This should indicate a middling ability to build scope and autonomy, although it should not be as difficult as it might be in Wisconsin.

This book is built on a variety of data to ensure that my conclusions are supported from different angles. Interviews and the archived files of state officials provide the backbone for the argument. Thirty-four out of forty interviews were with representatives of major, state-level educational interest groups (e.g., state teachers' unions or associations, school administrators' groups, school board groups, business associations; see Appendix C), state legislators with a particular interest in educational issues (as determined by committee membership), and current or former state education department personnel at all levels. Each interview was approximately one hour long and confidential. Interviewees were chosen because of their likely firsthand knowledge of the activities of the state superintendent and deep involvement in education politics. The remaining interviews, with former state superintendents, were one to six hours long and not confidential. The questions were tailored specifically to each superintendent's particular policy interests, political inclinations, and controversies during that superintendent's term. Semistructured interviews such as these allow interviewees to follow some of their own tangents of thinking while providing me a better basis for consistent analysis (Leech 2002; Rubin and Rubin 1995).

Governors' papers, the files of former state superintendents and other officials kept at state archives, self-published interest group reports, and major state newspapers in Georgia, Ohio, and Wisconsin provided context for the interviews. What an interviewee could not remember often appeared scrawled on a weekly memo that had been stuffed in a superior's folder twenty years earlier. I made extensive use of weekly memos to governors, internal agency memoranda, and contemporary interest group documents to fill in these gaps in memory. The danger of archives, of course, is that there is no way to know which documents have been omitted or which documents never made it into the record. This danger is mitigated by using multiple, roughly simultaneous sources. This I did both by using major state newspapers, *Education Week* (whose coverage of states is necessarily not consistent), and the files of multiple personnel with similar responsibilities; for example, I used multiple assistant superintendents in state education agencies, or both the governor's files and the governor's education assistant's files. To gauge the public perception of an agency's importance, I sampled newspaper coverage from large dailies in each state.

A rich portrait also emerges from quantitative analysis. I draw on three basic sources. First, I analyze Wisconsin's DPI, Ohio's ODE, and Georgia's GADOE budget requests. I trace agencies' budget abilities through twenty years of budget requests, gubernatorial allowances, and legislative adjustments. This results in one measure of how autonomous an agency actually is. The budget is also an accurate measure of the scope an agency has.[14] Second, I compiled the tenure and committee assignments of every member of the legislature in these three states. If education is a salient issue, then one would expect that legislators would be eager to serve on an education committee relative to, say, an ethics committee.[15] Third, I estimated the effect of both legislative salience and budget success on the rates of introduction and passage of education-related legislation in each state.

Plan of the Work

The next chapter, which begins part 1, lays out a theory of autonomy and scope, drawing on scholarship on bureaucracy, Congress, interest groups, and chief executives. I define my terms and explain that each of the factors that I posit influences both autonomy and scope. The third chapter sets out concrete expectations that I have for how the institutional, active, and passive factors influence governmental agencies.

Part 2 of the work presents evidence for the influence of each group of factors. In chapter 4, I trace the historical development of the scope of each state's department of education to show the roots of its institutional situation.

Chapters 5 and 6 explore active, endogenous causes. The former shows how each state's agency managed interest groups to further the agency's favored programs (or failed to do so). The latter tells the story of six state superintendents, each of whom harnessed a distinct leadership style to persuade the public, governors, and legislators to yield to the agency's direction.

Chapter 7 highlights passive, exogenous causes on agency autonomy and scope. It analyzes electoral challenges to agency clout through turnover in the governor's office.

Part 3 shows some effects of autonomy and scope. Chapter 8 looks at legislative salience over time and its link to bill introduction and passage. In chapter 9 I present the budget success of agencies over time.

A final chapter concludes by drawing on the themes developed throughout. Here I discuss the ramifications of agency autonomy for the stability of education reforms, which are notoriously difficult to move "to scale," and the prospects for the federal government to assume that state agencies are able to use their own clout to promulgate new mandates. Finally, I address the limits of using experts to shape policy in a democratic society.

2

Autonomy and Scope in Government Agencies

... while submission of an evaluation of progress and services to the state superintendent can provide useful information to respond to requests by the legislature and others, the department does not have staff to review or make effective use of them.

—Wisconsin Department of Public Instruction,
1997–1999 Biennial Budget Request

In the first chapter, I argued that agency autonomy is important practically because, as shown by others, the federal government expects local and state governments to be able to change course quickly if necessary to implement federal programs. Agency autonomy and sufficient agency scope are important to explain where actual, concrete policy comes from. Agency autonomy allows the agency to broaden its scope to fulfill a preferred policy goal. Although there will never be an agency that is fully independent of political influence—if one actually wanted such a nondemocratic creature—agency autonomy is a central component of building a functioning government.

In this chapter, I develop a theory to explain how an agency may leverage its existing responsibilities to increase its technical, political, and fiscal autonomy to answer the question: When can an agency change its principal's preferences for policy and oversight?

On its face, such a theory would appear counterintuitive, for two reasons. First, much principal-agent literature argues that principals have preferences and expend resources to ensure that agencies do not stray too far from their preferences (see, for example, McCubbins, Noll, and Weingast 1989). These efforts include institutional constraints through rules and procedures to prevent political gain by future politicians (possibly with different preferences) or another branch of government (Moe 1989). Or, a political overseer might create redundant agencies or bureaus to prevent any agency or political group from becoming too powerful (Ting 2003). Others argue that principals might also reduce suboptimal outcomes by increasing the supervisory powers of agency leaders and managers, whether by creating tighter controls over hiring and firing, pay, performance measures, or other institutional features (Kiewiet and McCubbins 1991).

Second, bureaucracies are often, perhaps exclusively, portrayed as unable to participate in policy creation at the top level, or as participating in a negative, ex post facto way.[1] This is the underlying assumption in articles where interest groups and others alert Congress to bureaucratic misdirection, malfeasance, or other unacceptable behavior.[2] Although the literature admits that agencies have considerable discretion, this freedom is often painted in terms of shirking or sabotage. Agencies are eminently able to *de*emphasize policies with which some bureaucrat disagrees.[3] Finally, bureaucrats are assumed to follow a principal's policy direction only because a payoff is impending.[4] In each case, bureaucrats are supposed to follow the policy direction set by their principal. The role of the principal remains clear-cut: it sets the goals and monitors the results.

A further complication is the definition of the principal. For federal agencies, scholars usually conceive of the principal as a congressional oversight committee, an executive-branch official, or perhaps the judiciary (see, for example, Canes-Wrone 2003; McCubbins, Noll, and Weingast 1989). State counterparts of each of these lie layered between the federal level and the agency. In some states (including Georgia and Wisconsin), the state education agency's relationship is further complicated because the state superintendent is a constitutional officer equivalent to the governor—that is, the state superintendent is not legally required to report to the governor.

Of course, the relationship between state government actors is complex. There is never a single principal in intragovernmental relations, but it does make sense to simplify the process. Not all of the possible principals are relevant at all stages of policy making. When designing the state budget, for example, the governor prepares a budget that the legislature can mark up or ignore. The state agency will want to be generously remembered in the governor's budget, but it will also need to convince state legislators of the importance of its budget items. In this light, there are two principals: the legislative budget committee and the governor. For designing state standards to meet requirements of the No Child Left Behind Act, the federal Department of Education is the principal. As such, I will follow the practice of federal principal-agent scholars and assume that the "principal" depends on the context.[5]

I believe previous research is convincing in the generic case. Agencies *are* subject to a principal's direction, even if bureaucrats have substantial discretion. But I argue here that agencies, with a particular combination of factors, are able to rise above this and shape the preferences (i.e., policy goals) of their principals. To do so, I argue that the agency may leverage its already-granted *scope* to gain more *autonomy*. Further, an agency's responsibilities increase recursively with its autonomy.

The mechanisms by which an agency increases its autonomy and widens its scope may be grouped into three factors: (1) *institutional* factors, (2) *endogenous* factors, where the agency takes an active role in pursuing broader scope or exercising autonomy, and (3) *exogenous*, or passive, factors over which an agency has little influence. Overall, autonomy is the independent exercise of choice, but I break it into three somewhat more concrete strands to gain some traction for the argument. It may rely on its *technical autonomy*. Technical autonomy is a combination of professional expertise and bureaucratic structure. Bureaucratic agencies are repositories for professional expertise simply by virtue of the long tenure that many employees enjoy and the detailed knowledge required to write regulations and enact directives of the executive or legislature. *Political autonomy* is the ability of an agency to shape or redirect gubernatorial or legislative oversight. Most political science research lies here. Finally, *fiscal autonomy* is the ability of an agency to control its own funds. The primary demonstration of this appears in the state budget process.

A Theory of Bureaucratic Autonomy

Bureaucratic autonomy, be it technical, political, or fiscal, is a direct function of institutional and endogenous factors and an indirect function of exogenous factors. These combine to give an agency resources to seek increased scope. The first move is an autonomous action by the agency—something outside of its current scope, but something that it would prefer to have legal scope to do. When the agency acts autonomously, exogenous actors note the action, and, if the agency has not overreached, they shift their own preferences toward the agency's preferred policy output. This is made formal by the legal extension (or statutory neglect) of the agency's scope to accommodate the new activity. The greater an agency's scope, the more room the agency has to act autonomously, and the more likely it is that the agency's preferred policy output will be implemented. That is, both scope and autonomy function as a continuum. This section considers these elements in greater depth. The following chapter suggests some concrete outputs that I expect will exist for state education agencies in particular. A schematic diagram of this theory appears in Figure 2.1.

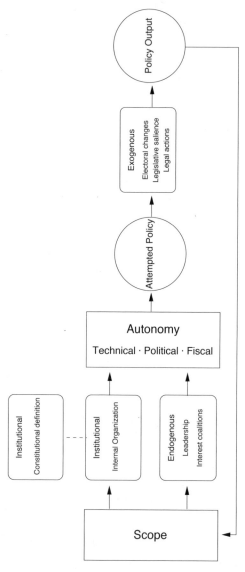

Figure 2.1. Factors Influencing Agency Autonomy and Scope.

Scope

For an agency to be meaningfully autonomous, it must have something meaningful to do. "Scope" is the set of tasks that an agency is expected to do by law accompanied by a budget sufficient to do these tasks. In the beginning, legislatures created all agencies; thus scope appears before autonomy. Legislatures, presidents, or other principals generate an initial set of responsibilities.[6] Because scope functions as a legal protection, agencies prefer to act within their extant scope. But when they *do* take steps outside of their scope, they prefer to have it added to their legal set of tasks. I assume that agencies seek to maximize scope.

Scope can best be understood by a nested definition. At the outer level, scope includes the number of policy areas an agency administers. In the case of education, agencies often handle student health, teacher licensure, building safety, and public libraries. Since the 1970s, many also handle curriculum standards and student evaluation. Some of these areas are not strictly educational (student health, for example), and some have argued that school readiness and children's socialization are more familial than educational. (This is one reason Head Start is not part of the Elementary and Secondary Education Act.) For example, Minnesota's education agency was at one time merged into the family services department, an indication that its education bureaucracy was much more limited than other states' (in that it was only one function of a noneducation-focused agency).

Within these policy areas, "scope" includes the specific actions that an agency has undisputed authority to take. I will discuss three. First, agencies must enforce the law and their own rules. (The autonomy exercised by writing a strict rule is meaningful only if the agency follows up with inspection.) This is especially true of regulatory agencies, but other agencies, including education departments, also have limited power to ensure that, for example, school districts are maintaining their school buildings in legal condition.

A second set of actions is collecting and publishing information for legislators and the public. In effect, this is the first "draft" of new public policies. With data collection and compilation, an agency can emphasize certain findings before anyone else has access to the data, and no one else can make informed decisions without access to this data. Neither the rise of the Internet nor the advent of legislative research divisions has made agency information collection passe. Someone with a day-to-day knowledge of a policy area is still the best source for data.[7] Although Wisconsin Superintendent Herbert Grover lamented to me about his inability to parcel out information to the legislature in the later years of his tenure (ending in 1992), DPI was still the source for raw data. And at the end of the 1990s, Superintendent Zelman's administration in Ohio (beginning in 1999) was just announcing a new initiative to *increase* data collection and processing to improve "data-driven decision-making." The state-wide set of almost micro-level funding and student data is only available at one agency, the Ohio Department of Education.

A third (informal) part of scope is to promote the interests of the agency's general policy area, akin to a state-level lobbyist. This responsibility is both to the consumers of the policy and to other interested persons. Because an agency will have to cooperate repeatedly with many of the same individuals over time, its leadership must be concerned about its reputation, and its reputation will be built on promoting policies that are seen by at least some actors as beneficial to the policy area—high-quality teachers, unadulterated foodstuffs, or monitored nuclear power plants. An agency with a solid reputation will be more able to act autonomously because all of the major players in the policy area assume that it is not working to fulfill an agenda built on pure political partisanship or favoritism.

Promoting the policy area is not the same as agency capture. Capture implies that the interests of a few large organizations control agency output. Recent work demonstrates that agencies may be more interested in preserving their reputations than building ties to large industries or interest groups. A fear of the fallout from poor results at the Food and Drug Administration and a concern for accurate forecasts at three federal macroeconomic agencies were better predictors of agency behavior than marketplace dominance or institutional ties (Carpenter 2004; Krause and Douglas 2005). The capture hypothesis is very suggestive about state education departments in the past, when state superintendents hosted (and sometimes were presidents) of state education associations, but the frequency with which agencies have taken on state university systems and changed teacher licensure requirements seems to indicate that departments now hold an independent conception of how education should work. In Georgia, for example, the state department supported and administered stringent school performance standards in the 1980s over the objections of teachers' groups and district administrators.

This definition of scope finds a loose analogue in the word "authority." Authority implies that an agency can define "good public policy" with few credible detractors. Scope is similar in that an agency has the legal *right* to draft and enforce regulations to mesh with its vision of good policy. Unlike authority, scope does not require an exclusive policy domain. Indeed, an agency's autonomous action may simply be to override a competing agency's definition of good policy. For example, high school graduation standards were within the scope of both the University of Wisconsin and the Department of Public Instruction until 1945. State Superintendent Charles Cary believed that the DPI was the proper source for these, as most children did not go to college (see chapter 4), thus he drafted standards that conflicted with the university's; a protracted governmental conflict followed, but Cary eventually won. The DPI did not have the "authority" to make the standards because they were within the scope of more than one agency.

Autonomy

What is autonomy? Some examples may be easy to spot: If an agency is able to create a kindergarten ability testing program with little input from the legislature, interest groups, or even the governor, then that is a meaningful exercise of autonomy. Awarding contracts without oversight (as happened in Georgia in the late 1990s) is a meaningful, if questionable, exercise of autonomy.[8]

Carpenter (2001a) argues that genuine agency autonomy exists not only when an agency can implement necessary rules but also when that agency can make policy that is beyond the *intent* of existing law. Politicians defer to agency activity when it is politically dangerous not to do so and when clients and politicians see the agency's freedom as beneficial to their policy interests. For Carpenter, bureaucratic autonomy exists when agencies act in a way that "neither politicians nor organized interests prefer but that they either cannot or will not overturn or constrain [an agency] in the future" (17). Further, he argues that autonomy can force legislators' hands to *create* new laws that justify the agency's policies. His definition of agency autonomy shifts the focus from authorizing laws to agency activity. Agencies build reputations for effective action over the long term, and their reputations depend heavily on the visions of their leaders.

Building on Carpenter's observations, I define autonomy as an agency's ability to choose *whether* to use current scope or whether to pursue *new policy directions* based on internal decisions. Whatever the action is, it is taken without the prior consent of political principals, but it *is* taken in the hopes of having the action added to its scope. Autonomy is the means to an end, that is, maximized scope. Autonomous actions may extend scope if the legislature goes along. (It is autonomy if an agency chooses *not* to enforce its regulations in a particular case, although this might be an example of "negative" autonomy.) Autonomous actions become scope only to the extent that political principals allow the actions to stand.

This is more expansive than Carpenter's definition, in that I argue that the agency can *shape* the preferences of political principals so that they agree and ratify its actions rather than having to *force* a policy change through constituent pressure. Said another way, I argue that agencies can play an active role in shaping preferences about what the agency should do. Carpenter's definition works well for his case study of the Post Office Department and the Department of Agriculture. Both departments had built a constituent base that clamored for services in such a way that legislators would have been foolish to ignore the department's innovations. But both agencies were headed by strong-willed leaders who had a vision for where they wanted to take their respective agencies. I argue that less well-situated agencies may find autonomy with weaker leaders, more attentive legislators, and (arguably) more controversial policy areas. Such agencies are less able to force policy changes and must instead shape preferences of key political actors.

As in Carpenter's discussion, an action is autonomous when the action first takes place—not when the legislature or governor ratifies the department's actions. By acting autonomously (that is, self-directedly), there is a possibility that an action will be rejected by a political principal. Autonomy has little meaning if there is no risk of failure: If department personnel already know they can do something with impunity, then the action is effectively in the agency's scope already.

Of course, it is in the agency's interest to succeed. To that end, an agency must monitor interest groups, incorporate discussions with legislators, and use department leadership effectively. Interest groups or legislators may sound the "fire alarm," bringing unwanted attention (from the agency's perspective) from legislators, who may then restrict the agency from further action in some policy domain. This point is parallel to that of Pious (1996, 89–96) regarding the powers of the president. He notes that presidents who use prerogative powers may find their actions "frontlash" to build support for additional presidential power. The actions may "backlash" to build presidential power, even though the individual president loses political clout. Or, finally, presidential prerogative may "overshoot and collapse" when it appears that the president has so exceeded an acceptable use of the office's powers that Congress or the courts may explicitly reduce the president's power. In each case, the prerogative action precedes a congressional or court response. Agencies are subject to similar effects.

This description of agency action contrasts with one often found in the literature on political control. Most research on political control of the bureaucracy uses "discretion" to indicate an agency's freedom of action. Studies often use a definition resembling this one: discretion is "making judgments regarding policy actions not prescribed in detail by formal rules or legislation" (Ringquist 1995, 339). Unfortunately, no law is so specific as to create the rational-legal bureaucracy outlined by Max Weber: Most policy actions are not described in detail. As defined earlier, discretion only focuses on the pseudocontractual arrangement between an agency and the legislature via statute rather than the actors and day-to-day situations in which bureaucrats find themselves. A better definition might be "making judgments where legislators intentionally left the law vague." Discretion may be thought of as dispensation for action within a legally constructed policy domain. Autonomy goes beyond discretion: it is the ability to independently enlarge, bridge, or create policy domains and to persuade overseers to formally incorporate these actions into the agency's accepted scope.

In the remainder of this section, I distinguish between three manifestations of autonomy: technical, political, and fiscal. I also indicate which other government actor might have similar scope to indicate why an autonomous action might be meaningful. Theoretically, these help distinguish which kinds of independent actions an agency might be more likely to take given a particular set of factors (institutional, active, or passive). For example, in a state that has an independently elected state superintendent, political autonomy might appear to be used more often than fiscal autonomy. In states where the governor's office prepares agency budgets de facto, fiscal autonomy will appear less often. Empirically, each of these three made separate appearances in interviews I conducted. My interviewees talked as if these three strands *were* independent. They would discuss their limitations in the state hierarchy of agencies, or the limitations of their knowledge of how effective the agency's administration was; then they would discuss their agency's difficulties with the legislature and governor, usually with some quip about the evils of politics; and then they would talk about the budget as routine, although nightmarish, paperwork. Some made weak links between two (particularly between politics and the budget) or all three, but most did not.

TECHNICAL AUTONOMY

All agencies have some measure of technical autonomy. Technical autonomy is the agency's ability to formulate policy with its unique access to information and to use its enforcement powers (however slight they may be, they have greater authority than a comparable private-sector organization). Technical autonomy gives rise to expertise that is often unparalleled in its policy area. It is most aided by the formal placement of the agency in government and its formal responsibilities. For example, an agency may determine how to measure graduation rates or what an appropriate application to open a charter school looks like. The rule-making powers implicit in technical autonomy have also created an example of shirking or even sabotage: a widespread complaint among proponents of the No Child Left Behind Act is that state departments have fudged test cut scores to make more children appear "proficient" or have altered teacher requirements to ensure that most of the teaching staff in the state are "highly qualified" (Hoff 2002).[9] This is probably the strongest form of autonomy, because it legally and logically falls within the purview of an agency.

Other agencies sometimes encroach on this power; in Wisconsin, the governor created a standard-setting commission in 1996 after he did not think the DPI's standards were rigorous enough (see chapter 7). Many states also have legislative reference offices that do research on behalf of legislators. The Government Accountability Office and the Congressional Research Service perform this function nationally. Although many times these offices rely on agency data, they are sometimes charged with doing independent research so legislators can enact law without (or in spite of) an agency's technical abilities (see, for example, U.S. Government Accountability Office 2008). Assaults on technical autonomy by other political organizations are the most serious because their actions suggest that an agency cannot be trusted with basic decision making in its own area of expertise.

POLITICAL AUTONOMY

This subset of autonomy casts a wide net, as political autonomy is the freedom from interference by the legislature, governor, and courts. The appointment power is the most direct control these three have over agencies' political autonomy. Governors in many states (including Georgia and Ohio) relished the ability to appoint members of state education boards to control state agencies. Many scholars of bureaucracy have noted the weaknesses of appointees, which makes this form of autonomy stronger. Appointees can change the level of agency output—until the appointee leaves and activity returns to normal (Wood and Waterman 1991, 1993). In addition, appointees have limited opportunity to lead an agency because they have little ability to either offer incentives or fire employees due to civil service protections (Johnson and Libecap 1994). They are also constrained by the agency's load of responsibilities, as they may be able to suppress an agency's output but not be able to emphasize one part of the agency's mission over another (Krause

1994). Finally, appointees may cease to be effective overseers (from the executive's point of view) if they adopt the outlook and preferences of an agency, whether out of frustration or desire (Heclo 1977). Scholars have also shown, indirectly, that changes in congressional preferences and judicial ideology may serve to guide agency work, although agencies sometimes fail to take the hint (McCubbins, Noll, and Weingast 1989; Canes-Wrone 2003). I expect that political autonomy is most influenced by forces outside of an agency's direct control, such as elections, legal challenges, and elected leadership. Nevertheless, agencies with active leaders may also be able to play the political game well.

Obviously, governors are the most able to impede an agency's political autonomy. In most states, they have the power to make appointments and sometimes remove them. In Ohio, Governor George V. Voinovich successfully convinced the legislature to allow him to appoint part of the state board of education because he though that voters would blame *him* for educational problems. But his move also cost the Ohio Department of Education political autonomy; some legislators and interest groups came to see the department as being "too tight with the governor" (see chapters 5 and 6). Because agencies exist in a political system, outside challenges to their political autonomy are not as damaging as those to its technical autonomy. In some circumstances, political shake-ups might push an agency to move closer to the preferences of an elected majority. Note that this is the reverse of autonomy: the political system is shaping the agency's preferences, rather than the other way around.

FISCAL AUTONOMY

Some agencies may be able to request funds in excess of either the governor's or legislators' desires (but not both)—and get them. "They were always jealous of me," Franklin Walter, Ohio's longest-serving state superintendent, told me. "I always got more money than the governor wanted me to get. We were the fourth branch of government. Completely independent." Most directly, fiscal autonomy is the degree to which an agency can request, receive, and spend funds based on its own recommendation. Although individual bureaucrats may not be budget maximizers due to institutional constraints, agencies as a whole can overcome these limits (Blais and Dion 1991; Niskanen 1971). Fiscal autonomy is even more apparent when funding changes exceed incrementalism.[10] At least four factors affect this form of autonomy: the source of funds, the structure and importance of the agency, the previous year's budget success, and, to a lesser extent, the political configuration of the legislature and governor.[11] An agency that can withstand the governor's budget wishes has a great deal of fiscal autonomy indeed. With fiscal autonomy, agencies can reshape a governor's program. For example, empowered by the Ohio Supreme Court's *DeRolph* decisions, ODE was able to suggest a school funding formula it found appropriate and to force Ohio to cut funding from several other major state programs (see chapter 5).

The Interaction of Autonomy and Scope

Government agencies, no less than any organization, are limited by the status quo. There are many explanations of the difficulty required to change: divergent preferences, multiplicity of opportunity to quash change (veto points), partisanship, and organizational culture, to name four (Krehbiel 1998, chapter 3; Scott 1992, chapter 12; Moe 1989). Bureaucracies store the policy decisions of the past and preserve them against the political winds of the present, often to the frustration of leaders. At least since Franklin Roosevelt, presidents have sought better ways to control the federal bureaucracy, usually to their own frustration (Light 1995).

Yet agencies can change, and many scholars have suggested how external agents shape bureaucracy. Outside of the formal governmental structure, social movements or interest group pressure may alter the behavior of an agency (Brehm and Gates 1997; Zald and Garner 1987). And within the government, a shift in congressional or presidential preferences signals an agency to shift at least its output level if not its preferences (Wood and Waterman 1991, 1993).

In this book, I argue that agencies themselves may initiate change by attempting to extend their scope through autonomous action. An agency may argue that the legislature should allow it to take the lead in creating or reshaping programs because of the importance or technical demands of its already-existing scope. For example, the responsibility to track individual student attendance or test scores may already be within a state education agency's scope. An agency may ask for more staff or more funding (say, additional computer support). The scope contained within this program implies that an agency may design (or buy) standardized tests, determine who may use the data, and how, when, or if to publicize the results. Or, an agency may be required to report on the condition of school funding in each school district. It may uncover funding inequities (in a way that the agency has defined) by acting autonomously; then it can seek new scope to implement a revised school aid formula. In an extreme case, an education agency may define its scope to permit an autonomous takeover of recalcitrant school districts (either for poor student performance or for delinquent use of school funds).[12] When an agency takes an autonomous action, its new task will lead it to demand a wide enough scope to do the task "right," according to agency leaders.[13]

This cycle may occur even when an agency is in a weak position. Variations on this chapter's epigraph appeared throughout the Wisconsin Department of Public Instruction's budget requests for the 1997–1999 biennium. The department had only narrowly escaped being gutted by the governor, and its budget was in trouble. Even under these circumstances, however, the DPI sought to convince the governor's office and the legislature's budget committee that it should be allowed to continue—or reshape—the programs it judged crucial to its mission. Of course, the degree to which agencies actually pursue this cycle is a question. Such a finding would add nuance to the standard view of agency behavior: bureaucracies may not shirk their responsibilities but seek them.

How, then, do agencies gain scope and autonomy? In the next section, I lay out the three major factors leading to changes in scope and autonomy. Throughout this chapter I rely on scholarship about the federal government. For reasons I gave in chapter 1, I assume that the underlying political processes are the same (other scholars have followed this path as well; see, for example, Nicholson-Crotty, Theobald, and Wood 2006).

Inside the Box: Factors Affecting Autonomy

In their quest for scope through autonomy, government agencies may find themselves aided by three sets of input factors over which they have more or less influence. These are found in the four rounded boxes in Figure 2.1. The first set embraces *institutional* factors, by which I mean both "standard" institutional features such as who appoints whom and also the internal management style (the "culture" of the organization). Agency leaders have great clout over the latter, and sometimes they have influence over the former, depending on whether the agency is defined constitutionally or not. Because the constitutional factors are difficult to influence, they are connected to the figure with a dotted line. Institutional factors may be thought of as "background" effects. The second grouping, *active* factors, are within the purview of agency actors by definition. They may be thought of as endogenous influences on the agency. These include anything that agency representatives do publicly to enhance their agency's position (and sometimes their own!), but I highlight leadership and interest-group coalition building here. The third group of factors is outside of the control of agency leadership. These factors are reactive to an agency's exercise of autonomy but directly related to its scope. These are *passive* factors that only affect the agency exogenously and include legislative turnover and the filing of lawsuits.[14]

Institutional Factors

Institutional factors, in the top box in Figure 2.1, work in the background because they set the rules of the game and the culture in which bureaucrats work. These can be difficult to change.

The formal structure and position of the agency in government is probably the most subtle, though highly influential, cause of an agency's level of autonomy. Important design elements for any public agency are the legal political entities overseeing the agency above (such as a legislature and a similarly charged federal agency) and administrators, employees, and beneficiaries below. In the federal case, many agencies are torn between reporting to Congress and responding to the president, although no one doubts that the agency has some responsibility to both. State-level education agencies have even more influences to consider: state legislatures, the governor, and the U.S. Department of Education above; and school districts, boards, and even parents below. Further, state education agencies are unique in the field of government agencies in that many state education agencies are defined by the state's constitution. Many state constitutions declare that education is a state responsibility and sometimes designate a state superintendent as a constitutional officer. Most states have boards of education, but some are elected, while others are appointed. Perhaps alone among state agencies, education agencies have multiple lines of accountability. Accountability is splintered among many offices.

One might expect that agencies with gubernatorial paternity would be more sensitive to the governor's political agenda. Conversely, insulated, independent agencies, such as the Federal Reserve, should be the most autonomous. Legislatively and executively controlled agencies should have the most limits placed on them. Nevertheless, scholars have shown at the federal level that the quality of work does not change depending on who oversees the agency because of reputational pressures (Krause and Douglas 2005). The ease of gaining wider scope may be simplified if, say, the agency is constitutionally independent than if it is overseen by the legislature, governor, or a state board. If, as Moe (1989) argues, agencies are designed to thwart control by another branch, then "independent" agencies or those with multiple principals should be able to circumvent these institutional politics (see also Calvert, McCubbins, and Weingast 1989). Institutional structure also has consequences for how an agency is managed. A study of the U.S. Environmental Protection Agency (EPA) shows how one of the EPA's multiple principals expanded and contracted the agency's tasks in response to the other principal's action. The result was that the agency had trouble determining where to put employee resources. The push and pull induced the agency to "hedge" its enforcement activities (Whitford 2005).

Constitutional structure is a background effect, as changes to state constitutions and the abolition of state agencies are rare. Yet the multiple-principal, quasi-independent status of many state education departments puts them in good stead to claim new scope through the exercise of autonomy.

Active Factors

Active factors, listed in the second box in Figure 2.1, are factors over which agency actors have direct control. They are endogenous. Skillful agency leadership may be able to overcome institutional limitations, for example, by using the news media, political relationships, and interest groups to argue for increased autonomy and wider scope. Failing at these, an agency will likely be reduced to cutting checks to spend federal dollars and other functional responsibilities.

LEADERSHIP

Leadership drives autonomy and scope because it is the most visible means to claim new activities. If an agency chief believes that something is crucial to the success of his or her agency's mission, then that chief will seek to convert the organization—and outsiders—to his or her view. Depending on the leader's style, he or she may aid or hamper autonomous action.

Leadership is distinct from management in that leadership helps organizations (and people) change, while management makes organizations understandable (Kotter 1990).[15] Commonly identified characteristics of leadership include inspiration and vision. These characteristics are also found in Weber's description of a charismatic leader: "Charisma knows only inner determination and inner restraint. The holder of charisma seizes the task that is adequate for him and demands obedience and a following by virtue of his mission" (1946, 246). If this is so, then leadership is difficult to transmit, which is one of Weber's observations. Charisma is fragile.

Most concede that charismatic leadership is difficult to come by yet believe that leadership is possible, even without the "gift." While Kotter views management as the glue, Pfeffer argues that leadership makes an organization coherent. The leader is a symbol who receives praise and blame when things happen to an organization (Pfeffer 1977). Such a function is important internally, because bureaucracies "work" only when "many bureaucrats share the principal's preferences" (Brehm and Gates 1997, 20). If a leader can take those preferences and advocate for them with the public, groups, and politicians, then his or her ability to gain autonomy and scope should be enhanced. If the agency is to work, then, a leader must be skillful at *shifting* the preferences of the principal.[16]

Even if an agency is in a weak institutional position, leaders have at least two potent abilities. The first is to set the agenda for their policy area. Although an agency leader has nowhere near the same exposure that the U.S. president has, comparisons between the two are instructive.[17] Research shows that the president can focus public attention by giving high-profile speeches (generally the State of the Union) (Cohen 1995). His focusing ability also extends to the media and sometimes to Congress. The same work shows that Congress never sets the agenda; this legislature only responded to other actors and events (Edwards and Wood 1999). Correspondingly, agency chiefs can set the agenda through high-profile local speeches and other public work. They are also in a good position to drive the legislative agenda if the analogy between the chief executive and an agency executive holds. Further, presidents with legislative experience may be more successful at setting the agenda and accomplishing goals than those without this experience (Edwards 1989).

With this in mind, I propose that three forms of leadership are available to agency chiefs: public leadership, which is essentially public relations; insider leadership, or one-on-one bargaining; and political leadership, in which the leader is in the thick of drafting bills, logrolling, and deal making.

INTEREST COALITIONS

Cognizant of their limitations, agencies may seek to collaborate with outside organizations that may have access to different clienteles than the agency normally would have. Although political science literature often considers whether and when interest groups "capture" agencies, I argue that agency leaders may find a number of advantages in partnership with such groups—and that the agency may actually lead interest groups.

First, an agency might use interest groups as a sounding board for ideas and to cultivate new policies. These groups are usually the elite groups in education: the teachers' unions, school administrators, superintendents, and school boards. This gives the agency the appearance of legitimacy both in the field and with some legislators. By deliberately consulting many interest groups, an agency can head off the accusation that it is captive to any particular group—not an idle threat, given the sheer size of teachers' unions in many states. Yet the number of interest groups is large and growing, and the arrival of business groups in education has helped break the one-time monopoly of education elites.[18] The agency can also use the groups to arrive at socially beneficial policies, at least as understood by these groups. Frequent interaction between the agency and a set of interest groups may give the agency a good sense of which agencies should be most trusted and listened to.[19]

Second, agencies may seek partnership with groups to ease policy implementation. State bureaucracies are rarely overstaffed, and many times they are forced to fall back on a cursory enforcement of many regulations to use the fewest employees possible. Membership interest groups can step in to aid an agency with its work. For example, one study found that the Occupational Safety and Health Administration (OSHA) cited more violations at sites with a workers' union. The authors made the argument that a union member walk-along helped point out violations (Scholz, Twombly, and Headrick 1991). In education, there exists a large literature studying how reforms "go to scale." The top difficulty is convincing practitioners to change (Elmore 1996; Smith and O'Day 1991; Pfeffer and Salancik 1978). In my work, Wisconsin teachers' unions have helped the DPI publicize how teachers may become "highly qualified" as required by NCLB.

And, third, good relations with interest groups may forestall complaints from legislators and groups about the agency. Some scholarly work shows that legislatures can use interest groups as a cheap oversight mechanism (Balla and Wright 2001). Groups monitor the action of a bureaucracy for slights to a group's membership, real or imagined. If autonomy precedes extensions of scope, then circumventing complaints should be a primary goal of an agency. If the agency is successful in incorporating groups into some part of the agency's decision process, then the groups are less likely to cause the agency trouble later. If not, the group may severely limit an agency's growth of autonomy. For example, Ohio's Department of Education was a strong advocate of charter schools in the 1990s, but the two major teachers' unions were strongly opposed to charter schools. Although the unions did not have much support in the state legislature, their persistent investigations of alleged wrongdoing by school operators weakened the resolve of the ODE (and perhaps helped tighten up still-existing charter schools). One longtime observer told me that the unions' opposition to charter schools helped reinforce a "bunker mentality" at the department. The result is that new charter proposals from ODE are viewed more cautiously by legislators.

Passive factors

Passive factors are those over which the agency has no obvious control. These are endogenous factors. Government employees are prohibited from campaigning for legislators and governors (although agency chiefs may not be), but the electoral environment has major repercussions for an agency's abilities. Congress may have limited ability to set the agenda, but legislators are still more receptive to some policy messages than others (Edwards and Wood 1999). Finally, agencies have little control over lawsuits in which they are a defendant; they have even less control over the outcome of court cases. (These appear in the last box of Figure 2.1.)

ELECTORAL CHANGES

Because an agency sits in a network of political institutions, electoral changes in the governor's office and in the legislature may limit an agency's ability to pursue autonomy. Because these are the legal arbiters of an agency's autonomy, they must be courted and won by agency personnel if an agency's scope is to be expanded.

The governor's office is the star of the state system. If one assumes that governors are parallel to the U.S. president, then they have the same tools at hand. Empirically, they sometimes have more power, especially with the line-item veto. Governors have at least three powers that may limit an agency's autonomy or scope, and how a governor uses these powers will shift significantly when a new governor is elected. First, the governor has a "power to persuade." While governors vary widely in their legal strength, if a governor continually presses on a topic, then the legislature is likely to take up the subject. If the subject appears popular, then legislators may steal it from the governor. On the other hand, if the governor is a supporter of some program in the agency, then her or his bully pulpit can only reinforce the agency's position.[20] Second, governors have appointment powers. For education, the governor appoints some or all of the state board in many states, and sometimes the state chief. Due to the inherent transience of appointments, noted earlier, this strong power may not have as deleterious effect as one might suppose (Dometrius 1999). Nevertheless, a governor with a legal mandate to shape an agency's leadership will constrain whichever actions an agency might take. Third, many governors have significant sway over the budget process, if only because they often have the de facto responsibility for preparing a budget for the legislature to mark up. Legislators tend to defer to the governor in the budget process.[21] Thus when a new governor comes to power, budget priorities change. This circumscribes the limits of an agency's push for autonomy.[22]

Turnover in the legislature may deprive an agency of friends or enemies. While state agency personnel are insulated from public opinion by civil service protections and public ignorance about agency activities, legislators are tuned to their constituents. If the public has a clear, pressing concern about some issue within the agency's domain, then legislators are more likely to write detailed legislation (Ringquist, Worsham, and Eisner 2003). Further, some legislators specialize in an agency's policy area. If the agency has a strong political presence, then legislators may be unable to foray into uncharted education territory.

Electoral changes may result in divided government—divided both between the legislature and governor, but perhaps also between the governor, legislature, and the agency if it is headed by an elected chief. The effect of divided government on legislative output is mixed, although it appears that *major* legislation has a better chance of passing under unified government.[23] Others have found that total state budgets tend toward party budget targets—with Democrats desiring a higher state budget and Republicans a lower one—and that unified government (after a period of divided government) prompts a rapid change in the state budget toward that overall target.[24]

State agencies with independently elected heads are subject to an additional layer of complexity because the agency may have a chief identified with a party different than the governor or legislative majorities. This creates five possibilities for divided government.[25] An agency may become identified with a partisan agenda in two ways: First, if the agency chief has a history as a partisan, then the agency is more likely to be identified as such. In Wisconsin's case, Herbert Grover and Tommy Thompson served in the legislature together but on opposite sides of the aisle before they became state superintendent and governor, respectively. Second, if the interest groups that the agency consults are commonly identified with one party or another, then the agency will likely be similarly identified. For education, teachers' associations have become identified with the Democratic Party because of their turn toward unionism in the 1960s and 1970s (West 1980). Obviously, if a state's agency chief is elected as a partisan, then the agency will be assumed to follow behind.

If the findings for state budgets hold for specific policy areas, then it should be more difficult for state agencies to gain responsibilities when they are on the opposite side of the aisle from the other players. A number of scholars have found that the governor's preferences are of prime importance, so an agency aligned against the governor should have the least success in gaining new responsibilities through the budget process.[26]

The agency's autonomous action might also be subject to more scrutiny under divided government, especially if the legislature is unified against the agency and governor. Much of this attention likely will come through the budget process. On the other hand, if the agency is not strongly identified with a party or if the legislature is split, then an agency's autonomy should be enhanced because its formal principals will not be able to agree on an acceptable level of agency output. This should lead to the incorporation of autonomous action into the agency's scope. Yet because divided government limits significant legislation, the level of agency responsibilities should remain stable.[27]

LEGISLATIVE SALIENCE

If legislative changes affect prospects for autonomy, then the salience of the issue must also change. As with the governor, if legislators in the right places have an abiding interest in responsibilities governed by an agency, then the agency may have more difficulty pursuing acting autonomously. Legislators may be "friends of education," but they will still have institutional interests in mind and are unlikely to abdicate much to agencies. Werner Rodgers, former Georgia state superintendent, told me that he wanted to keep the chairs of the Georgia House and Senate education committees—both longtime members—within sight. "Whenever they went out of state, they came back with a new idea—I didn't want them to go without me. I wanted to be in the middle of reforms. Who knows what they'd come back with for me to do."

Legislative salience may be defined as the interest of legislators in some policy area. Usually this interest is driven by constituent pressure or a high level of public disagreement (Bawn 1997). Others show that legislators will be highly motivated to intervene in issues that resonate strongly with the public, on which the public has clear preferences, and is not complex.[28] Although there is no opinion barometer for state legislators, a useful proxy for salience is legislative experience on education-related committees. If, as the literature often asserts, agencies are the experts and the legislature must tease out information, then expert lawmakers would serve as truth serum for bureaucrats. The legislators would know the right questions to ask and would know with whom to verify the information. Even absent an informational asymmetry, longer-serving legislators should have firmer opinions about the appropriate role and budget for an agency. In either case, an agency's autonomy should be straitened as legislators on a committee become more expert.

The importance of legislative salience to an agency's scope has been compounded by the dramatic increase in legislative professionalism over the last thirty years of the twentieth century. Particularly between the Great Depression and the 1960s, many saw state government as backwaters—so much so that the authors of the first federal Elementary and Secondary Education Act in 1965 felt compelled to provide funding through Title V to increase the capacity of state education agencies. The authors assumed that state governments would have few resources and little inclination to support state-level oversight of education (Murphy 1976, 1974; Halperin 1975).

A dramatic shift occurred between 1970 and 1990. State legislators over this time period generally became better paid, had more staff available to them, and had more time to spend in the legislature (Brace and Ward 1999; Mooney 1994). Although there is debate whether state legislatures are actually "professionalized" as compared with the U.S. Congress, there is no doubt that legislatures are far better equipped to handle day-to-day decision making than they were in the 1960s (Squire 1997; Fiorina 1997; Polsby 1968). In terms of political autonomy, this bodes ill for agencies: more professional legislators are able to make specific policy better. Further, the legislature is able to take on some responsibilities once reserved to agencies (such as commissioning independent policy studies).

LEGAL ACTIONS

A third exogenous contributor to agency scope is court action. Although agencies may appear as parties to a case as state education agencies often are for school finance cases, they have little control over the outcome of cases. The outcome can either ratify their autonomy or check it.

Unlike the legislature, the governor, or interest groups, the courts have influence only when outside parties ask them to, although agencies, no doubt, work hard to avoid legal pitfalls. In education, the two best-known examples are desegregation cases, in which courts have taken direct control of school districts, and school finance cases, which have spawned an entire academic discipline. In both examples court involvement is particularistic and spotty. In the Ohio school finance case that I recount in chapter 5, the court repeatedly refused to specify what a constitutional formula looked like, despite calling the existing formula unconstitutional. This was an open invitation to exercise agency autonomy once the court moved on to other cases.

Although legal actions may reshape an agency's scope (for example, by requiring that an agency track district racial composition, or by granting an agency a free hand to hire and fire teachers in financially strapped districts), there is no way to know whether a court will legitimate or proscribe an agency's autonomous action ahead of time. One might postulate that an agency that is frequently in court will have less opportunity to act with autonomy and thus have a narrower scope, but the number of high-profile cases is sufficiently low to make testing this hypothesis impossible in the short time frame I cover here. I have included this factor for the sake of completeness.[29]

Conclusion

I expect that both autonomy—the independent exercise of choice—and scope—the set of tasks given to an agency to fulfill—will enable an agency and its leaders to shape the preferences of its political principals. For education, this means that governors and legislators may be receptive to and even supportive of ideas from the department about student testing, teacher certification, and school finance.

In general, an agency can increase its autonomy in two ways—by selectively emphasizing mandates, a backdoor approach, or by persuading its principal that its policy success hinges on an increase in its freedom of action, a front-door approach. A backdoor approach may work for a while, but when an agency's actions attract attention, it is unlikely that the agency will be able to continue. The front-door approach may be more difficult politically, but the long-term benefit is a stable, increased scope.

I would expect that a rise in one stream of autonomy would appear at the same time as a rise in another stream. Nevertheless, a number of caveats are in order. First, particular circumstances may slow or stop the growth of one of the streams of autonomy. For example, tight budget times may prevent more money from flowing into an agency, however persuasive the agency chief is. Second, tight state budgets do not necessarily constrain the ability of a legislature to legitimate the technical autonomy of an agency. Wisconsin State Superintendent Grover successfully argued for a significant restructuring of the mid-level educational service-provision structure during the state's tightest budget biennium during the twenty years I studied. Third, note that the effectiveness of an agency's argument is partly conditioned on the "state mood" for state-level education. In the 1980s and 1990s, the tides of reform were very high across the country, allowing education agencies to incorporate the manifest enthusiasm for change in their appeals for autonomy and scope. Finally, no agency is able to control outcomes. In education, school district administrators, principals, and even teachers can change the best-intentioned program in unexpected ways, and many influences far beyond the control of any government official weigh on students from birth.

The next chapter presents the empirical expectations for each element that will guide the remainder of the project.

3

Expectations for Scope-Seeking Agencies

This chapter outlines my expectations regarding the factors that are discussed in the chapters that follow. I begin with the most basic, institutional factors, and then I move to active and passive factors.

Institutional Factors

The two major institutional factors that affect agency autonomy are the selection mechanism for the state board and the state superintendent (sometimes called the "commissioner of education," but I will refer to the top education spot as either the "state superintendent" or "state chief"). While the power to choose the superintendent and state board is the bluntest mechanism for influencing autonomy, who has the appointment (or nonappointment) power for these top posts is essential to both the policy direction of the agency and the quality of its leadership.

Of the many arrangements in educational governance, I expect that the "mediated" form of appointment will produce the best odds for the agency. The mediated form is the selection process in which the state board chooses the superintendent (these are found in the twenty-six states; see Table 1.1 in chapter 1). Why? Even if the board is appointed by the governor, the state chief is one step removed from the governor's whims and is therefore difficult to replace. Further, board members are not facsimiles of the governor. As U.S. Supreme Court watchers know, ideological commitments of justices on that bench are notoriously difficult to gauge in advance. Presidents Dwight D. Eisenhower and George H. W. Bush were distinctly surprised at the ideological leanings that Earl Warren and David Souter developed after they had been nominated and confirmed. Although state board members are usually easier to remove than Supreme Court justices, the principle is the same. Further, chiefs who are isolated electorally have the advantage of not needing to spend time or resources shoring up a political base.[1] As such, I expect that agency chiefs who are insulated from both electoral politics and gubernatorial discretion will be the most successful in pursuing agency autonomy and scope.

A second expectation follows from the previous one. The ability of the chief to command more scope will depend on how much credit the governor wants. An "education governor" might be very hesitant to share the limelight and perhaps attempt to run education through his or her office instead of the education agency. One whose interests lie elsewhere will probably leave the agency chief with a freer hand. Therefore,

> agency chiefs who are subject to appointment by the governor are least likely to enjoy autonomy, although their scope will depend on the governor's interest.

Chiefs who are directly elected have some advantages. They are able to claim an independent base of power from other elected officials, especially the governor, and thus they are not accountable to them. This puts the agency in a good position to be operated autonomously. Nevertheless, the agency chief will have to deal with another executive, leading to clashes over the policy direction of the agency. Because both executives will have to filter their policy goals through the legislature, it is reasonable to assume that the governor will carry more clout than the independent executive of a single agency. Because the agency chief has an excellent platform from which to argue that the "voters have spoken," the governor will likely work to limit the agency's scope to preserve her or his own prerogative in education. I expect that

> agencies whose chiefs are independently elected will enjoy autonomy, but inter-branch politics will constrain the agencies' scope.

These expectations are addressed in chapters 4 and 7 on each state's institutional history and on the role of the governor, respectively.

Endogenous Factors

The two endogenous factors I analyze here are the quality of agency leadership and how well an agency manages the relevant interest groups.

Agency Leadership

Leadership is persuasion—convincing subordinates to do the right work at the right time and shaping others' perspectives of the organization. Empirically, I encountered three distinct leadership strategies that state superintendents adopted to further their agency's cause—public leadership, insider leadership, and political leadership.

The first form, public leadership, is essentially public relations. Because many governmental agencies may have few or no natural supporters in legislative or executive branches, leaders hit the trail to build broad public support. Building public support this way can short-circuit the normal political process and allow an agency to pressure legislators and the governor—through the public—on the agency's own terms. Not only will this enhance the agency's autonomy (because the public expects the agency to be able to make a difference) but also its scope (because the leader has made an argument to the public about what his or her agency should do). This leadership strategy might be especially effective when the state superintendent is elected. Therefore, I expect that

> public leadership will enhance both the autonomy and scope of an agency by using the public at large to generate political pressure on other branches of government.

Second, a leader might use "insider" leadership by seeking to build support one person at a time. Unlike either public or political leadership strategies, insider leadership does not use political appeals but instead personal appeals based on perceived trustworthiness (such as, "In my twenty-year experience as a school administrator, such-and-such worked, so we should do it state-wide"). While this strategy might be effective for gaining autonomy at the fringes, inside leaders will not be effective at building the worldview of legislators and governors for trusting the agency with an expansion of autonomy. Instead, the insider approach may be effective in solidifying the existing scope or increasing it at the margin because the leader may directly bargain with political principals. If the agency is not politically popular, then insider leadership may be the only option available to an agency chief. Then the strategy may serve only to staunch losses of the scope. Further, if the people with whom the leader works are turned out of office or retire, then long-term benefits to the agency are likely to be lost. An insider strategy is highly contingent on the configuration of institutional and political variables. Thus inside leadership will fail to generate autonomy for an agency because it is highly dependent on frequent, individual bargains, although it may build or consolidate scope.

Third, agency leaders may engage in political leadership and use democratic politics to logroll, to lobby legislators, and to feed information to governors. Unlike either public or insider leadership, political leadership explicitly emphasizes partisan and electoral ties (e.g., "I'll make you the best education governor this state has ever had," or "The Democratic leadership supports me on this issue, so you need to too"). This strategy for leadership may be extremely successful as long as the political configuration is stable, or it may fail spectacularly. Political leadership will work best for securing a new scope for the agency, because a leader will be able to bargain for particular programs and build legislative coalitions for them. Agency scope gained in this way may linger because of the difficulty of changing the status quo after these are established. The effect on autonomy will be incremental at best and based on the success of the chief in gaining scope. The expectation is as follows:

> Political leadership will be most effective in securing increased scope for an agency when the agency has significant legislative or gubernatorial support. It will be less successful in building autonomy, because the leader's success is explicitly contingent on the political process.

Interest Group Environment

The second endogenous factor generating scope from autonomy is how well an agency can organize interest groups. In each state studied here, the state superintendent was deliberate in using these interest groups as a sounding board for new ideas. Corralling interest groups has become more difficult as a plethora of think tanks and business organizations has encroached on the territory of traditional educational elites in the last twenty years. While traditional groups may suggest ways to reduce paperwork or improve service delivery, the business community has been particularly vociferous in promoting student achievement tests and curriculum standards. I expect that how an agency chooses to interact with interest groups will influence its autonomy:

> An agency that pursues fewer interest group partners will have greater autonomy because it has fewer outside groups

to manage. It will be able to build a greater scope because it does not rely on outside groups to accomplish tasks.

On one level, this expectation is obvious: the fewer partners an agency has to keep happy, the fewer compromises the agency will have to make to keep each of those interests on board. The fewer interest groups the agency works with will also tend to increase the width of scope for the agency, because the agency should be able to demonstrate independence from strong interest groups. If the agency is the source through which education policy is made, then it is less likely that the legislature and others will try to pursue policy through interest groups. That scope will fall to the agency, as shown in chapter 5.

Exogenous Factors

Exogenous influences on agency autonomy and scope are those things that the agency has little control over. Here I consider both the agency's relationship with the governor and its interaction with the legislature.

Gubernatorial Turnover and Interest

At one time, governors were not very active in education in general. A mid-level DPI bureaucrat in Wisconsin told me, "In the '70s, if we could get the governor to mention the word 'education' in his state-of-the-state we were exhilarated." Now, of course, governors use the word all the time. Particularly in the late 1980s, state governors were instrumental in shaping and redirecting state educational policy toward more standards for student learning. Arkansas Governor Bill Clinton first gained national prominence at the "Education Summit" in 1990; many other governors (Lamar Alexander, Tennessee; George W. Bush, Texas; Roy Romer, Colorado) became education governors of one sort or another in the 1990s.[2] Although many of the education observers with whom I spoke were skeptical of their governors' true interest in education, the governors in Ohio, Georgia, and Wisconsin devoted a great deal of staff time to the subject. As such, my expectation, vetted in chapter 7, is as follows:

> The effect of gubernatorial turnover on an agency will be contingent upon the governor's interest in education relative to other activities of the administration.

Legislative Salience

State legislatures have become increasingly well endowed with staff, financial resources, and time in which to enact laws (Fiorina 1994). These increasing resources for legislators have not eliminated the traditional advantage of state agencies: information. Many states have created legislative reference bureaus. Although these services have weakened some of the informational gatekeeping that agencies once did, staffers still have to ferret out information from state agency databases. Thus even though the information asymmetry between agencies and legislators appears to be declining, state agencies can still use their power over information to retain technical autonomy (they still employ the specialists), to gain political autonomy (by helping interpret information for the legislature), and probably to maintain some fiscal autonomy to keep up their own data operations.[3]

Nevertheless, it is difficult to predict the effect of legislative salience on agency autonomy because of the feedback effect, noted in chapter 2. If legislative salience is low, then the agency's scope will be stagnant. It will have scope only from historical accretion. Its autonomy will be limited, because the legislature has not seen fit to give the agency much to do (although oversight will likely be low as well). On the other hand, if legislative salience is high, then legislators may wish to designate exactly what and how an agency works, thereby setting the scope for some policy area, resulting in narrow scope and limited autonomy.

In the short term, that is most likely: high salience will yield more legislation and more prescription and thus restricted autonomy.

In the long term, however, I argue that high legislative salience is more likely to result in an agency with broader scope and more autonomy. The reason for this is straightforward. Legislators devote limited time to any one topic, so even if they spell out work for an agency to do, that agency will retain that scope for a long time after interest in the policy has faded in the legislature and particular legislators have left. When legislative salience becomes high again, the agency will be able to enter the policy debate on its own behalf and to capitalize on its previously existing scope.[4]

The expectation for legislative salience is thus:

> As the salience of state-level education increases, the more likely it is that legislators will seek to reduce the autonomy of the state education agency in the short term.

Chapter 8 explores this short-term expectation using the number of bills introduced, the bill time to report from committee, and bill passage.

Effects of Autonomy and Salience

The policy outputs of autonomy and salience are potentially manifold. I emphasize the appearance of these through examples in teacher standards and licensure, school finance, and state standards and accountability, but I test one possible outcome directly in chapter 9: the state budget.

How close can agencies come to accurately reading the political environment? The answer to this question has a direct bearing on how well the agency can shape the preferences of its political principals. If agency budget requests are consistently very different than actual appropriations, then this indicates that the agency has little ability to act autonomously in fiscal matters. Legislators are not heeding the agency's requests for increases in scope. If an agency's appropriations come close to its requests, however, then the agency is in good stead to have its autonomous actions ratified by other political actors. I summarize this argument as follows:

> The difference between agency requests and actual appropria-
> tions will be smaller for more fiscally autonomous agencies
> and greater for less fiscally autonomous agencies.

The next chapter presents the historical background and unique strengths that each state department of education sought to use in the 1980s and 1990s.

Part 2

Historical Roots of State Involvement

I was the first elected state superintendent in over 60 years . . . and then I lost to a total unknown. It took everyone by surprise.

—Werner Rodgers, former state superintendent of Georgia

Georgia Superintendent Werner Rogers, of the epigraph, had good reason to be surprised: no election after 1933 was seriously contested. Elections merely ratified appointments that governors had made because a previous superintendent had died or resigned. Then, in 1994, Rogers lost to a Republican who was practically unknown, even in her own party.

Georgia's generally long-tenured superintendents who held their jobs through uncontested elections helped create a state department of education that, by 1994, had a broad scope of responsibility with wide latitude for autonomous action. The state departments of education in Ohio and Wisconsin were each resource-poor, responsibility-poor, and respect-poor throughout the nineteenth century and into the early twentieth century. Their narrow scope compounded the inability of superintendents to command technical, political, or even fiscal autonomy for themselves. Georgia's department was in the same position at the end of the 1800s, but the stable leadership succession helped build its position at the end of the twentieth century.

The history of American education has been told in many other places, but historians inevitably recount the story through the classroom (for examples, see Tyack and Cuban 1995; Ravitch 1974, 1983, 2000; Cremin 1980; Tyack 1974; and Bailyn 1960). State-level constitutions, departments of education, and offices of the superintendent were far away from classroom practice and, in some respects, still are. Nevertheless, state-level support for education has proven important to American education, and as legislators and others adopted that view, state education departments gained in stature.

In this chapter, I show how state departments were able to start the scope-autonomy cycle only when state superintendents and their legislative allies were able to argue that education was necessary for economic development. As corollaries, they argued that an unequal distribution of educational resources hampered economic development, and, later, that low educational expectations also hampered development. These arguments took many years of repetition before they became accepted by legislators, and they often become salient only after severe economic, political, or educational troubles were presented to political leaders.

To address these, this chapter is divided into two parts. First I present an overview of the roots of general state support at statehood in Georgia, Ohio, and Wisconsin. Then I sketch the development of each state education department from statehood to 1980. Developments after 1980 are covered in later chapters.

The Roots of State Involvement

Theorist Alexander Gerschenkron argued that each successive wave of international industrialization was only successful to the extent that the country could build on the technology that had been forged by a previous industrial pioneer. It would be fruitless for Prussia in 1871 to try to duplicate the steps of England's industrialization of the 1820s and 1830s, or Russia in 1917 to copy Prussia's. Although Gerschenkron was building a case for industrial development, a similar case can be made for the development of state educational bureaucracies (Gerschenkron 1962).

It comes as no surprise to students of American political development that early territorial legislatures blatantly plagiarized their most-recently settled neighbors to the east in the nineteenth century.[1] State education codes were no exception. Drafters of Georgia's education codes of the 1840s knew of Ohio's experiences and of Wisconsin's early steps toward a new education code, due in part to multistate educational associations. Wisconsin's constitutional framers explicitly sought to prevent the graft and corruption that they knew surrounded the sale of Ohio's Section 16 school lands. Legislators and common-school boosters all knew of Massachusetts' common school model.

Each state's education code has similarities—at the most basic level, by requiring localities to have some sort of school for a few months a year (usually two or three). Early politicians often sought to impose these borrowed education codes on political, economic, and ethnic cultures regardless of their differing beliefs about the role of education and whose responsibility education was. Wisconsin had large enclaves of immigrants that had little to do with the state's political system until late in the nineteenth century. Georgia had European settlers decades before American independence and a rapidly growing African population. Ohio in the early nineteenth century was a booming state with rich agriculture and manufacturing and mining industries that neither Georgia nor Wisconsin could match.

In all three cases, education reformers had an uphill battle to convince legislators that there should be a state role *and* that it should be expansive. Would-be educators in each state faced three challenges. First they had to convince legislators that education was actually a state matter. Particularly in Georgia, private tutoring was the received wisdom, and, indeed, for Georgia's planter class, this remained the norm for well over 100 years after American independence. For both Ohio and Wisconsin, territorial and then state legislators—almost exclusively from somewhere else, usually from Pennsylvania, New York, or New England—often had been educated in private academies, which sometimes had state funding and sometimes not. All of them had to confront the ethos that education was a family or community responsibility rather than the state's.

Second, education boosters had to convince legislators that education was a state responsibility at least on par with economic development. This meant that the state would have to provide incentives to recruit teachers and incentives for localities to maintain a standard, basic education that would attract, or at least not repel, economic investment.

Third, educators had to convince the legislators that local funding inequalities were a detriment to education. Usually reformers argued that the state should increase funding over and above what localities could or would raise. To the degree that policy makers accepted these arguments, state-led education became more explicit and less symbolic. State superintendents were often evangelists for education, and, later, state departments became their pulpits.

The Early Backdrop

Schools were an afterthought for the original legislators in these three states. Many European settlers came to the West looking for land, economic opportunity, or simply escape from the East through the early 1800s. Aside from the political elite, few had formal schooling of their own. Nevertheless, after the first wave of settlement, territorial and colonial legislatures sought to create a society comparable to the one they had left back East.

Georgia

Georgia is the oldest of these three states, and it was separated by distance and culture from New England and even from Thomas Jefferson's

Virginia. Unlike Wisconsin's or Ohio's school system, Georgia's schools modeled England rather than New England. There were no general state-supported or locally supported schools until Reconstruction.[2]

Early Georgia schools were largely for charity. Although a few German parish schools existed in and around Ebenezer in the 1730s, these quickly disappeared due to lack of support from a transient German population. The trustees of Georgia (in Britain) provided the first sustained support beginning in 1742. They allocated funds exclusively for "poor schools." Parents were leery of being labeled "poor," and the colony's administrators proved unable to compel attendance. In an attempt to remove the stigma from the schools, the trustees declared that schools would be available to "all the children of the colony," regardless of their income (Orr 1950, 9). This still had little effect. Some difficulty probably stemmed from the lack of regular schoolmasters in any part of Georgia until the 1750s. After that, the Crown provided funds for two.

After statehood in 1776, Georgia's legislature provided support for a number of academies in the form of land taken from the Creek and, later, Cherokee Indians and from British Tories. Most other expenses were supported through the monetary subscriptions of parents. Georgia maintained this system until the Civil War, and state support of private schools helped prevent the development of a New England "common school" ethos. Combined with de jure segregation after Reconstruction, Georgia never had strong proponents of local control and the "little red schoolhouse." (Only when Georgia was flirting with abolishing its public school system in the 1950s to avoid desegregation did "local control" become a rallying cry. Even then, it was the lingo of state officials opposed to privatizing schools, rather than local districts.)

Instead, education was the domain of counties. Georgia's colonial trustees had created a "county-unit" system of government to accommodate the sparse population. County officials became so strong by the 1830s that a proposal for a district school system funded by a property tax was scrapped primarily because it would subdivide counties—diluting county-level power. This county-unit system persisted throughout the twentieth century, although it grew substantially weaker after U.S. Supreme Court-ordered political redistricting and desegregation orders in mid-century. The effect of the county-unit system was to concentrate most political power into the hands of rural elites at the expense of urban residents and the poor throughout the state (O'Brien 1999, 3).

Curiously, teachers' associations, state superintendents, and other education reformers in Wisconsin and Ohio fought to create county systems like Georgia's. County-level boards were seen as a way to encourage the consolidation of small districts—tiny, really, because at the time of consolidation, in the mid-twentieth century, more than a handful of districts had fewer than twenty-five children. In Georgia, where county systems were created to solve that problem in the colonial era, county systems came to be seen as obstinate roadblocks to change and state-level political autonomy—first by Reconstruction governments in the 1870s, then by the U.S. Supreme Court in the 1950s, and finally by the state department of education and the governor in the 1980s. The county system was a major impetus for the strong state oversight that exists in Georgia now.

Ohio

Formally, public education began early in the Northwest Territories. The Northwest Ordinance of 1787 was arguably the most direct federal intervention in state educational policy making until the Elementary and Secondary Education Act in 1965. The ordinance set aside Section 16 (or one square mile of each thirty-six square-mile township) in what would become Ohio, Indiana, Illinois, Michigan, Wisconsin, and part of Minnesota for the support of schools.[3] The sale or lease of the land was supposed to raise money for schools. Northwest state education proponents thus had an early opportunity for fiscal autonomy. In fact, most early common-school boosters made explicit calls for a state superintendent to oversee the sale of these lands.[4]

Ohio legislators recognized that the federal land grants for education were a valuable revenue stream. Ohio was still sparsely populated, and not a few legislators saw gold in land speculation. Soon after statehood, the state legislature determined to lease the land for ninety-nine years at low, fixed rates. Even with these favorable land deals, lessors simply cleared the land for its timber, abandoned the plots, and defaulted on their leases—depriving the state of revenue—and left it to squatters who paid nothing. Although some legislators were on the take, many legislators came to believe that leasing the land was cumbersome and inefficient. In 1828, Ohio sold all of its Section 16 land for $4 million, mostly to speculators (Shreve 1989, 7).

The history of poor management of Ohio's sixteenth sections prompted two legislators to agitate for the sustained support of public schools. Following their advice in 1821, the Ohio General Assembly created school districts as a level of government beneath townships and allowed townships to tax property if they wished. This system did not generate the expected revenue, because most townships were hesitant to impose taxes, and the committee that the legislature had appointed to study the issue quarreled with township officials over who had the right to dispose of school lands. In 1825, the legislature made the taxes mandatory for districts (Ray 1943, 6; Shreve 1989, 8).

Ohio's first constitution used the Northwest Ordinance as its template, so it has always had a strong commitment to "encourage" education, as the ordinance stated. Yet after disposing of the school lands, the state legislature had more interest in the development of canals than in tax-supported education. Families were left to organize their own schooling, if any. The General Assembly wrote this local tradition into statute in the 1840s which later became a roadblock to state control. The legislature did try an experiment with a state superintendent in 1837, but legislators felt that his work was so little that it abolished his post and gave his responsibilities to the secretary of state in 1841. There would be no formal state advocate for the support or control of education for several decades.

Wisconsin

Although Wisconsin was also a part of the Northwest Territory, its education history begins with the French, who were in the area beginning in 1634.[5] French missionaries conducted some ad hoc schools throughout the next century and a half. The first sustained school for which there are records met at Green Bay, a city of 550, in 1817. As with Georgia, most early schools in Wisconsin were quasi-private. Green Bay schools were run out of the garrison or in connection with the Episcopal and Catholic churches. Although statutes in the Michigan Territory, of which Green Bay was part, required that property tax support schools, these were ignored, and both the nonsectarian and the church-run schools were supported by subscription. This left the schoolmaster to drum up students:

> Gentlemen—as I have mentiond to you boath, that I inted to keep school being the onley means for a Liveleyhood. I shall concider it a great Obligation if you will favour me in obtaining Scholars, which I promise to do & act faithfully my duty as a school Master toward them &c. (Jorgenson 1956, 9, original spelling)

These early schools were usually in French, or in both French and English. By the 1830s, however, the fur trading industry that was the basis of the French-speaking economy had substantially declined. A separate, New-England-influenced movement for schools appeared in the southeastern part of the territory. Wisconsin's settlers in the 1830s and 1840s were overwhelmingly from New England and New York, accounting for 88,000 of the territory's 135,000 citizens in 1850.

When Congress severed the Wisconsin Territory from Michigan in 1836, the territorial legislature adopted Michigan's school law verbatim. Towns (called townships in other states) were responsible for licensing teachers; financing for teachers and school buildings was the responsibility of districts (which had to contain at least ten families). The money came from a property tax that was proportionate to the value of the property and the number of children in the family (the rate tax), but a family could pay in kind or through labor instead of in cash (Jorgenson 1956, 17).[6]

By 1840, many town residents were unhappy with the Michigan school legislation—particularly the rate tax—and they petitioned the territorial legislature for a new law. In the same year, the legislature responded with a school act that required school funding to come from a county-wide property tax of two-and-a-half mills. It also did away with the child adjustment to property tax and the in-kind provisions. Further, in a radical departure, the law required education to run on a county level—anathema to the large majority of settlers from the Northeast who favored township-based government and taxes. In 1841, the legislature relented and returned taxing and decision-making power to the towns. Perhaps in spite, the legislature imposed a $200 limit on total district taxes for school buildings and a limit of zero for support of teachers unless three fourths of district voters approved of more (up to twenty mills).

Despite these limits, the legislature spent a significant amount of time through 1848 making exceptions to the tax limit as school districts clamored for the authority to raise more revenue. In fact, one historian notes, "Tax-supported schools were not created by territorial legislation; it would be much nearer to the truth to say that they developed in spite of such legislation." Indeed, almost three quarters of school funding in 1847 (some $8,000 total, or about $145,000 in 2006 dollars) came from local taxes (Jorgenson 1956, 37, 24, 31).[7]

The legislature shied away from school politics after the fight over county school systems. The new state legislature formalized district systems in the education code of 1849. With this code, the state, and the superintendent, created by the 1848 state constitution, surrendered most control over schools and their subject matter. In 1863, the state superintendent complained that each district had become "a separate independent republic, accountable to no higher authority, and dependent upon none, except in the matter of the examination of teachers and the annual receipt and expenditure of a small amount of money" (quoted in Jorgenson 1956, 98). In later years, unlike either Ohio's or Georgia's, Wisconsin's Department of Public Instruction was extremely hesitant to challenge local power. Rather, state superintendents often sought to prevent the DPI from gaining power at the expense of local autonomy. Instead, actions by outside groups (notably the state university and the teachers' lobby) forced the DPI to either take on more responsibility or die.

Departments of Education

In the nineteenth century, with the partial exception of Georgia, all three states had little political capital with which to build an autonomous bureaucracy with wide scope. Nevertheless, they were able to harness current events and their political history to gain scope, if not autonomy, in the latter part of that century. This section considers the changes to the formal organization of state education agencies.

All three of the states covered here had strong teacher-group support for a department, and most state superintendents berated the legislature for not providing more funds and personnel to the department. Local resistance and lack of resources often kept the state superintendent from effectively executing state laws. Still, even in the early period when state "departments" consisted of the state superintendent and sometimes a clerk, legislators turned to the department for its technical expertise and frequently made modifications to law based on its recommendations. As education became an economic issue in the first half of the twentieth century, legislatures expanded departments so that they could provide better oversight of districts, better support for school funding, and better information to the legislature. Each component is evidence of nascent technical autonomy and increasing scope.

Departments also became useful vehicles for later policy goals, whether equality or excellence. When legislators and governors began to seek "excellence" in education—as they did sporadically throughout the century and sustainedly by the end of the century—departments of education were well prepared to propagate standards and assistance to districts. In fact, it was the departments themselves that sought to equalize state education and urged legislators and others to address educational excellence and financial equality.

Georgia

Despite the long existence of formal education in Georgia, there was no early state-level interest in education aside from the maintenance of a school fund by the legislature. In 1851, a statewide education conference at Marietta suggested a state bureau of education and a state superintendent, but according to the gloss of one historian, it was tabled by a "determined stand . . . against the conservative idea that education should descend gradually from the higher institutions to the masses of the people" (Orr 1950, 159). The same group again recommended a state superintendent appointed by the governor in 1859. The recommendation was ignored.

Reconstructionist suspicion of local sympathies after the Civil War led to both a state department of education and a state superintendent. This arrangement laid the groundwork for a politically autonomous department later on—the state was seen to be the appropriate locus for education, not the school. Although the Reconstruction Constitutional Convention recommended a state board of education accountable to the legislature, called the Board of Regents, and a state superintendent in 1868, bargaining eliminated the board and created a post for a governor-appointed state commissioner. Two years later, the legislature created a state board of education, and a state superintendent, as well as county boards of education and separate boards to license teachers. The Georgia Teachers' Association made many of these recommendations (Orr 1950, 196).

Early superintendents fought for state teacher certification and an increased state school fund—a difficult proposition, given the economic malaise that clung stubbornly to Georgia from the Civil War through the 1940s. As the legislature recognized that Georgia's school system might help stave off population losses and business flight, superintendents slowly got their wishes.

In 1911, in tandem with major educational changes in other states, the state legislature fulfilled some of the earlier state superintendents' pleas and the proposals of the Georgia Teachers' Association. New legislation created a governor-appointed board and an elected state superintendent, granting the department an important degree of political autonomy. This board was responsible for allocating state money to school districts, for selecting textbooks, and for setting state course standards (Georgia Department of Education 1970, 13). The board also conducted teacher institutes throughout the state (Orr 1950, 270). To compensate the department for its widening scope, the legislature added three supervisors to help staff teacher training institutes (Cox 1967, 108). The following year, the "Stovall" constitutional amendment made state support of high schools constitutional, although not required (LaMorte and Meadows 1978, 8). The addition of high schools allowed the department to widen its scope and write rules without disturbing long-existing practices—there were none to disturb. Unlike in Ohio (as described later), Georgia's department emerged from the 1910s with both wider scope *and* greater autonomy.

Between the 1890s and the 1940s, Georgia elites watched with dismay as African American residents fled to the North. Although never willing to rectify social and legal barriers, they knew that blacks were Georgia's primary laborers; without them, Georgian industry would come to a halt. State superintendents took little exception to the separate-but-equal doctrine, but the department was able to use the racial separation to force improvements in local schooling for blacks. In 1911, State Superintendent Brittain created a Division of Negro Education, which persisted into the 1960s. It was headed by whites and was charged by the superintendent to "stimulate local interest" in school buildings, to improve elementary instruction with private monies, to improve one-teacher schools, and to emphasize industrial training and sanitation (Orr 1950, 323). Even though it was a gross duplication of effort, the division funneled money into black schools over the strenuous objections of county boards of education. By the 1950s, African American students had almost the same amount spent on them, per pupil, as white students, which was a significant accomplishment given strong local discrimination (O'Brien 1999, 18).

As desegregation took hold through the 1960s and 1970s, state politicians became more interested in education as a political issue. The department of education was a beneficiary of this attention, and in 1972 it emerged unscathed from Governor Jimmy Carter's overhaul of Georgia's government. The department was able to argue, beginning in the 1970s, that academic standards were the next step in state influence.

The difference in accountability between the board and the state superintendent had the potential to cause significant administration problems, and it did, twice. Georgia voters have elected only three state superintendents to a first term between Reconstruction and this writing: Mauney D. Collins, who served from 1933 to 1958; Linda C. Schrenko, who held the office from 1994 to 2002; and Kathy Cox, whom voters selected in 2002.[8] The sitting governor appointed the rest to fill the previous superintendent's term on resignation or death. Two of the three proved to be staunchly independent. Collins was a strenuous opponent of the governor's and legislature's attempts to close the public school system in favor of a state-supported private system in the 1950s, and Schrenko was a lightning rod for criticism from the board—so much so that the governor had to ask the entire board to resign (Ramage 1997).[9]

Ohio

From statehood until 1912, Ohio had an on-again, off-again relationship with state educational authority. Because local districts were responsible for funding education—to the tune of 96 percent in the 1930s—the legislature did not see much point in investing in a state-level superintendent.

An advocacy group organized in 1829, the Western Literary Institute and College of Professional Teachers, agitated for a state superintendent in Ohio, commissioning a study in 1835 to investigate "the expediency of employing superintending agents for the common schools" and a state education department (Ray 1943, 10). Knowing the Ohio legislature's weaknesses, the association argued that a superintendent could protect the ever-controversial school lands fund. Presciently, the institute argued that the superintendent should be nonpolitical and independent from the legislature and governor, foreshadowing the arguments in the 1950s around Ohio's proposed state board. The post was so important that "its duties can no more wisely be super-added to those of a Secretary of State, or any other officer, than those of the Mayor of London can be attached to the Premier of England" (quoted in Ray 1943, 17).[10] Even this early on, advocates for state-level education were promoting political autonomy.

The legislature indulged the institute, briefly. Samuel Lewis began his three-year term as Ohio's first state superintendent in 1837. Unfortunately for him, the legislature was preoccupied with economic development and speculation rather than education. Despite the legislature's creation of a "permanent" post, it abolished Lewis's office after his term expired. Nevertheless, Lewis was an effective advocate of teacher testing and increased district reporting. Had he been a better advocate for himself, he would have had a "department" with a scope remotely resembling that of the Ohio Department of Education in 1980. The legislature took both of Lewis's suggestions but gave these responsibilities to local and county boards. Teachers would be examined in reading, writing, and arithmetic before they were allowed to teach (Ray 1943, 70).

A post for an elected State Commissioner of Common Schools was recreated in 1853 by a law that imposed a one-tenth-mill levy state-wide for the support of libraries and school equipment. As before, a commissioner was responsible for inspecting the condition of schools and for spending "at least ten days in each judicial district in the state, superintending and encouraging teachers' institutes, conferring with township boards of education or other school officers, counseling teachers, visiting schools, and delivering lectures on topics calculated to subserve the interest of popular education," although he had no staff to do so (Ray 1943, 38). The commissioner also could require reporting from districts and would compile state school expenses to help the legislature develop a budget. By 1876, the commissioner would be able to withhold state monies from districts, although the state fund was very small relative to local funding until the Great Depression (Ray 1943, 44).

The Teachers' Association was dismayed by the elective nature of the post. It had argued that only an appointed chief would be above politics. Handed this loss, the association promptly nominated its state-wide representative, Lorin Andrews, as a "nonpartisan" candidate for the 1853 election. The Democratic Party nominated Hiram H. Barney (as a partisan candidate), who won the election. Handed a second loss, the association ended its brief stint in nineteenth-century electoral politics, instead becoming a de facto state education bureau, lobbying hard for more powers for the commissioner and lending him space in every issue of its *Educational Monthly* to write about educational needs in Ohio (Ray 1943, 25–26).

In 1892, the legislature increased the commissioner's staff from zero to two (Shreve 1989, 12). In 1900, the legislature expanded the department to four: the commissioner, a chief clerk, a statistical clerk, and a stenographer (Ray 1943, 48).

Although commissioners were unhappy with the size of their department, the staff was probably commensurate with its responsibility. Up until this time, Ohio's state department was chiefly a data bureau. A 1908 school fire that killed 160 students, however, prompted the legislature to take swift action to widen the scope of the state department to include the inspection of school buildings (Ray 1943, 51). This was the first in a string of significant increases in scope over the next twenty-five years.

Ohio's constitutional convention in 1912 provided two major changes to the state's educational landscape. First, the elected state commissioner ceased to be a statutory office and became a constitutional office. The convention changed the post's title to superintendent of public instruction and gave the governor appointment power. This revision was meant to take "politics out of education," although adding the post to the governor's cabinet would, in the 1950s, be seen as just as politically vulnerable as the elected post had been. (One of the oddities of this amendment was that the convention gave the state superintendent a four-year term, while the governor had a two-year term.) Second, the constitution was amended to explicitly guarantee state funding for education. The first change weakened the department's political autonomy, but the second built a foundation for greater department scope.

Lawmakers expanded the superintendent's inspection powers shortly after the 1912 constitution was ratified. Now, not only could the superintendent collect data, but he could audit school districts, approve state aid requests, fix the maximum price for textbooks, approve school curriculum and classes, and approve college and university curricula. The superintendent also had more mundane duties, such as "furnish[ing] boards of education with metal placards which are to be placed on the building, showing the grade or grades of such [high] schools" (Ray 1943, 54).

Superintendent John L. Clifton (1927–1931) was able to capitalize on a sense of optimism about government and economic emergency in the late 1920s. He multiplied his department's scope and the consequent technical autonomy as he added nine new divisions under his management: teacher training, music, licensure, scholarships, health and physical education, guidance, a state-run "School of the Air," educational research, and parent-teacher (Ray 1943, 101). Indeed, state-level educational boards for various topics multiplied both inside and outside the department: by 1942, one report found that Ohio had the most state education boards in the country (Ray 1943, 168).

Ohio's patchwork system of governance was the subject of repeated studies, which culminated in the 1953 Manahan Study (named for its chair). In addition to making recommendations about how to recast the department and superintendent's post, the Ohio School Survey Committee suggested that the state board take the lead in school consolidation, teacher certification, and curriculum standards (Ohio State Board of Education 1989, 25). Unlike previous studies of educational governance, the General Assembly took seriously this commission's recommendations.

One major suggestion was to make the superintendent appointed by the board. Between 1837 until the 1950s, most state superintendents served less than four years, leaving the department of education with little political support or political expertise (see Figure 4.1, next page). Like many other Ohio executive agencies, the department was the recipient of many patronage appointments. Its lack of political autonomy made making stable policy difficult.

In 1953, Ohio voters agreed with the commission by passing an amendment to their state constitution creating a state board of education. The amendment also made the state superintendent an appointee of the board, rather than of the governor. Armed with a revised constitution, the legislature created a board of twenty-three members with six- year terms, one from each congressional district. As was true in other states, much of the Ohio and national education establishment—including the Ohio Education Association, the Parents and Teachers Association, the Association of School Administrators, and the Council of Chief State School Administrators—supported a "nonpolitical" board to counter the influence of gubernatorial influence and increase their own (Ohio State Board of Education 1989, 2). In addition, some made the argument that a board would preserve expertise over several administrations of superintendents (Ray 1943, 205).[11]

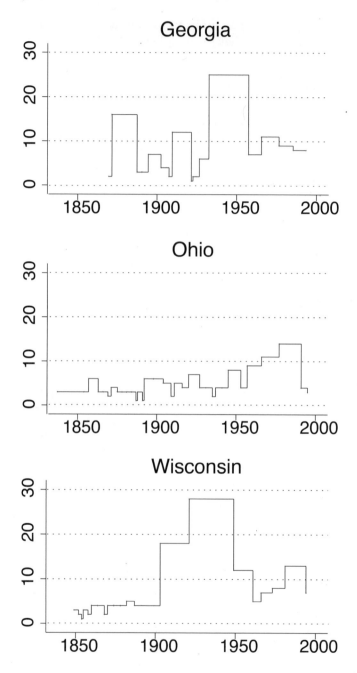

Figure 4.1. State Superintendents' Tenure by State, to 2000.

Figure 4.1 shows the effect of the change: a distinct increase in the tenure of state superintendents. While superintendents frequently served less than four years before 1953, the next three superintendents served nine years, eleven years, and fourteen years, respectively.

By the start of the 1960s, it became clear that the department's small staff would not suffice if Ohio's districts were to be held to the board's higher curricular and building standards. In the past, whenever the General Assembly had requested a report, the state superintendent had to round up volunteers to work on the research and writing. Although staffing at the department was only slowly increased, the state board was able to use some of its appropriation to add department staff—an element of fiscal autonomy. The legislature added enough staff so that the department, for the first time, was able to hold annual conferences for county educational personnel to help them identify ways their districts needed improvement (Shreve 1989, 66).

In the late 1970s, the state board sought to reorganize its thinking about what it and the department of education should do. In 1978, the board began creating specific district standards that emphasized student outcomes rather than district programs or processes. Using its technical autonomy, the department was charged to improve its over-sight of student outcomes, a process that reached its fruition at the end of the 1990s with Ohio's far-reaching student assessment system. Many of these goals found their way into the 1981 *Mission for the 80s: A Blueprint for Excellence*. The standards in this document were similar to those in other states after *Nation at Risk*. They included improving pupil performance on competency tests, reducing dropouts, increasing school funding, increasing programs for disadvantaged youth and those who were not performing well, and improving communication between the department, state board, local districts, schools, and parents (Ohio State Board of Education 1989, 84–86).

Wisconsin

Until the 1980s, Wisconsin's DPI was a remote agency that had little clout at the local level. State funding was low, state standards were extremely vague, and the state department had no supervisory power over the 6,000-plus one-room schools that were common through the 1950s. Nevertheless, Wisconsin's state educational apparatus has gradu-ally accrued powers, although the DPI was also the least able of these three states to rely on institutional resources to push for changes in local districts or the legislature.

After the fashion of the times, territorial legislator Michael Frank called for a state superintendent in 1840 and in 1841, but the territorial legislature defeated his proposals overwhelmingly, this despite the strenuous calls of schoolteachers and others that a state superintendent would help stop the wholesale waste and fraud surrounding the lease and sale of school lands that, proponents noted, had been epidemic in Ohio (Jorgenson 1956, 26). By the end of the decade, however, the delegates to the state's constitutional convention had become convinced of the value of such a state officer, and the second constitution—which has been in effect since 1848—provided for an elected state superintendent, a state school fund supported by federal grants and land sales, and town and city property taxation. It also provided that the state would withhold aid from any district that did not hold school for at least three months a year. Schools would be free and open to those between four and twenty years old.

Originally, constitutional delegates preferred that the governor appoint the superintendent with the approval of the Senate. The thinking was that the state should be free to appoint the "best man" from any state rather than an elected one, who would have to be from Wisconsin. "The state should no more be restricted in its choice of superintendent than colleges and universities are in their choice of presidents and professors," said a Milwaukee delegate (Patzer 1924, 23). Many delegates did not want some uppity Easterner to run Wisconsin schools. Democracy was better. The vote was honest (Jorgenson 1956, 62–63).[12] As adopted, the state superintendent was politically autonomous from the governor, and the constitution set his salary at $1,000, 80 percent of the governor's. (That is somewhat less than $20,000 in constant 2000 dollars. Only in 1903 was his salary was raised to $5,000, equivalent to $80,000 today [Patzer 1924, 23].[13]) The superintendent was to gather statistics, visit all common schools, proportion what state aid existed on a per-pupil basis, and ensure that schools provided reading, writing, arithmetic, grammar, geography, and spelling. Teacher certification fell to individual school districts (Clark 1958, 9).

Wisconsin's first foray into standardization came just one year later, when in 1849 the legislature empowered the state superintendent to seek uniform textbook prices.[14] His term was doubled to two years. As in other states, Wisconsin's budget provided no staff.[15]

As might be expected in a strong local-control environment, local superintendents frequently ignored the state superintendent's directives. The superintendent's office had limited scope, as shown by a charge in the state code to collect materials "without expense to the state." The situation was such that Lyman C. Draper, an early state superintendent, vociferously demanded that the legislature stipulate that town school boards remove recalcitrant local superintendents. The legislature passed a law to this effect in 1859, but it was entirely ineffective. No town superintendent was ever removed under the statute (Patzer 1924, 56).

Draper also argued for the expansion of his office's powers in other ways. He advocated paying districts state funds based on student attendance. This would encourage districts to reduce truancy. The legislature did not take him up on this proposal, but it did when he argued that the state would save dollars and administrative hassles by replacing superintendents with county superintendents. The move eliminated over 640 superintendents in 1861. Although Draper was unable to gain teacher certification or taxing powers, his successors only had to handle sixty elected county superintendents. The smaller number allowed the department to hold statewide county superintendent conferences with its minimal staff. The meetings enhanced the DPI's influence by informing county superintendents of the state superintendent's views on how schools should be run and what should be taught. This was the superintendent's first foray into managing interest groups (Clark 1958, 17).

Throughout the remainder of the century, the state superintendent butted horns with the state's ethnic communities, local districts, and the university. Ethnic communities resented and resisted state inspection of their schools, local control advocates kept state oversight entirely out of one-room schools, and the university set high school standards independently of the state superintendent.[16]

The DPI's first major expansion in scope came in 1913 at the behest of Progressive legislators in Wisconsin. During this year, the legislature placed the department on a line-item budget that protected it from the whims of the governor. It also appropriated funds for a significant increase in staff: two assistant superintendents, two high school supervisors, one supervisor of school libraries plus one assistant, two rural school supervisors, two grade school supervisors, three elementary supervisors, one director of educational measurement and statisticians, one publicity editor, one supervisor for deaf and defective speech classes, one director of special education, one assistant psychologist, one high school supervisor, and a director of manual arts, plus clerks and a stenographer (Patzer 1924, 212–13).

Two factors led to this expansion. First, a forceful superintendent had held the state superintendent's office for ten years (and would hold it for ten more; see Figure 4.1). A constitutional change in 1902 made the superintendent's office nonpartisan, lengthened the term to four years, and eliminated the constitutional salary cap. Superintendent Charles P. Cary (1903–1921) was a thorn in the side of the university, although he was often seen as a quixotic crusader who accomplished far less than he proposed. Nevertheless, his outspokenness prompted the legislature to appoint a committee to study the state's educational governance system in 1909. The committee recommended that the state recognize the superintendent as the head of the entire state education system—Cary's ultimate goal—but the committee recommended against any other reorganization. Only one bill came out of the committee, to create county boards of education to promote consolidation, and it was handily defeated (Patzer 1924, 365–66).

Second, after the crash in 1929, the legislature had a renewed interest in economy. It appointed another committee to study ways to save school dollars. Even though this new committee had the same information as the 1909 committee, it argued that Wisconsin's educational governance system could only have been drawn up by "a person with weak mental powers." It suggested that the state was wasting money on "numerous duplications, excessive overhead, pointless rivalry, minimum standards, and misplaced emphasis," at least partly due to the lack of any "single authority to impart either momentum or direction . . . to the State's work in the field of education" (quoted in Clark 1958, 1).

The committee recommended that the state abolish the DPI the two Boards of Regents, the Free Library Commission, and the Board of Vocational Education—the state's five major educational policy makers. These would be replaced by a single board of education overseeing these functions. The committee did not promise that the changes would cost less, only that the system would be more efficient, making higher curricular standards, consolidated districts, and more rigorous teacher certification possible (Clark 1958, 2).

Fortunately for the DPI, the committee's recommendations were tabled. The DPI *was* able to leverage the report to enhance its reputation and convinced the state university to cease high school inspections, a major coup for its technical and political autonomy and an increase in its scope. It built technical autonomy because DPI would now be able to build expertise and enforce its own conception of a high school education, and it gained political autonomy because it would not have to compete with the university in this policy area. In 1948, when another committee recommended changes strikingly similar to those of the earlier commission, the legislature only acted to enhance the oversight authority of the state superintendent (Porter et al. 1948). (A 1970 commission had similar recommendations, too, with no effect; see Kellett 1970.)

After the 1940s, the DPI's place in state education remained static. Perusing the state's *Blue Book*, roughly parallel to the *Manual* for the federal government, one finds little change in the description of the department between the 1950s and the 1970s, beyond noting the addition of federally funded programs. It picked up curriculum specialists in the 1950s and added staff through the 1960s to disburse federal money. In the early 1970s, the legislature added Indian Affairs and Handicapped Education bureaus. The organization of the department did little to leverage its responsibilities for more responsibility or autonomy. The DPI would have to rely on the force of personality in the 1980s to gain these.

Conclusion

By the beginning of the 1980s, Georgia, Ohio, and Wisconsin each had varying ability to argue for increased departmental autonomy. Georgia's department had the most resources. Not only could it argue that state level control could help mitigate race-based local decisions and that local economic disparities required state-wide finance distribution, but it also could argue that its experience in administering state-wide programs gave it the capacity to improve state-wide curriculum standards and broad-based student assessment. Wisconsin's department had the least. A series of superintendents who were intent on preserving local prerogatives and the legislature's inability to overcome the bulwark of local control validated legislators' skepticism that the DPI could perform. Finally, Ohio fell somewhere in between. Although the state's involvement in education began similarly to Wisconsin's, the depression and much higher economic development in Ohio pushed the state to increase its funding of education. Further, the creation of the state board and the appointment of the state superintendent ensured that whatever policy Ohio chose to pursue, a long-term expert could be at the helm of the education agency. Although the department did not have many technical resources until the late 1970s, its political autonomy and technical autonomy were very clear to the governor and the legislature.

5

Bringing Them to the Table

Managing Interests

There's no way to find common ground. What's the use [of working with ODE] if we can't go back and counter their arguments?

— Ohio lobbyist, on *DeRolph v. Ohio*

For many years, state education policy appeared to be a textbook example of an iron triangle. The state department of education created policy that the state teachers' and administrators' associations deemed helpful or necessary. In turn, those associations would provide political support in the legislature (e.g., for Ohio, see Hayes 1955). A cursory glance at the historical record does provide some support for this hypothesis. State education agencies organized and hosted professional conferences for teachers and administrators. State superintendents occasionally were also state education association presidents.

Such a view discounts both the role of the individual personalities who headed their state education departments and the independence that those departments used vigorously in the past. Given the small policy domain that education agencies had in the early years of tax-supported education, it was probably true that interest groups and education departments worked together because of necessity and shared beliefs. As departments grew in scope over time, so did their differences with interest groups. Thus they grew in autonomy.

By the 1980s and 1990s, it was clear that the iron triangle metaphor no longer worked for education policy. It is true that the number of state-level interest groups was small and well defined, and everyone in the field knew who they were, but state education agencies did not rely on them for favorable lobbying in the legislature. Instead, state agencies tried to leverage interest groups to shift the preferences of principals toward the agency's preferred policy *and* to enhance the agency's own autonomy. "Leveraging" interest groups did not always mean working *with* them. (ODE, for example, used some of them as a foil for its own plans, as shown later.) The "principals" that education agencies sought to sway were usually the legislature and governor, although the state court system fills this role in the school finance case described later. How successful the agency was depended on its existing scope, its political situation, and its institutional environment.

First, a department with expansive scope muffles the need for interest group support. Such a department can afford to lose interest group support in one area because it has any number of other policy areas to which to attend, and trouble in any one area is unlikely to generate significant, broad backlash from its principals. Further, if the department has a near monopoly on state education policy, then interest groups will have little choice but to contend with the department as it is.

Second, the political and institutional situation of the department may compound the influence of interest groups. Especially since the 1970s, educational interest groups have become more clearly identified with partisan agendas. The best examples of this are the National Education Association (NEA) and the American Federation of Teachers (AFT), both of which are aligned with the Democratic Party, or at least liberal causes (Archer 2002; West 1980).[1] The affiliation of administrator associations and school board associations is less pronounced, but collective bargaining with teachers' unions tends to push them away from a strong Democratic affiliation. Business groups, latecomers to the education area, are usually Republican-leaning.[2]

The partisan environment can be crucial. When key interest groups do not lean the same way as the governor, the majority in the legislature, or the education department, their influence will be muted simply because they do not have easy access to the natural influence that co-partisanship provides. Being on the "wrong" side can also stymie grassroots efforts. One union organizer told me that she had trouble convincing union members to vote against their Republican state representatives, who were securely in the majority. "We have [some noncentral city parts of the state] where teachers don't see that their representative doesn't vote for public education. They just don't think about that."

Third, institutionally, the more insulated the department is from electoral politics, the less likely a department will need to rely on interest groups' aid. For example, in many states, teachers' unions have the largest potential "grassroots" network of any group (Diegmueller 2002; Beilke 2001). If that network cannot directly support or oppose the state superintendent (because she is appointed by a state board) or persuade the governor to do the same (because the governor does not oversee the department of education), then this large network will have little practical significance in the short term. Political pressure on the department from principals is indirect.

Therefore, in an autonomous agency, interest groups will have influence only to the degree that the agency allows. These departments will be able to expand their responsibilities because they can "go it alone" without a need to build consensus among fractious groups. Conversely, less autonomous agencies will have to rely on interest groups to prop up what scope they have. Those departments will not be able to gain new scope, because they will have difficulty holding on to what scope they have. I expect that *an agency that pursues fewer interest group partners will have greater autonomy because it has fewer outside groups to manage, and it will have greater scope because it does not need to rely on outside groups to accomplish tasks.*

As I noted in chapter 2, interest groups have three avenues for influence on policy. They may enhance a department's autonomy by feeding it ideas that the group will support; they may cooperate in implementing department initiatives; or they may serve as informal overseers in place of the legislature. This chapter proceeds in three parts, with each part devoted to one of these avenues.

Ideas: Teacher Licensure Reform in Wisconsin

Superintendent Herbert Grover held meetings with Wisconsin's big education groups every Tuesday morning to keep them informed, on board, and in check. The most important of these groups was the Wisconsin Education Association Council (WEAC) under Morris Andrews, whose support for the DPI was crucial if other interest groups were to come along. Several of my interviewees had little but praise for Andrews for his ability to keep squabbling interest groups tacitly unified. Indeed, the power of Andrews was such that Governor Tony Earl charged Grover to "keep WEAC out of [Earl's] hair over the educator issue," according to an associate of Grover's. A major part of the "educator issue" was revising the state's teacher licensure system. The governor recognized that WEAC could pressure him, the principal, to rein in the DPI. It is a testament to the contingent nature of autonomy that DPI, an agency with little apparent autonomy, had the confidence of Governor Earl to manage the state's most powerful educational interest group.

In Wisconsin, teacher licensure has been clearly within the DPI's scope since 1939 (see chapter 4). As the DPI revised licensure requirements in the 1980s and overhauled them in the 1990s, its relatively weak autonomy was evident. Throughout the entire process, the department had to rely on the state's interest groups to draft the regulations and to overcome resistance in the field.

Institutionally, Wisconsin has an independently elected superintendent, which pushes the office into the political fray. Although nominally nonpartisan, in the early 1980s the state superintendent was a former Democratic legislator. The governor and the majority of state legislators were also Democrats. The DPI's scope was relatively narrow—essentially teacher licensure, curriculum guides, operating the state's public library system, cutting federal checks, and boosting the image of public education (student testing and state standards appeared later). In the 1990s, Superintendent John Benson was in the same institutional arrangement without the partisan support. Therefore, the expectation here is that interest groups would play a large role in shaping policy because the DPI did not have the political autonomy necessary to ignore elections. Further, the DPI could not afford to lose on one of its few responsibilities; the DPI would *have* to pursue interest groups to ensure compliance in the field.

Prior to 1980, the DPI had no "native" teacher preparation standards. Instead, it used the recommendations developed by the National Association of State Directors of Teacher Education and Certification (NASDTEC) and enforced them as law. In 1979, however, the state legislature demanded that the DPI develop its own standards and suspended DPI's ability to use the NASDTEC recommendations. As a result, newly elected Superintendent Grover had an opportunity to reshape the rules from the first day of his term. The rules were clearly within the DPI's scope, but even so, the department was in no position to draft the rules alone. It could anticipate complaints from the teachers' unions, and the state's university system proved recalcitrant.

In late 1982, Grover appointed a twenty-three-member Task Force on Teaching and Teacher Education to draft the state's licensure rules; members of interest groups from the business group Wisconsin Association of Manufacturers and Commerce to the Wisconsin Federation of Teachers were represented, as well as the university. The department made it a point to emphasize that representatives from every major educational group in Wisconsin were included in its drafting process (Teacher task force 1983). "The unanimous support of major state education interest groups lends credibility to the whole effort," wrote Grover in the DPI's monthly newspaper (Grover 1985c). The DPI codified the standards in PI 3 (for "Public Instruction chapter 3.")

Despite Grover's announcement that the rules were being improved, the department's first attempt encountered skepticism in the legislature for relying on the very groups that would have to "buy" the standards. Key legislators thought that the department had relied too much on groups interested in preserving the status quo. Too little had changed from the NASDTEC standards. Cal Potter, the chair of the Assembly Primary and Secondary Education Committee, complained in August 1983 that the changed sections of the teacher rules were, "essentially, simply renumbered." He wrote, "The purpose of this letter is to *strongly urge* that such revision be promptly undertaken. The purpose of the revision should be not only to improve the clarity, style and format of the rules, but to also revise and update the *substance* of the rules" (Potter 1983, emphases in original). Grover admitted that the previous "revisions" were the "combined efforts of teachers, representatives from teacher training institutions, consumer groups, and department staff," but he assured Potter that he would instruct the State Superintendent's Advisory Council for Teacher Education and Certification to "complet[e] a comprehensive review of this section of the administrative code" over the next year (Grover 1983a).

The task force did substantially what Superintendent Grover had promised. He *was* able to keep the support of WEAC by explicitly involving Morris Andrews and others in the revision process. But when the DPI began to tinker with course requirements, he brought vehement criticism from the University of Wisconsin. Reminiscent of the battles between Superintendent Cary and the University of Wisconsin in the 1920s (see chapter 4), the university initially refused to take orders from the DPI. Grover said, "Rulemaking authority is important stuff—I held hearings [on PI 3 and 4] in the summer when all the professors were away, and I had the rules in place by the fall." Relishing the thought, he added, "Were they mad!" Grover recalled that he told the dean of the school of education that he could do whatever he wanted with the UW–Madison College of Education, but that the DPI would refuse to grant licenses to any of his graduates. One former DPI employee remembered, "The Board of Regents tried to frame the issue as a legal problem, but it never asked a lawyer. We had six system campuses with us; we had all the interest groups. That was a battle royale." In the end, the university backed down.

Grover's experience with PI 3 and 4 demonstrates some of the power and weakness of relying on interest groups to perform basic department responsibilities. Although no interest group except the university questioned the right of the DPI to issue teacher licenses, the department had to run all proposed changes through a panel of interest group representatives, and it was only able to bargain with them after a legislator issued a veiled threat. The DPI's political autonomy was weak because of its dependence on regular interest group meetings to ensure field support. The department displayed limited technical autonomy given that interest groups, and WEAC in particular, staffed the Superintendent's Advisory Committee to rewrite the rules. It is also significant that Grover's "battle royale" was over a settled area of responsibility, and not a new front. The DPI's responsibilities were under attack, and it had to rely on other groups to give its actions legitimacy.

Superintendent John Benson, Grover's successor, would follow the same path when he tried his hand at strengthening the licensure system. Although Benson's revisions were perhaps more substantial than those of the 1980s, the DPI still had to rely on WEAC and other groups for political legitimacy.[3] John Benson combined the substance of PI 3 and PI 4 into PI 34, his most enduring administrative project. He appointed a task force to improve teacher licensure a year after his election; the panel had a rough outline of PI 34's teacher standards within eight months. This first task force recommended that "statewide committees . . . be broad-based in order to achieve the collaboration that the Task Force has emphasized throughout the Report" (Wisconsin Department of Public Instruction 1995, iii).[4]

Benson took the task force's advice. Interest groups dominated the committee writing the rules for new license tiers. Ten interest groups were represented on the new task force; of the fifty-one members, thirty-three were interest group representatives, and nine were DPI staff. WEAC supplied eight representatives and the Wisconsin Federation of Teachers two more, making the state's teachers' unions the largest contributor to the project.[5]

Wisconsin's new teacher certification system was meant to address frequent criticism—by no means unique to Wisconsin—that teacher certification did not prepare teachers for successful careers. Part of the impetus to alter the requirements so soon after Grover left office was that teacher preparation had become a national issue in the early 1990s. Benson's original panel studied standards proposed by the National Board for Professional Teaching Standards, the Interstate New Teacher Assessment and Support Consortium, and the National Council for Accreditation of Teacher Education before settling on state-specific standards (Wisconsin Department of Public Instruction 1997, 1995, 2, 5).

PI 34 created three levels of teacher licenses: "initial," "professional," and "master." The greatest differences from the old licensure rules were the requirements for a professional development plan (for initial and professional licenses) and a committee of mentors to approve license renewal and, when applicable, to approve the professional development plan. This plan is supposed to list identifiable activities to improve a teacher's compliance with the state's new teacher standards, shown in Table 5.1. Abstractly, the change was one from "an input system that focuse[d] on course and credit completion to an assessment system that emphasize[d] successful demonstration of the required knowledge, skill, and disposition" to teach (Wisconsin Department of Public Instruction 1997, 5).

The initial license is available only for a teacher's first five years. If a teacher does not fulfill his or her development plan by the end of the term, then the teacher will lose his or her license. Otherwise, the teacher will be promoted to a ten-year, renewable professional license. An initial teacher's committee is comprised of a teacher from his school, a district administrator, and a representative of a college with an education program. Once promoted to a professional license, a teacher's committee must be composed of three licensed teachers. The license is renewable as long as the committee agrees that the teacher meets the professional development plan.

The top level, the master's license, is not required, but it has its perquisites. This license is a renewable ten-year license, and no mentor committee is required. Nevertheless, a teacher must have a master's degree and must have held at least one five-year professional license. Three teachers and (at the state superintendent's option) a school board member assess master teachers for "exemplary classroom performance," improved student learning, and a "contribution to the profession." Each of these assessors must be nominated by educational interest groups and must be trained by the DPI (Kiel 2002).

The substance of the task force's initial report gained the respect of James Cibulka, a prominent critic of the DPI, however, he still slighted

Table 5.1. Wisconsin PI34 Teacher Licensure Standards

1. Teachers know the subjects they are teaching.
2. Teachers know how children grow.
3. Teachers understand that children learn differently.
4. Teachers know how to teach.
5. Teachers know how to manage a classroom.
6. Teachers communicate well.
7. Teachers are able to plan different kinds of lessons.
8. Teachers know how to test for student progress.
9. Teachers are able to evaluate themselves.
10. Teachers are connected with other teachers and the community.

Source: Wisconsin Department of Public Instruction (2003).

the department's preparedness to implement the recommendations. "DPI [has not] developed any overall plan to encourage and coordinate the most effective use of staff development as a policy lever that can help the state's educational system make a transition to a 'high-performance' orientation" (Cibulka 1996, 17). Another observer I interviewed was more pointed in his criticism of the DPI's ability to implement policy. "Education policy [in Wisconsin] has a whole cesspool of political legitimacy problems" because of the DPI's heavy reliance on interest groups to carry out its work.

Some of that morass is broader than teacher licensure, but the new regulations provided a new focal point for conflict. The Wisconsin Association of School Boards (WASB), for example, recommended that boards see PI 34's mentoring requirement as part of a teacher's existing responsibilities, not as an additional task that would require changes in pay or time. The WASB also suggested that teacher mentors could *not* participate in teacher evaluation or supervision—if this were to happen, then the mentor would have to surrender membership in the teachers' union per Wisconsin labor law (Wisconsin Association of School Boards 2000, 2). One DPI official with whom I spoke was unrepentant about the cost of PI 34, however: He estimated that the mentor program would cost only about $2,000 per new teacher and noted that federal ESEA Title II was supposed to cover teacher development costs. This was less than 0.1 percent of current payroll. (Many districts used Title II funds for class-size reduction instead, which was also a legal use of these funds.) School district administrators were also made subject to PI 34 certification, which upset their interest groups as well, according to an observer. "DPI added administrator certification to PI 34 at the last minute, but administrator certification is something else altogether" than teacher certification, he said.

In PI 34's design, some interest groups were "more equal" than others. As might be expected, the state-level teachers' union, WEAC, had significant clout in the design of the regulations. Benson said that WEAC had initially been suspicious of changes particularly regarding who would evaluate teachers and the design of the salary schedule, but "once we got over the hurdles, they got out in the country preaching PI 34," he said. When PI 34 came up for legislative review, both the DPI and WEAC asked organizations to register support for the measure (e.g., Wisconsin School Counselors' Association 1999, 3). Further, the teacher organization spent a significant amount of effort promoting PI 34 throughout the state and showing how teachers could meet the new standards. WEAC also promoted the seminars of DPI's Kathryn Lind, the director of teacher development, in its member materials (see Haas 2003). The

DPI has been very favorable about this assistance; indeed, Jack Kean, an assistant superintendent at DPI charged with PI 34, promoted WEAC's Professional Development Academy to a state-wide meeting of CESA administrators in 2002 (Cooperative Educational Service Agency #7 2002). Note that this is not far removed from the state-department-sponsored professional conferences of the nineteenth century.

Although PI 34 has received the praise of many groups concerned about teacher licensure in Wisconsin, the DPI's process in designing and executing PI 34 did little to expand the agency's autonomy or scope. Benson's accomplishment in PI 34—which became effective under his successor, Elizabeth Burmaster—is notable because the DPI persevered, even though the political configuration was against the department. Governor Tommy Thompson and the legislature were pursuing their own vision of education reform. That vision did not include the DPI. Benson himself was proud of the consensus building he encouraged, telling me that, "I don't take any credit for PI 34—well, I take a little bit of credit for bringing people together." In so doing, however, the DPI reinforced its image of catering to the teachers' unions.[6] This provided fodder for the department's principals to roll back its autonomy.

Teacher licensure under both Grover and Benson confirms the expectation that autonomous and responsible agencies will not need to rely on interest groups to do their work. The department's political autonomy was low; and, unlike either Georgia or Ohio, the DPI was forced to rely on outside groups for a policy area that was clearly within its purview, and had been for sixty years. The DPI's work on PI 34 continued only because of the heavy involvement of interest groups.

Implementation: Georgia's Kindergarten Assessment Program

In 1988, the Georgia Department of Education introduced the Georgia Kindergarten Assessment Program (GKAP) after two years of development. Unlike Wisconsin's teaching standards, the Georgia department did so without extensive interest group input. After the test's debut, the department was hit with vociferous criticism of the exam. Although interest group pressure forced GADOE to retreat and retool the exam, the department was successful in maintaining the kindergarten assessment, an expansion of its responsibilities. Interest groups persuaded neither the legislature nor the governor, the principals, to rein in GADOE's activities. Instead, the legislature strongly sided with the department.

Interest groups were furious at being excluded from the design phase of the exam and were determined to put their mark on the

implementation phase. Georgia's institutions—an elected state superintendent—would seem to make the department more susceptible to interest
group influence, but GADOE had inherited extensive responsibilities over
its 125-year existence. Even the state chief was partly an inheritance;
most chiefs were "elected" only after having been appointed to the post
to fulfill a vacancy created by preelection retirement. Therefore, GADOE
should appear insulated from interest group influence.

Governor Joe Frank Harris was elected in 1984 on promises to
enhance Georgia's education system. Harris made good on his promise
in his first year in office by signing the Quality Basic Education (QBE)
Act in 1985. Indeed, he even had the cover of the state's fiscal 1986
budget emblazoned with the words "The Year of Education." Two
of QBE's basic goals were to lower tenth-graders' failure rate on the
state's Basic Skills Test and to ensure that students could fulfill state-
board-created standards in reading, math, and other areas the board set.
Both of these goals were to be measured with assessment testing. These
tests were not written in the governor's mansion, however. They were
the product of Assistant State Superintendent Werner Rogers and others under Superintendent Charles McDaniel. (McDaniel died in 1985;
Harris appointed Rogers to the job.)

GADOE had been handed a blank check in QBE. The act itself
was largely the product of GADOE. "Literally, when a page was written
in the governor's office, I'd take it over to the department to review"
before returning to the governor with corrections, one department
employee remembered. After QBE, "Joe [Frank Harris] pretty much
left us alone," the employee said. Werner Rogers backed up this statement, saying he had had significant "hands-on experience" with the
governor's office for QBE.[7]

The law gave GADOE broad responsibility to design the state
standards and the assessment tests. As a by-product, the law strengthened the department's technical and political autonomy. Among QBE's
provisions was a charge to the department to develop an assessment of
first-grade readiness in order to "identify as early as possible areas of
need" in kindergarten students, according to Superintendent Werner
Rogers. The kindergarten test was to be the first such exam mandated
in the United States. Students would be assessed for their skills on a
uniform exam. The child's score on the test would only be a part of
the promotion decision: for example, if, in her teacher's judgment, the
child was ready to move on despite her test score, then the child would
take a second, locally created assessment (Gold 1988).

The department of education was well prepared for such a task.
As early as 1980, then-Superintendent Charles McDaniel informed the
governor that he was developing a student assessment to be given in

the first, second, third, fourth, sixth, eighth, and tenth grades. McDaniel argued that "the State fulfills its responsibility for assuring an adequate educational opportunity for all students by establishing standards of performance" and measuring them consistently. McDaniel did not roll out the complete program at the time, but his department continued to explore student assessment—before the governor gave it the directive to do so (McDaniel 1980).

Even if outside groups had sought to circumvent the department, they were in a poor position to evaluate the state's educational status. In 1983, R. Scott Bradshaw (1983), GADOE's curriculum director, sent a searing note to the Legislative Educational Research Council denouncing a report it prepared for the House Education Committee's Subcommittee on Educational Accountability. The subcommittee had been called to "review the current status of curriculum in Georgia, including . . . the relationship of the curriculum to the state testing program," but no one had asked the department for its expertise. Instead, the committee had called an advisory committee consisting of the state's prominent interest groups. The querulous advisory committee met only once. Neither did it lend much support to the subcommittee's project, according to a department official. Bradshaw targeted the council for suggesting that the curriculum guides should be monitored by the state ("for the most part, done," 1) and excoriated its report for suggesting that a norm-referenced test should be used to test students' facility with state standards ("not sound psychometrically or from a commonsense point of view . . . naïve," 2). The department favored criterion-referenced tests, which it was developing at the time. In short, the interest groups the committee called upon appeared to be unaware of the extensive work that GADOE had already done (see also Georgia House of Representatives 1982).

By 1985, then, GADOE was technically well prepared to handle a kindergarten exam. Originally, it had proposed a shortened version of the California Achievement Test (CAT), which had been used in that state since 1980. GADOE's decision was part practical and part political. Practically, using an off-the-shelf exam would save the department considerable money, especially given that the exam had already been field tested in California on kindergarteners for more than six years. Politically, a test "practice" administration in 1987 showed that Georgia kindergarteners scored above the national norm for the exam—which would automatically generate good press—and that the exam's results correlated "very well" with teachers' judgments about promotion to first grade. Further, many local school districts already used the CAT in their own promotion decisions (Georgia Department of Education 1988; Gold 1988).

The decision to use the CAT was internal to GADOE, which conducted field inquiries about the CAT while field-testing the exam, but it had not needed to rely on outside groups to design the test. Instead, the department was able to enlist its own considerable technical expertise to evaluate and execute the CAT. Even the state board of education was not privy to the design of the test; instead, it was only asked to approve GADOE's proposal to use such a test, which it did, 7–1 (Gold 1988).[8]

The reaction to the exam was immediate. It was manifest that GADOE had decided on the exam by relying on its political autonomy. The most vociferous criticism came from a national group, the National Association for the Education of Young Children (NAEYC). The NAEYC called the exam "educationally and psychologically harmful" (unlike Bradshaw's opinion), especially because promotion decisions were informed partly by a student's test performance. GADOE estimated that 10 percent of kindergarteners would fail the exam, which the NAEYC found unacceptable. "Regardless of the nomenclature, children are really aware that that's the dummy group," noted Susan Bredekamp, a NAEYC director (Cohen 1989; Gold 1988).

But local groups bashed the exam as well (the major opponents are listed in Table 5.2). The central complaint was that the CAT did not "reflect the broad, developmental scope of the kindergarten instructional program," and that using the test placed "unnecessary emotional burden on teachers, parents and especially students." Both of these are generic complaints about standardized tests (Georgia Department of Education 1988).

Another critique, however, challenged the core of GADOE's autonomy and whether the exam fell within the department's scope. The school districts and the teachers' associations challenged the right

Table 5.2. Major Interest Group Opposition to the Georgia Kindergarten Assessment Program

Georgia Association of Educational Leaders
Georgia School Board Association
Georgia Association of Educators
American Federation of Teachers
Georgia Association of Young Children
Professional Association of Georgia Educators
Georgia School Superintendent Association
Georgia Association of Curriculum and Instructional Supervisors
University of Georgia Faculty Senate

Source: Georgia Department of Education (1988).

of GADOE to set standards for kindergarten promotion. Even though Georgia education never had a strong ethic of local control (see chapter 4), superintendents and teachers were not averse to using a local-control argument. The animosity that GADOE attracted from districts was not solely over the kindergarten test; QBE also gave the department significant authority to inspect school buildings, teacher licensing, and other district-run operations. GADOE could withhold funding if it found a district wanting, and school districts uniformly resented this expansive authority (see chapter 7).

The department's internal opinion was that the responsibility for setting standards for promotion was "clearly assigned to the state," according to QBE. The statute read that students "must have achieved the criterion score or scores established by the State Board of Education on the school readiness assessment" (Section 20-2-151(b)(2)). The department held that only legal changes outside the control of GADOE could give local districts this authority (Georgia Department of Education 1988).

Nevertheless, the uproar was such that Rogers publicly backed down and proposed that GADOE offer districts seven different kindergarten tests from which they could choose—the department would still create them and would still set the cut points. This compromise did not sit well with the legislature. Representative William C. Mangum Jr., chair of the House Education Committee, was an early convert to Rogers's point of view about the appropriateness of the kindergarten test. He fumed, "They told me at the time that they had piloted this for two years and interviewed over 4,000 teachers and everything's ready—and then the first year we had the test and all of a sudden everything's wrong." Mangum introduced a bill to require GADOE to impose a single, statewide exam on kindergarteners. The House easily passed the measure, 136 to 34. (The Senate Education Committee buried it.) Thus GADOE was caught between interest groups and districts wanting to strip the department of autonomy and certain legislators seeking to strengthen both (Cohen 1989).

Chastised by both sides, Superintendent Rogers withdrew his multiple-test-choice offering and the CAT—at least under that name. Unlike the CAT, the new GKAP exam would be explicitly linked to Georgia curriculum, but Rogers still directed the department to contract with the same assessment company that had developed the CAT, IOX Assessment Associates. This California company had developed high-stakes, criterion-referenced exams for other states, including Texas and California (as it continues to do) (IOX Assessment Associates 1989).[9]

Unlike the first GKAP attempt, GADOE found it politically expedient to include interest group advice, although its input was limited. All of the department's promotional materials for the revised GKAP emphasized that *Georgia* teachers and *Georgia* experts sat on the test design committee. For example, GADOE, with the help of IOX, developed a videotape to distribute to schools in advance of the new exam. Superintendent Rogers appears in the opening sequence to build support for the test, and he says, "We are very proud of this program for two reasons: first, because it effectively answers the assessment requirements that brought it into being, and second, because it is a *Georgia* product." At the end of the piece he again emphasizes outside input, saying, "It is based on our state Quality Core Curriculum [so] it assesses those things that are already *part of* the instructional program, and it allows teachers to observe and document capabilities *as your child attains them.* . . . In closing, let me thank you for your role in the essential partnership between parents and teachers" (Walton 1990, emphases in original).

The extent to which Georgians were actually involved in the test design process, however, is not clear. GADOE tenaciously held on to its prerogative to design the exam. In his interview with me, Rogers strongly emphasized that GADOE brought in a state test director, that GADOE contracted with James Popham (of IOX), and that GADOE designed the exam. Documents from the assessment division show that GADOE "coordinated" the three standard test-design committees: a twenty-member advisory committee, an eighteen-member content review committee, and a seventeen-member bias review committee. Members of these committees were not a random sample of Georgia educators, and all of the fieldwork was done by IOX. The test was also constructed unusually fast, weakening the practical value of any input Georgia participants might have had. IOX charged a premium for its involvement, because, "given the particularly short time line involved in preparing, pilot-testing, and delivering a version of KAP [*sic*] by October 1989, the project will unquestionably cause an unanticipated diversion of IOX personnel resources" (Bernknopf and Blount 1989; IOX Assessment Associates 1989).[10]

GADOE did hold hearings around the state in the spring of 1989 to gauge reactions to the first administration of the GKAP, which led to changes in how the next exam was presented to districts and to the increased visibility of the role of the teacher's judgment. A letter to district superintendents from Paul Vail, the associate superintendent in charge of the exam, noted that

> the assessment program is designed to provide a basis by which a *teacher* can obtain and evaluate relevant and reliable

information about a student's capabilities. However, once summarized, recommendations relative to a student's placement are made by the *teacher*, utilizing his/her professional judgment to interpret the available information. (Vail 1990, emphasis added)

Although the original GKAP allowed a teacher to contradict the test's assessment of a child's readiness for first grade, the test was on equal footing. Now the teacher was making the actual promotion decision regardless of the exam. (Obviously a teacher who consistently placed students contrary to the exam's results would raise the suspicion of GADOE, who maintained final legal authority over promotion decisions.)

The new test relied more heavily on a teacher's judgment in other ways as well. Although the exam was explicitly criterion referenced, the test did not include a "paper-and-pencil" assessment. Instead, a teacher was required to conduct a "structured assessment activity" (SAA) for each component of the exam over the course of the school year. The SAA covered five areas: communication skills (including "emergent literacy"); logical and mathematical skills; personal responsibility ("initiates independent activities"); motor and manipulation abilities; and social interaction (Vail 1990).

The department estimated that this new exam would require one hour of time for *each* student. These changes were made to counter the NAEYC's charge that a kindergarten test was "not developmentally appropriate." The latter two words would appear repeatedly whenever the department sent materials discussing the new exam. The department emphasized that it was "developmentally appropriate." According to Rogers, the NAEYC was mollified: " 'If you have to do this, which we oppose, you've done the best job in the country with something that will work with kids' " (see also Vail 1990).

Therefore, GADOE enhanced its technical and political autonomy while maintaining the kindergarten test within its scope—all in the face of interest group opposition. GADOE was forced to retreat from its original, less expensive proposal for political expediency. But the department tailored the exam to fit Georgia's QBE standards better and continued to reiterate the importance of the test in determining readiness for first grade. The uproar over the first rendition of the exam neither stopped the test nor changed its authors. Georgia continued to use Rogers's GKAP until 1998, when it was revised. Kindergarteners are still assessed with a criterion-based test (Georgia Department of Education 2005). Interest groups were called for input for appearances only.

Oversight: School Finance and DeRolph v. Ohio

A third avenue whereby interest groups may limit an agency's autonomy is through their function as overseers. When groups pursue this strategy, they act as an external audit and raise hackles with legislators through their members or with the courts when the agency does not fulfill what the group thinks is necessary. Many of my interviewees made some mention of flawed performance of their state education agency, usually with some comment such as (from Ohio), "ODE doesn't really do its job. It won't rein in abuses of the charter school law. . . . We've had to set up a hotline to report problems." According to this source, the hotline was well used.

Although interest groups may seek to rein in agencies through political pressure directly (as when the state superintendency is an elected post) or indirectly by using friends in the legislature, this section addresses the most direct means that interest groups may use to squelch autonomy—the courts. Here I discuss the four *DeRolph v. Ohio* school finance cases that dragged on for ten years.[11] The Ohio Department of Education was a primary defendant in the lawsuit. Although the department lost some autonomy in the early stages of the case, the loss was temporary, as legislators and others realized that ODE's responsibilities had given it substantial, unrivaled technical expertise. Even hostile interest groups had to defer to its knowledge, as they learned when they provided erroneously derived data to the court. When its expertise again became central, ODE regained its political autonomy. The department had ample existing responsibilities, and the state's political configuration was such that the superintendent was isolated from the electoral realm, and many of the interest groups in the suit were commonly affiliated with Democrats—then far out of power in Ohio.

"Do you really want to know? I'd rather spare you brain damage," one lobbyist in Ohio told me when I asked about some intricacy of *DeRolph v. Ohio.* As with all school finance cases, the ends are simple, but the means are tortuous. School finance has a scholarly cottage industry of its own, and I will not attempt to weigh the merits of Ohio's school finance system, or the results that came out of the four *DeRolph* decisions. Instead, I will detail how a coalition of prominent Ohio interest groups tried to litigate the legislature and ODE into acceptable finance reform. Along the way, I show how the use of political oversight damaged ODE's political autonomy yet enhanced its technical autonomy. As department opponents tried to cut the department, they found they could not present a credible alternative. This pruning of the department actually led to later strengthening.[12]

The facts of the case are straightforward: in 1991, Nathan DeRolph (then a sophomore in high school) and five southeastern Ohio school districts filed suit in Perry County Court alleging that the state's method of funding school districts was unconstitutional. Ohio's constitution guarantees a "thorough and efficient" system of education, but the districts provided evidence that many Ohio school buildings were in very poor shape and that per-pupil spending in Ohio ranged from $3,000 to $11,000. Further, plaintiffs argued that high school systems could not adequately prepare students for college. The Perry County Court found in favor of the plaintiffs, only to be overturned by an appeals court. The group appealed again, and by this time the original five districts had grown to over 500 (out of 614 school districts). The group challenging the state was now headed by former assistant state superintendent William Phillis, erstwhile candidate for state superintendent (see Table 5.3).[13]

The state's supreme court finally received and ruled on the case in 1997. It found, 4–3, that Ohio's funding system was unconstitutional, and that "the General Assembly . . . must create an entirely new school financing system." The court stayed its ruling for one year to allow the legislature to appreciate the gravity of the task. This is known as *DeRolph I* (677 N.E.2d 747).

This decision criticized the state on four counts: the existing school funding formula was based on overbroad assumptions, the formula was too tied to property taxes, the state's mandatory school loan program created cycles of district dependency, and the state did not provide sufficient funding for school buildings. The court also declared that funding

Table 5.3. Organizations and Interest Groups Directly Involved with the Ohio Coalition for Equity and Adequacy of School Funding

Buckeye Association of School Administrators
Cleveland Teachers' Union
Coalition of Rural and Appalachian Schools
Murray State University
Ohio Association of Colleges for Teacher Education
Ohio Association of Elementary School Administrators
OAPSE-AFSCME/AFL-CIO
Ohio Coalition for the Education of Children with Disabilities
Ohio Education Association
Ohio University

Source: Ohio Coalition for Equity and Adequacy of School Funding (1997). Includes ex-officio members.

should be such that a district could meet all educational mandates. To add insult to injury, the court refused to say what it would consider an appropriate remedy—except that what existed was illegal.[14]

The ruling took both sides by surprise: "The Supreme Court's ruling . . . was more extreme than any close observer predicted. Even parties sympathetic to the plaintiffs were surprised. . . . Anybody watching the Statehouse knows 'there's trouble in River City,' " wrote an advisor to the governor six days after the ruling (Steiner 1997). No interest groups, plaintiffs included, had a comprehensive plan to address the court's demands, although the Coalition for Adequacy and Equity did have a four-page list of demands beginning with variations on "The state shall" (for samples, see Table 5.4). Nowhere do they suggest how

Table 5.4. Selected "Components of School Funding Reform" from the Ohio Coalition for Equity and Adequacy of School Funding

- A State Commission (the "Public School Facilities Commission") shall be established to develop objective criteria for the determination of necessary school facilities additions or renovations, to assess and prioritize the current facilities needs of school districts, to approve funding for and to coordinate and monitor the process of restoring and replacing Ohio's public school buildings. . . . Such surveys will be updated on a five-year cycle. (A.1.a. and b.)

- The existing Classroom Facilities Act will be phased out and all remaining school district indebtedness to the State for school facilities will be canceled. (A.2.d.)

- The State shall provide additional opportunities for staff development and assume financial responsibility for that development . . . the following areas of instruction must be covered . . . identification and implementation of effective teaching methods . . . alteration of curriculum and teaching methods to meet changing demographics and the world of work. (B.1. and 2.)

- The Ohio Department of Education shall implement a process that determines a student cost foundation level which has a direct relationship to the cost of providing a quality basic education program. (C.1.)

- School districts which should be included in the determination of the cost of an adequate education shall meet the following set of criteria: districts with a cumulative percentage . . . of at least 75 percent of the eligible students passing each part of the 9th Grade Proficiency Test and urban districts . . . where the cumulative percentage of eligible students passing each part of the 9th Grade Proficiency Test meets or exceeds the state-wide average. . . . (Appendix)

Source: Ohio Coalition for Equity and Adequacy of School Funding (1997).

the state should raise funds, however (Ohio Coalition for Equity and Adequacy of School Funding 1997).

The coalition and the court were in for rough treatment from some of the state's newspapers. Particularly troublesome was that the coalition wanted the state to fund a system that—vaguely, in editorial opinion—allowed children to "participate fully in society" and offered "high-quality educational opportunities." One opined that

> local taxpayers and state legislators can be tough judges. They are asking lots of questions these days about the performance of schools. They increasingly have been demanding performance and accountability. They want to see results for bigger investments of tax money. . . . [This] is a major reason education lobbies . . . have appealed to the courts for bigger infusions of cash, rather than dealing with those tougher arbiters, voters and legislators. (Judicial lawmaking high court wreaks havoc on Ohio schools 1997)

At first glance, the ruling appeared an unequivocal victory for the plaintiffs and an affirmation of the power of interest group oversight being able to curtail ODE's autonomy. Upon closer inspection, however, the decision actually *increased* the department's technical and political autonomy. Now it was being given a court mandate to act, limiting the normal political checks on its activities.

ODE saw a silver lining and put a decidedly positive spin on the ruling. Through a press release, Superintendent John Goff shaped the ruling into an argument for increasing the emphasis on the department-designed proficiency tests, saying, "For the last several years, the State Board and I have focused on raising standards and improving the performance of our educators, students, and schools. I was glad to see the court agrees that if we just talk about money, we can never resolve the school-improvement debate. *We have to talk about results*" (Ohio Department of Education 1997, emphasis in original).

The system-wide response to the initial ruling seemed to justify this optimism. Although the ruling presented an opening for state legislators to tinker with the funding formula that had been virtually the department's exclusive domain, the composition of the resulting school finance task force was decidedly advantageous for the department's technical expertise. Five politicians (two representatives, two senators, and the governor), the state budget director, and the state superintendent comprised the task force. Only the last two could be expected to have a full handle on the complexity of the state budget and the current funding formula.[15]

Indeed, although the coalition claimed that "Ohio's public education system is suffering from years of neglect by the state government," it recognized that the state, through ODE, was best equipped to rearrange the state's funding system (Ohio Coalition for Equity and Adequacy of School Funding 1997, 4). It did not call for the court to calculate the finance levels—it demanded that ODE do that, and even specified that ODE should use its existing school finance database to do it. Undoubtedly, the long service of the coalition's executive director, William Phillis, in ODE's school finance division, influenced this view (see Phillis 1991).[16] One of my interviewees from an interest group (not a party to the lawsuit) told me that whatever the plaintiff's demands, ODE had the upper hand: "They have the information everyone needs on school performance and finance. They have a simulation system for school finance that can play around with different variables. No one else has that. And they've been doing a better job of data organization than in the past."

Perhaps for political reasons, the state hired John Augenblick from Denver, Colorado, to assist ODE in designing a funding level for "adequate" quality education (rather than creating the formula in-house). His methodology became a major bone of contention between the coalition, other interest groups, and the state. Expanding on a formula outline developed with ODE in 1995, Augenblick identified a set of empirically determined measures that would indicate a "successful" school district (see Table 5.5). Next he identified existing school districts that matched the criteria. Finally, he used those districts' spending levels to suggest a base figure.

As might be expected, districts that spent more than Augenblick's figure ($4,350 per pupil) were irate. Some argued that the Augenblick formula would result in counterintuitive redistributions of state aid. One pair of authors noted that a particular well-to-do district would receive a 12.5 percent increase in state aid—the same increase as a school district at the 40th percentile. Others attacked it because it was "not grounded in extant state policy" (to which Augenblick responded that his recommendations used the state-board-approved proficiency exams). The executive director of the Ohio School Boards Association warned that most districts were adamantly opposed to the formula, and that they were working to defeat a sales tax increase meant to increase school funding based on the formula (Bainbridge and Sundre 1997; Augenblick 1997; Price 1998).

Despite the outcry from districts—and despite the defeat of a referendum to raise the sales tax to fund the plan (80 percent against)—the legislature generally adopted his recommendations and set the foundation level of funding at $4,063. Unfortunately, the legislature did not

Table 5.5. Variables in Ohio's Initial Funding Formula in Response to *DeRolph*, 1995

Input Measures

Average daily membership divided by the number of Advanced Placement courses

Number of high school courses offered

Cost-adjusted average teacher salary

Beginning-teacher salary

Pupil-to-teacher ratio

Pupil-to-administrator ratio

Pupil-to-support-staff ratio

Percentage of pupils in extra-curricular programs

Output Measures

Percentage of 10th-graders passing the 9th-grade proficiency exam by the fourth try

Percentage of 12th-graders passing all parts of the 12th grade proficiency test

Number of dropouts per pupil in secondary school

Source: Ohio Department of Education (1995).

appropriate enough state funds to cover more than $3,851 per pupil.[17] Reflecting the department's wishes and the governor's blessing, five additional bills set down tight financial, building, and academic accountability requirements for school districts.[18]

The academic requirements were even tougher than those of the later federal law, the No Child Left Behind Act: districts would have to meet academic performance standards in return for state foundation aid (which had been a major initiative of Superintendents Ted Sanders and John Goff). A letter to the House speaker from John Goff shows that the testing system was going ahead, despite the court challenge. In fact, the court's decision is invoked almost as an afterthought. He wrote, "At a time when additional dollars are likely to be added for public education, it is critical that the state has also set high expectations for Ohio schools" (Goff 1997).

The bill and this letter are significant because, despite the court's strongly worded missive and intense scrutiny from the coalition, the school boards association, and teachers' unions, ODE continued to pursue an accountability policy and a school funding formula without their input. And it succeeded. ODE's political autonomy had not been damaged so as to stop the accountability measures, and its technical autonomy was recognized as supreme, even by the plaintiffs.

The state's initial attempt to satisfy the court was decidedly unappealing to the interest groups that had brought the case. In 1999, they convinced the Perry County Court that the state's new efforts were just as bad as the old system had been. The county court complained that the state had merely imposed more mandates on school systems without providing sufficient funds, a claim only strengthened by the failure of the state to fund the base level of its own formula. Curiously, it also held that the state's focus on performance ignored "input" measures (Hogan 1998, 357–58; Drummond 2000).

Predictably, the state appealed the Perry County court decision to the state's supreme court. The supreme court again ruled with Perry County. The state had failed to address significantly any of the arguments the court had made against the state in the initial *DeRolph* ruling.

The formula struck down by the court was ODE's own, and of recent vintage too. Although ODE again developed three new models for the legislature—all variations on the Augenblick model, and all requiring compliance with performance standards—the Senate Education Committee chairman noted that ODE was no longer the only game in town, saying, "We're all working on the same chapter, maybe not necessarily on the same page." In this environment, ODE temporarily moved toward the background. The department had convinced the legislature and governor but not shifted the opinion of the court, the important principal in this case.[19]

Of particular interest is the Ohio Federation of Teachers' (OFT) proposal. It was the most wide-ranging proposal (outside of the coalition's) that pulled in multiple parts of its broader legislative agenda (such as calling for caps on the number of charter schools as a funding solution). Perhaps because of its breadth, it suffered from a lack of technical expertise. A pair of analysts critiqued the effort as a "half-finished product . . . the proposal looks like the product of a committee process in which no editorial supervisor reconciled different proposals from different members." Further, all of the proposals depended on ODE's numbers—none of the interest groups or legislators could produce work without them. This is evidence of a high level of technical autonomy (Driscoll and Fleeter 2000).

In addition, both the coalition and the OFT proposals lacked the political autonomy that ODE had. Both were constrained by their membership and others' perceptions of a "hidden agenda." Ohio's state treasurer noted after the first *DeRolph* ruling that "the legislative challenge would be easier if education leaders resistant to change would stop misleading us to believe that student interests always come first, as if there were no bureaucratic or professional staff interests at all." ODE was a major player because it had to be. Outside interest groups could not match its status (Blackwell 1997).

None of these back-to-the-blackboard proposals passed. Instead, in December 2000, the Ohio General Assembly passed a bill tweaking some of the reserved-revenue requirements and eliminating a requirement for district rainy-day funds that it had passed earlier. It did not touch the earlier performance requirements, which one of the bill's sponsors credited with improving the state's reading programs. In addition, Governor Taft's 2002–2003 budget adopted part of ODE's suggestions. It also tried to comply with the court's ruling by raising the per-pupil foundation level by cutting $1.4 billion from higher education, mental health, women's shelters, prisons, and other state programs (Welsh-Huggins 2000; O'Brien 2003, 412–14, n. 127, 132).

When the case returned to the court in June 2001, the state had cut deeply into other programs, but state tax revenue was falling. Two of the members of the court who had sided with the original majority against the state were tiring of the case. These defections allowed *DeRolph III* to provide specific guidance to close the case: fully fund the parity-aid program for poor districts (passed by the legislature in response to *DeRolph II*) and tweak the formula to raise the baseline. Chief Justice Moyer wrote, "We have concluded that no one is served by continued uncertainty and fractious debate. In that spirit, we have created the consensus that should terminate the role of the court in this dispute" (*DeRolph III*, 1190).

But the court misstepped. Although it sought to end the case, it turned out that the court had believed the research from the coalition without considering information generated by the state budget office and ODE. Due to faulty data the court used, the "small fix" would cost the state $1.2 billion *more* than the $1.4 billion in additional funding it had just squeezed out of a turnip. One editorialist opined that the court's new opinion "deserved diatribes against their inconsistent, illogical reasoning. And, in what stands as perhaps the sweetest sort of justice, it now looks as though the court's majority didn't even understand what it did" (School funding chronology 2001; Sheridan 2001).

By now, the court's position was untenable. There were no longer four votes to do anything. In response, the court ordered a mediator to bring the coalition and the state to an agreement, but intransigence on the part of the state and the coalition halted the mediation in March 2002. A former ODE official told me, "There's a fundamental lack of trust, and I could never figure out what to do to overcome that." From the other side, a lobbyist argued to me that the problem was less about trust than power. ODE had it. Outside groups did not: "There's no way to find common ground. What's the use [of working with ODE] if we can't go back and counter their arguments?"[20]

Although the coalition formally continued to keep up a drumbeat against the state, judicial patience had flagged. When the case came up a fourth time, it offered a perfunctory opinion that the system remained unconstitutional but then declared that the problem was legislative. The court would hear no more of the *DeRolph* cases. Despite this, in May 2003, after the coalition asked the court again to condemn the state's work on finance, the court killed the case permanently, saying the state's judicial system had had enough of the case. The majority opinion complained that the coalition's request was "an ill-disguised attempt" to thwart the legislative process (Candisky and Leonard 2003). William Phillis, head of the coalition, complained: "We have a legislature that won't obey court orders and a Supreme Court that won't enforce court decisions" (Farney 2004, 28).[21]

The moral of Ohio's school finance case is that courts are a poor venue to challenge the technical expertise of state agencies. In the end, the coalition had to swallow an assessment program that ODE likely could never have enacted without the court mandate to do *something*. Further, the department was able to completely ignore interest group input in crafting its responses to the court; both its institutional isolation and the support of its non-court political principals ensured that it was independent. The department had autonomy and broad scope already; it did not need to rely on outside groups for support.

Conclusion

In terms of policy output, both Ohio and Georgia were able to establish a new policy—a new assessment, new requirements for receiving state aid—while Wisconsin was only able to strengthen its existing licensure system with ideas that many interest groups already had experience with on a district-level basis.

This chapter showed that government agencies that possess wide-ranging responsibilities can avoid being captured by interest groups if they do not *have* to work with them. In Ohio, the department studiously avoided entanglement with interest groups, and despite temporary setbacks, it maintained and even widened its scope. In Georgia, GADOE engaged interest groups on a very limited basis, maintaining its autonomy and successfully implementing a program that many state interest groups did not like but came to accept grudgingly. In Wisconsin, the DPI's limited responsibilities left it with little option but to seek interest group partners, and, as a consequence, it had little credible autonomy, and its scope continued to be fairly restricted.

Interest groups do serve vital purposes in democratic discourse, not least of which is their ability to transmit the wishes of their constituents to legislators and to bureaucrats. Vice versa, interest groups can help smooth the implementation of new policy if their members are hesitant to change. In the aforementioned cases, department personnel saw interest groups as stalwart defenders of the status quo. Governmental agencies, in the right institutional situations, and if entrusted with broad enough scope, can overcome interest group resistance to create change.

6

Leading by Example

State Superintendents' Influence

> The charismatic leader gains and maintains authority solely by proving his strength in life. If he wants to be a prophet, he must perform miracles; if he wants to be a war lord, he must perform heroic deeds. Above all, however, his divine mission must "prove" itself in that those who faithfully surrender to him must fare well. If they do not fare well, he is obviously not the master sent by the gods.
>
> —Max Weber, "The Sociology of Charismatic Authority," from *Max Weber: Essays in Sociology*

The role of leadership is both strikingly clear and impenetrably foggy. Titles such as *Leadership for Results* and *In Search of Excellence* in any bookstore confirm that received wisdom about personal causation in organizations is deeply embedded in American culture. Of all the ways an agency may gain autonomy and responsibility, the style of leadership is the most active. Not only is it the easiest to control (at least for the leader), but it is easier to connect what a leader does to what happens at an agency. Although leadership is filtered through many other facets of politics, my interviewees ascribed a great deal of weight to the agency's top leadership. Yes despite popular belief, the effect of leadership on an organization's outcomes is unclear, and the research is decidedly unsystematic. When can any leader, strong or weak, overcome the limits of diffuse organizational structure?

It is my contention that the public nature of bureaucratic leadership is in fact a unique source of strength unavailable to private organizations. As Haass (1999, 9) observes, public agencies cannot "go out of business" in inhospitable environments. That is, other parts of the public system *must* cooperate at some level with the agency. Therefore, while agency leaders may not have a strong hand in dealing with internal organizational difficulties, the astute leader can challenge lawmakers to rewrite the agency's scope to fit with the leader's autonomous activity. More directly, when can state superintendents use their leadership post and its limitations to gain legal, political, and fiscal autonomy for their state education agency? This chapter suggests *how* those state education agency leaders have cajoled lawmakers and governors to do just that and suggests whether they were effective.

To do so, I construct a three-part typology of leadership drawn from the literature and from my analysis of how state education chiefs used their agencies' expertise and political situation—between legislators, governors, and stakeholders—to leverage changes in education law to their favor. They were not uniformly successful, but each demonstrated that the post as leader could be used to reorient both their agencies and the legislation that empowered them. These chiefs adopted different leadership strategies to suit different political situations, and I argue that the particular leadership style that they adopted gave their agencies greater (or lesser) autonomy to implement existing state education reform legislation and greater (or lesser) success in acquiring new scope to ratify those autonomous actions.

It should be noted that "leadership" here does not mean leadership in *schools* but in instituting *policy* at the state level. For this to happen, the governor and legislators, the political principals of the agency, must be convinced of the merits of the leaders' proposals. Certainly district superintendents, school principals, teachers, parents, and peers have a tremendous influence on the actual performance of policy inside the walls of the classroom (see Elmore 2000), but these stakeholders are not likely to hold as much individual clout in state politics as state superintendents and state education agencies do. (Also, this chapter does not consider how state superintendents convince their own state agencies to go along with decisions; see Lusi [1997] for a treatment of how two state departments of education implemented new legislative mandates internally.)

Bureaucratic Leadership

State agency leaders are a different breed of leader than presidents or governors, general managers, or CEOs. Not only do they have civil-service employees that cannot be easily rearranged or laid off, but their superiors, and perhaps they themselves, are elected by a population that pays only part-time attention to performance. They are expected to make decisions in public, follow the party line (if any), effect change, fulfill contradictory laws, and manage federal demands.

The literature on how leaders lead is large but tends to highlight idiosyncratic factors (see, for example, Ingraham, Sowa, and Moynihan 2004; Frederickson and Smith 2003, chapter 5; Copland 2003). In response, scholars of educational leadership have downplayed individual, directive leadership in educational organizations, because when individual leaders are successful, "they are recognizable only because they are the exception[s]" (Copland 2003, 375). If leadership is a rare Weberian personality trait, then many government leaders are without hope. The view that I find more convincing—the one I adopt here—is that leadership is a strategy adopted by an organization's chief. Such a strategy can influence both the agency at large *and* the preferences of its political principals. Such a view is supported by scholars who argue that "leadership" is a characteristic of an organization that no one person has (Ogawa and Bossert 1995; Sergiovanni 1984); those who define it as the shared adoption of norms and goals by many persons in the organization (Copland 2003; Bennett et al. 2003); and even those who suggest leadership is a normative, almost pastoral, quest to critique and alter the outlook of both teachers (or other employees) and of society by personal example (Dantley 2005; Greenleaf 2002; Starratt 1996). Others have characterized it as salesmanship (Cameron 2000; Ashford et al. 1998; Neustadt 1991). In none of these definitions is leadership endemic to an individual, but an individual *does* characterize the task. Even in the institutional view of organizations, individuals may lead when they can share the structure or resource flow to gain compliance to their wishes (Ogawa and Bossert 1995; Moe 1989). Therefore, individual leaders can adopt a strategy to bring others around to their view of a desired goal. Individual leaders may try and fail and still "lead"—a situation that appeared in all of the case studies here.

Beyond the basic challenges to leadership found in all organizations, state agency leaders, such as state superintendents, also face other barriers to the effective enactment of new policies. Many government agencies may have few or no natural supporters in the legislative or executive branches. Departments of education are no exception; though they advocate for public education, the many local organizations that create public education (schools and districts primarily) tend to view the state with wary eyes; only rarely do they lend their lobbying support (Glasser 1990; Pfeffer and Salancik 1978; Berman et al. 1978). State superintendents must consider not only resistance from teachers, district superintendents, and other educational stakeholders—the traditional sources of push-back (Elmore 1996; Glasser 1990; Pfeffer and Salancik 1978)—but they must also maneuver competing demands among state agencies, political parties, and political interests unrelated to education.

Three leadership strategies characterize the state superintendents in the discussion that follows. Which strategy state superintendents chose was empirically related to the policy topic's public salience, the likely response from direct stakeholders, and the expected feedback from other state-level elected officials. These were the key variables.[1]

A first strategy, which is here called public leadership, is essentially public relations writ large. One way to short-circuit the normal political process is to go directly to "the people" to build public support (Nicholson, Segura, and Woods 2002; Edwards 1989). If the superintendent can build a "mandate" for new ideas, then the state education agency may be able to pressure legislators and governors—through the public—on the department's own terms. Public leadership would be expected to be most useful when the leader was an outsider relative to both the agency's stakeholders and the current political rulers *and* there was reason to believe that the issues at stake were salient to the public (see Ringquist, Worsham, and Eisner 2003). The chief has to rely on public perceptions to bring about change to the policies the leader wants to pursue. Public leaders must be energetic and vigorous, and they must seek wide publicity. As shown later, such a strategy of leadership is time-consuming and often egoistical, leading to the neglect of internal department politics (as shown in an earlier chapter). Leaders like these can be lightning rods for critics, both within and without the department. This public pressure may be able to generate change by forcing the hand of other branches of government. Although the riskiest approach, such visible leadership may also generate the greatest gains. Thus I expect that *public leadership will enhance both the autonomy and responsibility of an agency by mobilizing the public at large to generate political pressure on other branches of government.*

Second, there is insider leadership. Akin to "distributed leadership" (Bennett et al. 2003; Leithwood 1992), a state superintendent might seek to build support for a new policy program by building support one person at a time. As the education literature on distributed leadership argues, such distributed leadership also enhances departmental "buy-in" so that a policy survives at least its initial implementation. Leaders who adopted this strategy would be much more likely to lead the agency from within, to make one-on-one bargains with political figures, to have an open door policy with staff, and to fit generally what the management books call "Theory Y" leadership.

While such a strategy might have reduced the need to use the superintendent's office as a bully pulpit, the lack of a formal means of communication and policy selection greatly increased the temptation for the parties who made agreements in private to defect from them in public (McCarty and Rothenberg 1996). Part of their problem was that, without public support, individual bargains have little long-term credibility as either side could renege easily. Perhaps not incidentally, all three met stiff passive resistance to their leadership. Such a strategy might also open up leaders to the charge that they are ineffective public figures and inept politicians.

Private, insider leadership is the most effective when the education agency has a high level of the "whole-organization leadership" that Ogawa and Bossert (1995) describe. More particularly, it may also be effective if the superintendent wants a policy change that will have little resonance with the public (so public leadership would not be an option) but the agency has existing scope to perform the change (so political leadership is not necessary). Insider leadership is also attractive if a leader's desired autonomous action could be damaging to the department's standing if the proposal was floated publicly first. This strategy should appear when public salience was low *and* stakeholders and other government entities were initially opposed to the state superintendent's proposals. Thus I expect that *insider leadership will fail to generate autonomy for an agency because it is highly dependent on frequent, individual bargains, although such leadership may build or consolidate its scope.*

Third, state superintendents may engage in political leadership. They may use democratic politics to logroll, to lobby legislators, and to feed information to governors. This form of leadership may be extremely successful as long as the political configuration is stable, or it may fail spectacularly when the political winds change. Political leadership publicly and explicitly links policy to partisan ends. Because of the nature of their work, legislators and governors have interests far broader than education policy, and effective state superintendents would seek to show how some change in the scope of the state agency would benefit these other political interests (Malen 2001; Mazzoni 2000).

Because the legislature and the governor (and non-education interest groups) have no formal tie to the superintendent, superintendents must lead "among equals." And unlike either public or insider leadership, political leaders must be able to "understand the language of multiple professional communities" and political constituencies (Honig 2006, 361). In this way, political leaders are classic "boundary spanners" (Weatherly and Lipsky 1977). Further, boundary spanners are, by definition, not part of the policy area's technical core (therefore they can take a longer view of an issue), and their formal role in policy making and implementation is informal and malleable, depending on the policy environment (Honig 2006; Kingdon 2003). Leaders adopting this strategy would be well suited for autonomous action under the right political circumstances.

State superintendents might choose this form of leadership if public salience is expected to be low (so public leadership would be unattractive) and *either* the department's stakeholders *or* other elected officials were resistant to change. Further, political leadership may be the only option if the agency's legal existence is under attack by the governor or other legislators—a situation that appeared in all three states used here at some point in the time period. Thus I expect that *political leadership will be most effective for securing increased scope for an agency when the agency has significant legislative or gubernatorial support. It will be less successful in building autonomy because the leader's success is explicitly contingent on the political process.*

The remainder of this chapter explores how superintendents used each of these strategies in their own political situations to further his or her agency's autonomy and scope. Although each superintendent did use multiple styles of leadership at different times, each was characterized by a dominant mode.

Public Leadership

Two primary reasons for resorting to a strategy of public leadership emerged from my work. First, superintendents may adopt this strategy when they are in a weak position, as when they do not have support from the legislature, the governor's office, or even from stakeholders, or their department had little scope on the state level. In these situations, agency leaders can try to make an end run around both the statehouse and the governor's mansion. If executed carefully, the agency's leader may be able to force her or his policy onto the legislative agenda. (How can a state agency chief not have the support of the governor? A handful of agencies, departments of education among them, have chiefs who are elected or appointed by various configurations of legislators, boards, and voters. These arrangements may deprive agency executives of their natural base of support in the executive branch.) As discussed later, Wisconsin Superintendent Herbert J. Grover had a department with narrow scope *and* little state support; and Georgia Superintendent Linda Schrenko had a department with broad scope but with political enemies.

The second reason for this strategy stems from self-inflicted problems. Even in states where the governor is influential in choosing leaders (whether through outright appointment or deep informal involvement),

agencies may take actions that prompt widespread outcry from stakeholders or the public. This puts the agency leader in an awkward position, as
the governor and legislators seek to distance themselves from the agency.
In this case, the leader will have to resort to public leadership to keep
her or his chosen policy on track, or worse, to keep her or his job. Ohio
Superintendent Ted Sanders provides an instructive example.

Wisconsin: Herbert Grover—Little Scope and Little Support

Herbert Grover was something of a showman as Wisconsin's state superintendent. "He was a volcano of motion and emotion," one longtime
lobbyist remembered. He was capable of working through the system:
he knew the limited scope of his department but constantly reminded
the legislature that the DPI was vital to Wisconsin. In his view, it and
the school districts it represented were chronically underfunded. He
pounded the pavement between his office and the state capitol, two
blocks away. He filled legislators' in-boxes with missives urging support
for the department's priorities.

But Grover was not content to work the formal channels of political
argument. More effectively than either his predecessor or his successor,
he toured the state making seemingly outrageous claims to hook the
media. On one occasion, he proclaimed that he would not send any
one of his six children to the DeSoto district public schools because
their curriculum was below DPI standards. Of course, this statement
was made in front of local newspaper cameras. "I had teachers crying
on the phone to me," Grover told me.

All of this served him well as state superintendent, and during his
tenure, it served his department as well. Many of the educators and
educational representatives with whom I spoke remembered Grover in
halcyon terms—even if they had been enemies when he was superintendent. Grover's public leadership had two qualities that were particularly
useful to his department's autonomy and scope. First, he was a tireless
correspondent, answering the most mundane pieces of mail. This gained
him a statewide reputation that emphasized his and his agency's constitutional independence from the legislature and the governor. Second,
he inundated local media with appearances, articles, editorials, and press
releases (and a healthy dose of compliments). Grover carefully watched
the responses too: "After one particularly blistery editorial complaining
about all the mail the newspaper was getting from DPI, we took the
Dunn County News off the press release mailing list," Grover wrote to
Representative Richard A. Shoemaker. When the DPI had a plan, no
paper in the state could plead ignorance (Grover 1985b).

Grover used his pen to push his vision for Wisconsin education whenever *anyone* wrote so little as a postcard to him. He responded to a class of fourth and fifth graders from Poplar, Wisconsin, that had sent him a calendar they had made, saying it would be "displayed proudly" at the DPI (Grover 1984d). To one letter writer, he replied with his philosophy of education and his department, "[T]he institution of education is responsible for the maintenance of the cultural heritage and improvement of self and society . . . without a conscious effort to teach and learn these things . . . [*sic*] a free republic will not long endure." He ended by arguing that the DPI is empowered, essentially, to preserve Western civilization according to the Wisconsin statutes (118.10) (Grover 1983b). To another correspondent who complained about poor vocational education but doubted that the DPI would care about his opinion, Grover replied with a two-page, single-spaced letter explaining how the DPI was enhancing vocational education in rural school districts. He ended with a pointed coda: "I read all my mail, John, and try to personally respond to it" (Grover 1984d).

Grover also used letters to round up support specifically for his programs, as he did when campaigning to reorganize the state's midlevel education service agencies. In one response that he sent to several district administrators, he linked a recent reorganization of the DPI with the need to reorganize regional service agencies (Grover 1982b). He also took on a local school board member's complaint that the move to larger service agencies would strip local control, saying that larger agencies would take more administrative burden off of (especially) small districts so they could exercise local control more effectively (Grover 1982a). Further, Grover never let a complaint go unanswered, even if he had to handle it with a bit of humor. In 1985, he (with the support of Governor Anthony Earl) sought to raise the base teacher salary to $18,000. One particularly negative letter received this response:

> In an enterprise as labor intensive as education is, it is absolutely necessary that the persons entering employment be of the highest possible quality. To not get these quality persons means we may pay a somewhat less bill [*sic*] for a vastly inferior product. . . . At any rate, I appreciate your writing to me on this matter. Thus far, this item has received no legislative support, so apparently you have little worry that this item will survive the complete budget process. (Grover 1985a)

Although I do not claim that Grover's extensive personal correspondence generated a new scope for the department, it did allow him to claim a "mandate from the people" when he *was* arguing for more scope. Indeed, a person was far more likely to get a personal response from Grover than the governor, as a look through Governor Tommy Thompson's correspondence archives confirms. (In fairness, the governor also received vastly more mail.) Grover was a former state legislator; this experience had taught him the value of constituent service. One former DPI official told me that Grover probably spent too much time answering correspondence at the expense of other policy-related activities, but Grover did not appear to be hurt by this.

What did allow Grover to leverage his program for the DPI was courtship of the news media. Table 6.1 (next page) shows how extensive Grover's personal correspondence was throughout Wisconsin and how much of it was seeking goodwill with notes of congratulations. He was friendly with the editor of his favorite newspaper, the Madison, Wisconsin, *Capital Times*, so he usually had a reliable organ for his views there.[2] Still, he actively sought coverage in every paper in the state. He made special trips to talk to editorial boards throughout the state and always sent a follow-up letter to reiterate his views. For example, he wrote to the editor of the Marshfield, Wisconsin, *News Herald* a day after his visit to expand on his description of a public-private partnership for a vocational education program that the DPI was starting in Janesville. He ended with a request for good coverage: "I know that the success of programs in education demands the support of the public, and you are a key link to the public" (Grover 1982a). He also sent congratulatory letters to all winners of journalistic prizes—even if the prizes were not education related. Finally, he boasted to me, "I was in the newspaper every day of the week."

Grover was able to capitalize on his political autonomy through his media coverage and his official personal correspondence. A longtime lobbyist noted, "Grover had it right—he could impact change. . . . He was loud and out there. For better or worse, when he wanted to do something, he'd have his arms flailing. He was loud. But he could bring everyone to the table." Grover's careful cultivation of state news and personal constituents enhanced the DPI's autonomy by ensuring that the DPI's view—independent of the governor's, or any legislator's—was heard. The effect of Grover's media use to bolster his department's political autonomy may be seen by the editorials that legislators frequently sent to him from their home district newspapers.[3]

In addition, his media use allowed him to easily take on recalcitrant public officials by propping up the department's meager responsibilities at the district level. For example, Grover relished his press releases of poor graduation statistics. He said, "Some superintendents came to me

Table 6.1. Correspondence with Journalists by Superintendent
Herbert Grover, 1981—1984

	1981	1982	1983	1984	Total	Pct.
Original from Grover, with . . .						
Information for a						
possible story	—	7	2	3	12	5.1
Response to a story	—	7	7	10	24	10.2
Thanks for the . . .						
Interview	—	12	14	20	46	19.5
Positive coverage	3	7	9	12	31	13.1
Favor*	—	—	1	4	5	2.1
Congratulations	6	34	12	61	113	48.1
Other	—	1	2	1	4	1.7
Total	9	68	47	111	235	100.0

Note: This does not include press releases, newsletters, and other material that the DPI
sent out regularly. Because archival sources are likely to be incomplete, these numbers
are only suggestive. Only his first term is shown because there exist only very few
copies of letters to the press in the archives for his second and third term.

*"Favors" include sending Grover information, participation in an event, or a personal
favor.

Source: Compiled by the author from Wisconsin Historical Society archives, Correspondence of the State Superintendent, Series 651.

and said, 'You aren't going to release that [to the press] are you? We
can't let that out!' But I did. And it made them change. Openness is
antiseptic." He released a study on the (in)effectiveness of the old mid-
level service agencies and he was sure to note that fact to legislators.
Similar tactics helped Grover win acceptance for both minimum state
standards (which had never existed in Wisconsin) and a competency test
to measure students' abilities. (Grover, uniquely among the education
agency officials I interviewed, credited the federal *Nation at Risk* with
helping him leverage the standards.)[4]

In sum, Grover's public leadership—particularly his use of the media
and personal correspondence—was a significant boost to his legislative
efforts to enlarge the Wisconsin Department of Public Instruction's
responsibilities and to reinforce his own ability to use the DPI autonomously from the governor.

Ohio: Ted Sanders—Broad Scope and Alienated Supporters

Sometimes public exposure and a full-court media-relations press only
serve to staunch the loss of agency autonomy when its leader has made

a politically or publicly unpopular policy choice. That is, superintendents may resort to a public leadership strategy when other state-level officials seek to abandon them. Ohio Superintendent Ted Sanders was by nature a political leader. He was superintendent from 1991 to 1995, a Republican in a state with strong Republican representation in the legislature and with a Republican governor, and, despite the formal independence of the state board of education from the governor, Governor George V. Voinovich had prevailed upon the board to hire Sanders. Sanders was careful to build political legislative support (see chapter 7). Unfortunately for Sanders, many of these legislative friends did not believe he had been transparent enough when pushing his academic standards plan. Public salience and stakeholder groups worked against him, and the department appeared to lose autonomy.

The Ohio Department of Education was responsible for developing state proficiency exams and for helping frame the state's standards with the state board. A cornerstone of Sanders's tenure was the introduction of so-called outcomes-based education (OBE) to help students prepare for Ohio's ninth-grade proficiency exam. Although Ohio had a ninth-grade exam in the 1980s, neither Voinovich nor Sanders thought that the curriculum it tested was very well defined. Both Sanders and Voinovich were familiar with the National Governors' Association education publication "Time for Results" (1986), then in currency, and Voinovich wanted to tighten up the curriculum to claim credit for what he hoped would be an improvement in test scores. Sanders saw OBE as one way to do both.

Outcomes-based education was an attempt to create concrete standards without resorting to achievement testing (Spady 1994). As an educational method, OBE requires students to be held to curriculum rubrics that define what and when students should be taught subjects (not unlike curriculum standards). Students repeat school activities, usually with no penalty, until they demonstrate "mastery" of all subjects on the rubric. Sometimes there are multiple levels of mastery. Many states adopted variations on OBE in the early 1990s, including Colorado, Minnesota, and Pennsylvania. Although the repeat-until-replete component drew criticism from those concerned about real-world job situations, the most stinging criticism was generated by some unfortunate terminology adopted by Ohio to implement the education model.

Ohio's OBE initiative created standards to define "what students should know, be able to do, and be like" (Sensky 1993b). The first two were noncontroversial, but the third phrase nearly brought down the department. The most explosive criticism was that the department was "telling our kids what to believe," but OBE came in for other complaints as well. One of the governor's advisors noted four other criticisms that set off the "firestorm" surrounding OBE. Opponents rallied against OBE's estimated cost (to permit students to work at their own pace); teaching methods (the rubrics would become a ceiling, so gifted students would be ignored); state control of curriculum; and the perceived strike against family control over education (Sensky 1993b). The regulations were also unclear as to how it would affect private schools: "Many private school supporters believe this is just a new way for the NEA and others to win control over their systems. . . . [OBE] forces them to teach to the test rather than teaching the particular philosophy of education advocated by that private school" (Sensky 1993b).

From the governor's point of view, however, the bigger problem was poor leadership by the superintendent. Governor Voinovich wrote a terse memo to Sanders as the controversy erupted.

> I am a little upset, frankly, that I was not tipped off that all of this Outcome Based Education has been controversial in other states. . . . I feel like I've been blind sighted [*sic*] and, quite frankly, am not very happy about it. I think it's imperative that you put together a very understandable document on what this is all about, so I understand it. I think it's important the Governor understands it. (Voinovich 1993b)

Sanders initially resorted to an insider leadership strategy by shoring up individual support for his chosen policy path. He met with state senators, representatives, and (perhaps most importantly) the governor to defend the department's choice of OBE, and he tried to clarify that "and be like" meant good citizenship, a goal that had been implicit in Ohio's school code for many years. But once he lost control of the issue, Sanders realized that the public—whose children would be affected by the department's new policy—could not be converted by talking to their state representatives. Prompted by this realization and the governor's anger, Sanders went public. He addressed school conventions, school boards, and parent meetings, and he met with the (Ohio) House Republican Caucus to quell the controversy. Sanders despaired to the governor that he was "encountering this issue in nearly all my public appearances, and know firsthand how unpleasant these critics and their criticisms can be" (Sanders 1993c). Those unpleasant encounters were sometimes extremely uncomfortable. John Goff, who was an assistant superintendent in the early 1990s, remembered being on the road with Sanders to promote the program: "Ted and I were in a church in western Ohio talking about the new standards. They were mad. I wasn't sure we were going to make it out alive—and not metaphorically. The standards said they would set what students would know, be able to do, and 'be like.' Including that phrase was the worst thing we ever did."

Despite Sanders's attempt to publicly redefine the offending terms, his critics were dissatisfied. After the chair of the House Education Committee declared that "O-B-E is O-U-T," Sanders wrote an unambiguous reply to depict OBE as only one model on the road to "performance-based" education (Sanders 1994). He tried to show that school-group stakeholders would actually have the final say about OBE. Sanders noted that the department developed OBE only as "one of several research-based school improvement models that school districts *may choose* to adapt through the venture capital grant process," and that OBE would require "*approval of their elected local board of education* and expressed interest by the majority of the school's staff" (Sanders 1993a, emphases in original).

This proved insufficient. In January 1994, Sanders gave up. He wrote a memo to the legislature that said in no uncertain terms that the department would not condone OBE in any form (Sanders 1994). In an ironic outcome, OBE, which was meant to replace fuzzy process standards with observable activities, was skewered as abstract. One newspaper editorialized, "The last thing Ohio needs is an approach to learning that sets abstract goals for kids. Kids need a concrete education" (Outcomes: Ousted 1994).

The issues that OBE stirred up did not disappear after Sanders "[drove] a stake through its heart" (Sanders 1994). In March 1995, a large consortium of private schools continued to object to the existence of a state test on the same grounds as they had objected to OBE (Ross 1995). But the wringer that Sanders and ODE had been through prompted the governor—suspicious of the department from the start of his term—and legislature to pull up on the department's reins. (Sanders had been picked by the governor in part to keep tabs on the department [Gallagher 1990].) Although Voinovich and Sanders remained on good terms after Sanders left, he had become a political liability for the governor and the governor's plans for Ohio's education system. Sanders left for greener pastures at Southern Illinois University in July 1995; this departure presented the governor with an opportunity to push through part of his headline reforms to give him appointment powers for nine state board members. In an attempt to forestall the governor, Cooper Snyder, the Senate Education Committee chair, argued that "reform comes from the Governor and Legislature through leadership. . . . Such things as proficiency tests, technology, equity funding, etc. have been accomplished with or without the State Board" (Snyder 1995). Although the department continued to develop the tests and create a student performance model that department staff were proud to tell me was more rigorous than No Child Left Behind, policy direction came from outside of the department, and the department's political autonomy was damaged.

Sanders resorted to public leadership as a last-ditch effort to quiet political dissent over OBE, yet his public leadership did little to dampen the opposition. Indeed, his road trips served to inflame other criticisms of the department's policies, especially over the mere existence of the state test. Sanders's *public* leadership had also made him a *political* liability for the governor, which weakened the superintendent's ability to switch back to a political or even an insider leadership strategy.

Sanders's public approach was able to staunch the department's loss of autonomy only because he could legitimately argue that he had both the responsibility to write the state exams and because he had the political autonomy to retreat from the department's unpopular stand. This is shown by the governor's criticism of Sanders—Voinovich was looking to Sanders for educational direction. Although the governor took steps to circumvent some autonomy of the department, the department continued to exercise the responsibility gained for it under Sanders. The Ohio Department of Education's pursuit of tight state standards proceeded along *very* similar lines and even became tougher under Superintendents Goff and Zelman.

Georgia: Linda Schrenko—Broad Scope and Active Opposition

Although Ohio's rear-guard public relations efforts helped stem the loss of autonomy, in Georgia, Superintendent Linda Schrenko's attempt at public leadership backfired and destroyed a relationship with the state's largest newspaper, harmed her relationship with the governor, and cost her her rapport with the state school board. Given her combative nature, Schrenko is an excellent test case for my hypothesis that public leadership will generate political pressure on other branches of government to effect changes. Her public leadership consisted of cultivating an outsider image to overcome board and legislative opposition for her agenda.[5]

Georgia Superintendent Linda Schrenko was the quintessential outsider. She was a Republican in a state that in 1994 was still dominated by Democrats (as it had been since Reconstruction), and she was the first woman elected to statewide office. Both of these characteristics guaranteed that she would be breaking new ground. She saw her outsider status as an asset and argued that the political establishment was consciously unfriendly to her (Jacobson 1999; Ramage 1997). Although she was a longtime classroom teacher, she also argued that many educational stakeholders and their interest groups were opposed to her ideas. Thus she adopted a public leadership strategy.

Superintendent Schrenko's cultivation of an outsider image was deliberate. She espoused local school control in a state with a centralized system. She emphasized no-frills, "back to basics" reading and math education. She strove to cut the staff in the department of education to hamper what she saw as administrative excesses. And she sought to disassociate from the "liberal" national educational establishment (which included the Council of Chief State School Officers and the Parent-Teacher Association). All four of these were aimed squarely at Georgia's traditional school arrangement and her predecessor, Werner Rogers.

The hints of Schrenko's public leadership strategy came during her first campaign for election. Believing that conservatives and disaffected classroom teachers were outsiders in the educational "establishment," she cultivated their support by railing against Rogers's support for certain health classes and campaigning against the department of education (Jacobson 1999; Lindsay 1995).

To gain conservatives during her election campaign in 1994, Schrenko accused Werner Rogers of supporting what he told me was "appropriate sex education and AIDS education." This helped Schrenko target him as being too liberal for Georgia—and when combined with Georgia's low education rankings, this allowed her to question why Rogers was spending time on controversial subjects rather than on "basic" education. Further, Rogers had refused to fill out a Christian Coalition position survey because he claimed he could not explain his position on the survey (White 1994; Schrenko 1995). Even a decade later, when he talked with me, he was still amazed at how much this political oversight helped defeat him.

Second, Schrenko ceaselessly campaigned against "bureaucracy" at GADOE. In doing so, she tapped a long-simmering frustration with Georgia's landmark Quality Basic Education (QBE) standards package, passed in 1985. QBE covered facilities, curriculum, and performance standards for school districts. The state could take over districts that failed these standards. It also required paperwork—lots of paperwork. Department staff began receiving irate calls about the yard-long "standards box" that schools filled for QBE (personal interview). Indeed, the governor had a form letter to respond to educators like this one who complained about the law:

> Georgia Educators are drowning in the bureaucratic paper-
> work of your QBE Act. Many excellent educators have been
> driven to the point of resigning to seek better jobs with less

paperwork and better working conditions. . . . Please pay
us what we are worth and GIVE US TIME TO TEACH!
(Jones 1988)

Governor Joe Frank Harris always pointed to Rogers as being responsible
for fixing the problem: "Dr. Werner Rogers is looking at the requirements behind the paperwork in order to see which can be simplified
or abolished" (Harris 1988). Rogers continued to promise to reduce
paperwork through his tenure. (In fairness, Harris thought the complaints
about QBE's allegedly arduous workload on teachers were "disgusting"
[Harris 1985].) Rogers was also the recipient of these complaints, especially after the *Atlanta Journal-Constitution* ran the critical 1989 article
"Lost in paperwork, teachers lack time to help children."

Schrenko was able to capitalize on the support of both of these
groups plus the general Republican fervor of 1994 to best Rogers in
November. (Rogers, a Democrat, was joined in defeat by three other
Democratic state officers.) She also governed as an outsider; she never
developed close relations with the teachers' groups or superintendents,
and she had an openly hostile relationship with the state board. At first,
many people gave her the benefit of the doubt. "People just didn't know
how to deal with a lady Republican," a veteran lobbyist told me. "It
wasn't even the Republican part. You see, you are in the South, and a
woman is supposed to be genteel-like. . . . But by the end of her term,
people had learned."

Partisan politics can hamper the enactment of reforms, education
and otherwise (Superfine 2005; Bowling and Ferguson 2001). But
electoral surprises can "shock" other players into cooperating, at least
in the short term. Schrenko's surprise win over Rogers in 1994 gave
her initial clout with the Democratic governor and legislature, especially
because she could claim a mandate from the public.

Schrenko's public leadership ensured that the legislature and governor would have to work with her on her own terms. She had courted one
key variable of leadership, public salience, helping her chances of success
in the short term. She successfully used her department's autonomy to
push through a phonics reading program whose effectiveness was questioned by the state board, to cut more than $20 million over her terms
from the department's budget, to fire dozens of longtime employees,
and to restructure the state's student testing system (Cumming 1998a,
b; Salzer 2000b; Measure accountability with state examinations 1999).
Although Schrenko might have been able to expand the department's
scope, her campaign promise was to cut the department, and so she
did—even as she successfully expanded the department's autonomy.

Schrenko quickly adopted a public leadership strategy. She was frequently on the road speaking to teachers' groups and community groups; by the end of her second term she was logging more than twice the miles in travel than the governor (Salzer 2002). She publicly attacked the national Parent-Teacher Association as being too liberal, supported a Bible-class elective for Georgia high schools, and proposed a tight school conduct code with little political or school board input. She terminated forty-five employees—including top advisors—soon after she came to office (White 1995b). She drew opposition from local superintendents because she often bypassed them and worked directly with schools (Loupe 1997; Puckett 1999; Loupe and Soto 1997; White 1995a). Late in her term, Schrenko gained the support of both teachers' associations when she strongly supported teacher job protections against the governor's attempt to eliminate them (Salzer 2000c). (One of my interviewees, a well-placed critic of Schrenko's, nevertheless noted that "teachers did appreciate the focus she placed on the classroom.")

She had above-average success—but not because she became an able manager of the department Rogers had left her. Instead, her program's compatibility with the governor and her loud public leadership pressured the governor and legislature to follow her changes.

Schrenko did have a working relationship with Governor Zell Miller for a while—both were classroom teachers—but Miller began to distance himself from her as her fractiousness became more public. Schrenko's educational priorities were close to Miller's. Indeed, Miller could claim compatibility with both Superintendent Rogers and Schrenko. When talking with me, Rogers spared no praise for Miller's HOPE scholarship program for economically poor Georgia students. Miller also was committed to reducing paperwork and reducing budgets in the department of education, something on which Schrenko campaigned. Although Schrenko's program was aided by the governor's parallel interest, her public leadership forced Miller to work with her in a way not of his own choosing. Miller's distancing may be seen in the increasingly cool way in which he referred to the superintendent in his speeches. In January 1995, he asked the legislature to "help Superintendent Schrenko and me perform radical surgery on the education bureaucracy of the state" (Miller 1998, 186). In 1996, Miller called her "our hard-working and forward-thinking superintendent" who was "leading the way in cutting back administrative overhead" (220). A year later, however, he would not directly link himself. Instead, he noted that "Superintendent Schrenko proposed that we redirect $60 million . . . to reduce class size" (274). Miller would only say, "I agree this is a good idea" (274).

Schrenko's downfall was that she never developed close relations with stakeholders, such as teachers' groups or local superintendents, and that she had an openly hostile relationship with the Georgia State Board of Education. Her interaction with the public was positive, but the interactions with both interest groups and other government officials were decidedly negative (and sometimes even with her department: "People would come back from lunch and find packing boxes all ready for them," a longtime GADOE employee told me). Worse, Schrenko's public leadership made Governor Zell Miller backtrack publicly on his appointments to the state board of education. Although initial meetings with the board were cordial, personality, policy, and political conflicts destroyed any amity that might have existed for the new chief. School board meetings became so contentious that Miller had to ask the entire state school board—which he had appointed—to resign. One board member said Schrenko had appointed "paranoid" advisors (Jacobson 1999). The new board was much more to Schrenko's liking, and she found a staunch ally in former state Senator Johnny Isakson and now board member. Isakson told a reporter that a friendly board was particularly crucial for Schrenko, saying, "Her predecessors were really close to their Democrat governors, . . . which made it easy for them to do their jobs" (Ramage 1997). Isakson was able to soften Schrenko's image with the board and to prevail upon her to temper her policy. When Isakson left to fill Representative Newt Gingrich's seat in Congress, the *Atlanta Journal-Constitution* editorialized that newly elected Governor Barnes, a Democrat, would find him "downright difficult to replace. He has a unique blend of attributes that made him the right person to oversee the school board and work with state School Superintendent Linda Schrenko" (Head 1998).

The pressure she generated outside of the legislature cost her department some of its important scope and much of its autonomy toward the end of her two terms. In June 1999, Governor Barnes named an Education Reform Study Commission to vet his reform proposals, the most controversial of which was to shift most of GADOE's work to a new, gubernatorial-controlled agency called the "Office of Accountability." Schrenko understandably argued that her department could handle all of the governor's reforms, as did Republicans in the statehouse (Cumming 1999a; Salzer 1999b, 1999c). Barnes won the battle and GADOE lost most of its work to the governor's agency because Schrenko had few friends in the legislature. Interest groups, remembering her past slights, generally were skittish to rally around her. Thus Governor Barnes was able to replace members of the state board with members hostile to

Schrenko (so hostile that even the *Atlanta Journal-Constitution*, no fan of Schrenko's, lambasted the board). Schrenko said of the board, "The original board was obnoxious, but it wasn't malicious. This board is both obnoxious and malicious" (Salzer 2000d; Education battlefield 2000).

Schrenko's public leadership caused two problems that contributed to this long-run situation. The first was that she bashed legislators who had redirected funds to Atlanta schools, alienating an important pocket of Democrats that might have been supportive of Schrenko's early-education initiatives (Schrenko blind to own failings 1999). She had had decent support from the legislature under Democratic Governor Miller, in part because he decided that her plans for GADOE were similar enough to his that he could work with her. But when Governor Barnes, also a Democrat, signaled to the legislature that he had his own vision of education, the Democratic-controlled legislature was ready to follow its highest elected official. Second, one of Schrenko's public strategies was to flaunt her membership in the GOP. "Everything was political with Schrenko," a department employee said, a sentiment echoed by many others; the *Atlanta Journal-Constitution* opined that she had "politicized rather than energized" GADOE. Her Republican membership probably did not hurt her—she was elected twice in a state where Democrats were losing seats at all levels of government—but it did hurt the department when it needed support from the (still) majority Democratic Party against the governor. Whatever her commitment to the party, she saw this as part of her outsider persona, not as the road to political success: she had criticized Rogers, the previous superintendent, as being part of the good-old-boy Democrats of yore (White 1994a).

Superintendent Schrenko's public leadership *was* able to generate support for changes to classroom funding, organization at the department, and opposition to Governor Barnes. Unfortunately, her harsh personality and brash politics left everyone with a bitter taste in their mouths after she lost her bid for governor in 2002. She left her office having waged an all-out "war" with Governor Barnes's school board, and Barnes had lost his job in part because he infuriated educators. Indicative of her demise, Schrenko became increasingly hostile to the news media in Georgia. In 1999, she cut off all verbal communication with the state's largest newspaper. She required the paper to submit written requests for information or interviews from GADOE (Cumming 1999b). Further, in October 2002, just before she left office, she sent a feisty e-mail to an Atlanta television station, saying, "Now I am leaving office and I ain't coming back so all of you unbiased media types can just go [deleted] yourselves and make my day" (Jacobson 2002). In short, her public leadership imploded on her and her department—as it did with Herbert Grover's Wisconsin DPI after he left. Public leadership may temporarily expand a department's autonomy and responsibility, but only as long as the leader has credibility herself or himself and has a powerful foil. Public leadership does not make friends.

In each of these cases, agency leaders had strong ideas about what policies their department should pursue. Yet a public leadership strategy was unable to sustain their favored policies in the short term. Adopting this strategy did not work well to convince other political leaders, or other stakeholders, to follow the lead of the agency. In some senses, resorting to public leadership is a reflection of the failure of "normal" political channels. The bureaucracy is not *supposed* to have to "go public." If its leaders must, then the agency suffers from weakness.

Insider Leadership

Insider leadership—"hidden-hand" leadership—could be considered the normal strategy of agency leaders. When leaders used this strategy, there was little fear of alienating stakeholders or political principals. The listening public will not hear of the agency's endeavors, and interest groups will find it best to work "through the system." There is no media to corral, no campaigns to orchestrate, and no ambiguity about who is responsible. As long as the superintendent's supporters are influential, insider leadership is perhaps the most powerful. And, if it is conducted in the same manner as district-level distributed leadership, then it may keep stakeholders involved and satisfied with the decision-making process. Insider leadership may be particularly useful when—as is often the case—the autonomous action the leader is enacting does not have great public resonance or a broad constituency. Such leadership may be an appropriate strategy when a leader is actively seeking to *avoid* public exposures: if the leader can consult with the movers and shakers in advance and work out criticisms over some addition to agency scope, then both may arrive at a policy closer to their ideal outcome without the associated political costs.

In my work, an insider strategy was adopted for part of the terms of Ohio superintendents Franklin Walter and John Goff. In Ohio, a report on ODE complained that Walter *was* ODE and that staff had to go through him for every decision. John Goff was well liked by his department and worked well with a few allies on the state board, but he seemed unprepared for the state board's spotlight that would force him to switch strategies.[6]

Ohio: Franklin Walter—Active Solicitation of Support

The effect of insider leadership on departmental autonomy was most apparent in the differences in the enactment of the strategy between Walter and Goff. Although both men were able to gain autonomy and scope for their department, both had a falling out with the state board and lost their positions. Both illustrate the tenuousness of using the insider approach to leadership.

Walter was Ohio's longest-serving superintendent. He took the position just as the department of education's school district computer network came online in the late 1970s, which allowed the department to gain a handle on the 600-plus semi-autonomous school districts in the state. The state board of education appointed Walter during a policy lull between two major curriculum reforms and teacher licensure studies conducted in 1974 and 1985. Walter was able to use this situation to his advantage.

Walter relished his success. When he spoke to me, he said more than once that ODE was the "fourth branch" of government. He was able to do things even when he was opposed by the state board, the governor, or state legislators. Late in his term, Governor Richard Celeste complained that the superintendent had undercut his support in school districts because they followed Walter's education agenda rather than the governor's (Celeste says Walter turning districts against him 1989).

In his interview with me, Walter said his success stemmed from his constant cultivation of personal support. Not only did he attend every state board meeting (which John Goff did not), but he met individually with them almost every week. (This had some immediate results. The board deferred to his choices for assistant superintendents at ODE.) He presided over monthly meetings with every major educational interest group in the state. He met twice a year with Ohio's district superintendents (Celeste says Walter turning districts against him 1989).

There is nothing that Walter did that other superintendents could not do, but he had amazing political energy to keep all of these contacts up. A longtime Ohio bureaucrat who had worked with Walter told me that Walter was a "master of playing the board," all the more remarkable because "ODE has multiple constituencies. There is the state board, the Governor ('the 800-pound gorilla'), school districts, the relevant Assembly committees, and the public. . . . I was asked by [a legislator] which one was ODE's priority. I had to come back and say, 'Well, they all are.'" Walter could keep them all number one. A lobbyist reminisced, "I hate to sound like everything was rosy in the good old days, but Frank was really the best of the last four superintendents.

He could convince the education community that he was constantly fighting for them."

Walter's insider strategy was to be able to preserve the scope of his agency because *he* was the source of agency information for virtually every outsider. Indeed, this was one of the primary complaints contained in Governor Voinovich's audit of ODE; no one seemed to know what ODE *could* do, because only Walter knew its true scope (or at least that was the perception). According to the audit, one of the department's major problems was that, "when in doubt, Department staff consult the Superintendent, even on as minor an issue as delaying the start of a new hire by a few days" (Governor's Task Force on Education 1991, 25). Walter's ODE was also able to act autonomously, as shown by Governor Celeste's complaint about district push-back to his plans. Although ODE under Walter did not engage in high-profile education reform like Sanders (a cost of engaging with an insider strategy), it was able to hold its own.

This deliberate strategy possibly also cost him his job when the political winds shifted. He told me that he was wistful for the time "before governors were interested in education." Walter had been able to command the respect of the education community. But when Governor Voinovich came into office, he had strong business support—a group Walter was not prepared to handle. Voinovich was able to grab the reins from Franklin Walter by commissioning an audit of ODE in 1990. Agency audits were nothing new, but Voinovich's audit was conducted by the executives of big Ohio businesses (see chapter 7). The audit had its (perhaps) intended effect. Walter's credibility was damaged. He was unable or unwilling to shift strategies by the early 1990s. Although it was his poor health, most likely accelerated by a very public confrontation with the state board president, which prompted him to resign, the audit made it clear that Walter would not do for the new regime, and he had no personal points with Voinovich. Walter was unable to hold his post when the political winds changed—the greatest risk of insider leadership.

Ohio: John Goff—Passive Coalition Building

Ohio Superintendent John Goff took on an insider leadership strategy. Goff was well liked by his department and worked well with a few allies on the state board (interviewees described him in terms similar to Wisconsin's John Benson: likable but not politically astute). While he was unprepared for the bright spotlight that the public and the board would place on him, he used private leadership to convince both stakeholders and legislators, and, eventually, the courts that his department's autonomous adoption of Ohio's proficiency exams was the best policy.

Goff, in office from 1995 to 1998, was mindful of the negative publicity that his former boss, Ted Sanders, had received while on the road defending the department. Goff knew that direct, public outreach could complicate the political needs of the Ohio Department of Education. He also knew that he had not inherited Walter's mantle, and he could not make personal connections weekly. "The political side of the job gave me trouble," he said to me. "I think five or seven of the board members got reasonable attention. I think the others felt left out." Goff also got into trouble with conservative educational groups when, with Superintendent Sanders, he helped create and promote Ohio's outcomes-based standards. Goff recognized that his opportunities for political and public leadership were limited: "We were ratcheting up the cut points on tests and improving the curriculum guides the whole time [I was superintendent], but we still don't have the ear, the mind of the education community out in the country," he told me.

Despite the challenges that Goff faced, he was able to capitalize on some of his strengths, notably his long experience in educational administration: he had been a principal, an assistant superintendent of Dayton, Ohio, and the superintendent of Kettering, Ohio, before moving to ODE under Walter. His basic strengths were that he knew the inside workings of ODE, and he had seen ODE from a district's perspective. While under Sanders, Goff had directed not only the school-finance litigation efforts but developed Ohio's new school standards and improved its efforts at cooperation with school districts in spite of the finance case (Goff 1995a).

Goff's expertise was invaluable for adopting an insider, private strategy. "Goff needs no breaking in," opined the *Akron Beacon Journal* (Goff steps up 1995). Indeed, Ted Sanders noted that it was Goff who was responsible for leading much of the reorganization at the department during his tenure and believed that Goff could provide "a new level of empowerment of individuals, less bureaucracy and operating mode that involved everyone, and a new culture of openness" (Sanders 1995b).

John Goff adopted an insider leadership strategy at the start of his term. As he recognized, this was his strength, but it did not bode well for the department's political autonomy and had little effect on its technical autonomy or responsibility. Goff was able to claim credit for winning a court battle that forced all schools—public and private—to take the state tests; for completing a landmark study of what the business community expected of students; and for creating a state-wide ombudsman position to take complaints about ODE and local districts. But he was unable to weather the political turbulence that plagued his term. The storms were not his own fault; three of Goff's biggest problems were spillover conflicts: an attempted takeover of the Cleveland school district, the long-running *DeRolph* school finance cases, and resentment of the state board.

The first was Cleveland. In an ironic twist, Governor Voinovich's home city also had long been home to atrocious bookkeeping and segregation problems in addition to academic troubles. In 1991, Superintendent Sanders threatened to take the Cleveland district to court to propose a balanced budget. (Cleveland's budget was subject to state oversight due to a desegregation order from 1976; see News updates 1991.) In 1992, the district appeared close to satisfying the federal judge overseeing its desegregation order, despite strenuous opposition from a handful of longtime district board members. Nevertheless, in 1995, the federal judge ordered the state to take over the district for desegregation purposes—and gave ODE the power to set aside any state law that stood in its way (Schmidt 1992).

Goff tried to work one-on-one with the interested parties, but he found them disinclined to cooperate. Despite the wide scope and broad autonomy handed to the department by ODE, the Cleveland case hammered Goff and ODE (see Goff 1995b). Goff admitted in 1997 that ODE could not force parties in Cleveland to agree on reforms. "It is almost impossible for us to move quickly," he told a reporter (Olson 1997). The state legislature became skeptical of ODE's abilities, and the state school board became restive over the whole issue.

Part of the problem may have been Goff's insider leadership strategy. Sanders suggested that Goff adopt a public strategy in a private letter to the governor. He argued that Goff would have to convince Cleveland that "a four-alarm fire bell is sounding. They [the school district management] continue to believe that the sound is from an alarm clock. . . . The whole community must get actively involved and sustain that involvement for years to come" (Sanders 1995a). If it worked like Sanders thought it might, then a public strategy would have forced Cleveland municipal and school leaders to answer the public for poor bookkeeping and scores. Then the attention would be off ODE and on local officials. ODE would be able to provide "necessary" changes rather than the appearance of heavy-handed oversight.

The second storm was the long-running *DeRolph* school finance cases described in chapter 5. It was during these five cases that Goff most adroitly deployed an insider, private leadership strategy. He could press the department's significant informational advantage over stakeholders and legislators even if he could not (or would not) meet with them regularly. Although the initial ruling appeared to be a defeat for Goff and his department, it actually increased his ability to act as an insider. Prior to the ruling, the Ohio Department of Education was only one of several political actors competing in the school finance policy realm. After the court's first decision, however, ODE was given a mandate to act. Goff did not have to compete for attention anymore—he had a mandated audience. Although Goff did issue press releases about the case, he did not "go on the road" as he had with Ted Sanders and OBE. Instead, he put far more energy into one-on-one communication and careful control of the department's data. He justified autonomous activity by his department as a response to the court, even though many of those activities predated the decision. He wrote the following to one legislator:

> The adoption of the standards by the end of 1997 will put in place a framework for increased performance and accountability for schools as the state response to the recent Ohio Supreme Court school funding decision . . . as enacted appropriate mechanisms for ensuring a return on that [school funding] investment. (Goff 1997)

Although the school finance controversy enhanced the standing of ODE in the long run (as shown in chapter 5), Goff's reliance on insider leadership did little to dispel complaints about the department's reticence in this or other areas. Recall the interview with the plaintiff's lobbyist in the school finance case: "There's no way to find common ground. What's the use [of working with ODE] if we can't go back and counter their arguments?" This is a symptom of insider leadership.

A third storm was the simmering resentment on the part of some state board members over the governor's appointment powers. Several of my interviewees thought that the appointed members "ran the board" because they had the support of the governor and did not have to face reelection. Nevertheless, the elected members still made up the majority, and one elected member was unusually problematic. Diana Fessler, who was later sent by voters to the General Assembly, seemed to enjoy roiling the state board, ODE, the governor, and just about everyone else at some point. Few people with whom I spoke had words of praise for her, although one lobbyist admired her independence. "One thing is certain about her," he said. "She's not in anybody's pocket." Although the most contentious member of the board, she did express the frustration borne out of friction between the elected and appointed members.

In the summer of 1996, the state board held an all-board retreat. At the retreat, members were meant to learn how to communicate better with one another, trust each other, and generally improve intra-board relations. Fessler found this dishonest. Her concern flowed from her position as an *elected* representative: "*As an elected official, it is my responsibility to speak on behalf of those who elected me, not to be an echo of the Board.* . . . The discussion [at the retreat] of speaking with one voice included the absurd notion that the Ohio Department of Education's 500-plus employees . . . and the nineteen member State Board of Education are just one big happy family" (Fessler 1996, emphasis in original).[7] Although Fessler represented the extreme manifestation of the tension between the appointed representatives (who could be expected to share similar views) and the elected ones, many of my interviewees saw this conflict. Lobbyists for groups that felt on the outs thought the tension was more obvious.

Although Goff inherited all three of these problems, and although he was lauded for his hard work on "unsolvable" problems, he was forced to tone back the expansion of the department's autonomy, just as had happened with Walter. At the beginning of his term he was talking about augmenting business partnerships, but by the end, the department was only talking about expanding the testing suite. Nevertheless, he *was* able to prevent the loss of responsibility; his expertise in leadership was widely regarded, and even after the state initially lost the school finance case, legislators—from the minority party even—were requesting detailed information from ODE (see, e.g., Goff and Sheets 1997).

For Goff, this tension helped undercut his position at ODE. Because the state superintendent serves at the pleasure of the state board, Goff could only tenuously act autonomously—he could be sure that someone on the state board would not like his actions. Because he did not invest as much personal time with these political principals, his insider leadership strategy was incomplete. The high-profile conflict with the courts and Cleveland under Goff's watch reverberated at state board meetings, and Goff could not know who would be incensed or how those conflicts would pan out at meetings, according to one interviewee. Of necessity, his response to the board was reactive.

Although Goff's insider leadership in each of these trials got the best of him, and the board let him go, the department lost neither no technical autonomy nor responsibility. The direct result of seven years of personal leadership with the governor's imprimatur, ironically, gained the department political autonomy from the governor. In a curious turn of events, the state board denied Voinovich's successor any role in picking Goff's replacement. The board had had enough of gubernatorial intervention. His successor, Susan Tave Zelman, picked up where he had left off, but without the political baggage that had clung to Goff from his time under Sanders. Curiously, despite this precaution by the board, a highly placed interviewee still complained that the board's pick, Zelman, was still "too tight with the governor."

Despite the weaknesses of Goff's insider leadership, he maintained and even strengthened his agency in a way that would likely have been impossible if he had chosen a public or a political strategy. Unlike public leadership, Goff did not court public opinion or try to make repeated appearances in the news media in his efforts to link funding to performance. Given that his department's ability to shape the reform agenda was grounded in a legal action, public support may have had a limited effect. Unlike political leadership, Goff did not rely on old political contacts and instead dealt with legislative leadership from both parties, and he kept a tight hold on the department's natural advantage, the availability of data, rather than using it for political advantage. More generally, insider leadership appears to be the strongest form for maintaining scope, though not for autonomous action, because the agency leader is working from an already strong position. This strategy does not have to seek or maintain other support, at least in the short term.

Political Leadership

Finally, political leadership could appear to be a perversion of the civil-service ideal of a neutral administration. Yet agencies *do* operate in political environments that are run by elected overseers who have political goals at heart—even those state education agencies with appointed boards and chiefs have an elected governor with goals (see Redmond-Jones and Malen 2002). Political leadership allows agency chiefs to exploit the vote-seeking tendencies of their political overseers. How is this different than public leadership? A public leadership strategy tended to appear when state superintendents were isolated from their stakeholders, on the one hand, and from their political principals, on the other. Political leadership appeared when a superintendent was deserted by only *one* of these groups. State superintendents who were seeking policies to tighten an existing standards regime sought to use this strategy. Georgia Superintendent Werner Rogers, described later, provides a case for this form of leadership.

A second reason for political leadership was less rosy from the point of view of state superintendents. As governors in these states became attuned to the political benefits of being an "education governor," they sought to increase their influence on state education departments. Yet because superintendents in these states were not appointed by the governor (or confirmed by the legislature), they had a potentially unique independence of leadership. State superintendents were jealous of this independence, and when governors sought to encroach upon their authority, agency chiefs would appeal to political allies to bolster their institutional claims. These political allies were often stakeholders who were opponents of the governor and the legislature, or simply opponents of restructuring the state bureaucracy. I return to Wisconsin Superintendent Herbert Grover for his use of a political strategy. But manifestations of this strategy were successful in securing broader scope for their agencies, and they effectively used their political skills to ward off challenges to their agency's autonomy. Nevertheless, when the political winds changed, neither was able to maintain his gain in autonomy.

Georgia: Werner Rogers—Isolation from Stakeholders

Even though Rogers was not as voluble as Grover, he was as adept at bidding the legislature to do his will. To me Rogers proclaimed that he adroitly avoided politics—although his actions indicate that he was, in fact, in the thick of the political process. He was very successful in securing new responsibilities for his department, however, the department held steady or lost some autonomy because of strong resistance from educators in the field. While Grover was successful partly because of the political skills he learned while a legislator, Rogers's success with the strategy stemmed from three characteristics: his close relationship with the previous superintendent, the tight connection of the department to the governor, and his superior technical knowledge when the chairs of the education committee of both legislative houses changed.[8]

Rogers came to the department as an assistant superintendent when the governor appointed Charles McDaniel state superintendent in 1977. Rogers's division was in charge of writing the state's 1985 school reform package, quality basic education (QBE), and Rogers was dispatched to the legislature to interpret the department's work for the legislature's floor leaders (McDaniel 1983).

The political skills that Rogers developed working with the legislature and Superintendent McDaniel put him in good stead. McDaniel died unexpectedly at his desk in 1985. Shortly before, Rogers had appeared on the *Today Show* with Albert Shanker, the head of the National Education Association. "That showed I could hold my own in front of a camera. That's one of the skills I'd tried to cultivate," Rogers said. A copy of the show made its way to the governor's office, and, with a recommendation from Bill Gambill, another assistant superintendent (and, incidentally, the governor's brother in law), Rogers got the job. Governor Joe Frank Harris said later that Rogers had the experience of "working within the structure of the state. And I felt at the time that it was more to our benefit to choose a person with experience within the reform [QBE] that was in progress . . . and could elect [*sic*] the organizations throughout the state [to] continue implementation." That is, Harris thought Rogers could guide GADOE politically (Cook 1987).[9]

Second, Rogers also benefited from the favorable position of GADOE in Governor Harris's policy book. He was supportive of the department from the first day of his term. In a pointed letter to the president of the state's largest teachers' organization, the Professional Association of Georgia Educators, Harris stated his alliance with the department:

> I do not know how many more times I have to say this to you, nor do I know how many more time my staff and representatives of the Department of Education must attempt to convince you that we are going to continue to improve education in Georgia. . . . I regret that since the legislative session, you have chose to break from our group on more than one occasion in an attempt to distance yourself so as to criticize me and the Department of Education. (Harris 1985)

This was more than rhetoric. When Rogers was in the hot seat over the department's kindergarten-completion test plan (discussed in chapter 5), a teacher recertification plan (discussed in chapter 7), and the amount of QBE paperwork, the governor would never fail to defend Rogers and the department.

Third, Rogers's technical expertise helped improve his situation with the legislature when longtime education members retired. Institutional politics often replaced partisan politics in Georgia because of the long Democratic domination of the state. The House in particular was often hostile to the governor and was sure to appoint an education committee chair "not in the pocket of DOE," according to one of my sources. Although McDaniel was careful to emphasize that GADOE would strive to answer legislators' questions promptly, he was a jealous guardian of the department's data (McDaniel 1982). At one point, he upbraided the commissioner of the department of administrative service for releasing information to a legislator without his consent (McDaniel 1985). Rogers, on the other hand, had detailed personal experience with the department's major responsibilities and had personal relationships with legislators. In 1987, the House had a new education chair, and Rogers was ready to accommodate, knowing that he could shape the agenda by being quick to respond (Georgia Department of Education

1987). While McDaniel's letters answering legislators were often short and perfunctory (although to the point), Rogers frequently spent three to four single-spaced pages explaining the position of the department. At one point, the House and Senate Education Committee chairs asked Rogers how they could help publicize the department's agenda.[10] They would frequently talk with Rogers, and more than once asked him to personally apprise them of the department's activity (see, e.g., Magnum and Foster 1989). Many people were impressed by Rogers's technical knowledge. After Superintendent Schrenko won the 1994 election, one board member reminisced about Rogers, calling him "crisp[ly] responsive" (Ramage 1997).

Rogers could credit his choice of a political leadership strategy for many of his successes in buttressing his department's autonomous actions with a newly legislated scope. In addition to maintaining QBE despite fierce criticism, Rogers could claim credit for two major enhancements in the department's scope during his two terms in office: creating a kindergarten completion test and implementing a school-readiness program for three- and four-year-old children.

I described the development of the kindergarten test in detail in chapter 5, but the relevant facts are that Rogers built a kindergarten test within the QBE framework to ensure that children were ready for school. Rogers was able to introduce the program in 1987 and sustain it through some ferocious opposition from interest groups, including all of the teachers' associations, the school boards association, and the National Association of Educators of Young Children (Georgia Department of Education 1988). In 1989, he recommended changes to the exam to mollify school districts. To me, Rogers claimed that even the NAEYC thought he had done a good (technical) job (see chapter 5). The education chairs of both houses of the legislature denounced these changes—even though the state board unanimously followed Rogers's decision (Gold 1988; Foster and Magnum 1989). Rogers's political leadership was instrumental in hanging on to his department's responsibility for the exam; both Governor Harris and the state Senate refused to step in (despite a 136–34 House vote to kill Rogers's changes) (Cohen 1989).

Second, Rogers was able to add a Head-Start-like school-readiness program, "Family Connection," to the department's repertoire. Schools in Georgia implemented full-day kindergarten only in the 1980s (there was no kindergarten in the 1970s), so the pre-K readiness program came with little experience with the full-day program. Like the kindergarten exam, the Family Connection program was an expansion of departmental responsibilities—this time into the private sector. The program provided money to any private or public entity that would provide basic health care, adult and some child education. Private day-care providers initially opposed Family Connection (who thought department of education funds would put them out of business, Rogers said), but they became big supporters of the program because it offered guaranteed funding. Rogers noted that although there was some "forced collaboration" in some of the initial school districts, the program completely covered the state in the next ten years (Georgia Family Connection Partnership 2005). The state again did not step in to quell dissent, a testimony to Rogers's political success.

Despite Rogers's success in building his department's scope, his department did sustain an attack on its autonomy, although with minor damages. In 1988, the Georgia Association of Educators (the state's NEA affiliate) filed suit against the department, alleging that GADOE was subject to the Administrative Procedures Act (APA). This 1971 act required that all rules issued by the executive branch be sent to the secretary of state and include a public comment period. Since the act's initial passage, the department of education and the state board had refused to comply with the law, believing that Georgia's constitution suggested that they were independent from the governor and his executive branch. Rogers maintained this tradition and was adamant that complying with the law would compromise his agency's constitutional independence. When a county judge ruled against the department, he was unable to garner legislative support for legislatively exempting GADOE (Ruling threatens legality of Ga. school regulations 1988). The ruling came at a bad time for the department, as school districts were lamenting QBE's allegedly onerous paperwork and arbitrary regulations. One longtime department employee noted that "QBE just about killed everybody" with simply fulfilling the department's responsibilities—but both powerful legislators and the governor had stood behind the department through the QBE crisis.[11] Although Rogers reluctantly complied with the APA, there is no evidence that GADOE has been actually hampered by the requirement. All of GADOE's post-1971, pre-1988 school regulations were sustained. But Rogers's political leadership can be seen at work even here. Had legislators or the governor seen a serious threat to GADOE regulations (especially QBE or the kindergarten test), it is likely that they *would* have stepped in, given their staunch support of the department's activities in these areas.

Unlike Wisconsin Superintendent Grover, Rogers could build political leadership in a "nonpartisan" environment. Republicans were not a force in Georgia politics prior to 1994, so Rogers could appear to avoid partisan politics while still being offered legislators political policy benefits—Georgia's well-tooled funding and accountability program.

Wisconsin: Herbert Grover—Isolation from Political Principals

Wisconsin Superintendent Herbert Grover is clearly the best example of political leadership among the superintendents I studied. Grover was adamant that his post was, and should continue to be, a nonpartisan office. Although he was an identifiable Democrat from his days as a legislator, Republican Governor Lee Dreyfus was a "father figure" to him, according to a longtime acquaintance of his. In addition to his loud-and-out-there public leadership, Grover succeeded at advancing the DPI's agenda because of his persistent cultivation of personal contacts with legislators, his political autonomy from the governor, and his eagerness to demonstrate the DPI's technical competence to legislators.

In 1981, when he first ran for the office, Grover's biggest liability was that he was known as a politician rather than as an educator. In fact, more than five dozen legislators signed a petition to support him, which signaled his legislative connections, according to one of my interviewees. But Grover's political liabilities turned out to be less consequential than those of his competition. He ran against incumbent Barbara Thompson, who was "known as a do-nothing by Dems, and Republicans thought her something of an embarrassment," recalled one Grover acquaintance. She also had failed to aid the teachers' union in the Hortonville strike six years before. By 1980, the teachers' union had regrouped after its loss at Hortonville and was ready for support at the top—but so were school district administrators, whose organization also supported Grover.

His political connections served him well. Grover was determined to take the DPI, "the sleepiest shop in town," and turn it into a strong agency. More than one person thought that he was trying to use the DPI as a stepping stone to the governor's office.[12] Whatever his aspirations, Grover's correspondence with legislators ranged from the personal note to a detailed exposition of just what bill a legislator should introduce. Grover tried to head off issues before they became legislative questions, as he did to a question from Representative Barbara Ulichny about increasing handicapped aids as recommended by a school finance commission. Grover wrote, "I do not support this recommendation. I have made no request in my proposed 1985–1987 budget . . . I don't think the Gov will include the task force recommendations, [so the] issue [of] 'I think' is moot" (Grover 1984a). He also would preempt legislation that might impinge on the DPI's technical and political autonomy. To Senator Joseph Czarnezki, who was drafting a bill requiring new teachers to pass a certification test, Grover wrote, "I intend to propose, under my s. 115.28(7) authority, a rule requiring that applicants to teacher education programs in Wisconsin pass a basic skill tests . . . I believe this action may make your proposed legislation unnecessary" (Grover 1984c). Finally, he might respond point by point to challenges to his proposals, especially if he felt out of the loop. Assembly Speaker Tom Loftus (no friend of the superintendent's, according to Grover) sent a letter to Governor Anthony Earl complaining about an increase in funding for the DPI's new competency-based testing program. Grover, who only received a carbon copy of the letter, replied with a dense, three-page defense of the DPI's responsibility for administration of the program (Grover 1984e).

Grover's second advantage was his relationship with two of the three governors with whom he served. The first, Governor Dreyfus, was already a Grover supporter. One interviewee said that there was an unwritten agreement between Grover and Dreyfus that "You're the state superintendent, but make me the best education governor ever, OK?" Dreyfus let Grover have the reins. For example, Governor Dreyfus vetoed a bilingual education program on Grover's advice (Stockinger 1981). Governor Anthony Earl, a fellow Democrat, likewise was willing to cooperate with Grover's proposal to reduce the number of district service agencies and to put his (Earl's) own educational excellence program on the back burner to let Grover's state standards bill pass instead. "Superintendent Grover felt that providing more school aid across the board [to implement state standards] was a bigger priority than starting most of [the governor's Educational Excellence] programs," said Nancy Wenzel, the governor's education advisor (State legislatures pass education reforms as 1984 sessions end 1984).

But the political autonomy that Grover enjoyed ended once a governor with the same self-assuredness came to office in 1986. Governor Tommy G. Thompson, who became the state's longest-serving governor, had an education program parallel to Grover's in many ways—better and more student testing and tougher teacher certification standards—but Thompson wanted his fingerprints to be on the work, not Grover's. However, Republican Thompson was also suspicious of Grover's work at the DPI. Grover had little to worry about at the time because the Democrats had a 59 to 40 majority in the state assembly, but he should have been forewarned when Representative Tommy Thompson wrote him an ominous note in 1981. "I am concerned," Thompson wrote, "because I feel the Legislature already has mandated too many public school activities and programs (and costs thereof)—leaving school boards and local taxpayers to pick up the tab" (Thompson 1981).[13] One of Thompson's hallmark education reforms of the early 1990s, two-thirds state funding of local education, was primarily a way to reduce property taxes. Thompson and Grover butted heads many times. Thompson wanted school choice (which became vouchers), while Grover strongly opposed them and lost; Thompson wanted to cut property taxes, while Grover opposed the move, although he was a proponent for more state funding. Grover won his increase in state funding, but school districts were saddled with a levy limit, a pet project of Thompson's.[14] "Bert forgot who was governor," said a longtime associate, "He thought he could develop the same kind of relationship with the governor [as with Dreyfus and Earl], but the agenda had changed. It all unraveled very quickly." "Thompson was as headstrong as Grover," said another, but Grover could always at least stand his ground. "When DPI lost Grover, they were unable to challenge the governor."

Even under Thompson, however, Grover was able to push a revised school aid formula to speed up school building and repairs, part of the agency's oversight responsibilities. "Our prisons are in better shape than our elementary and secondary schools," Grover said (Mathis 1989b). Although Governor Thompson only included half of Grover's request for school building aid, aid nevertheless materialized. Grover said that he was also able to swing help from another state agency to force school districts to upgrade their buildings or risk being condemned.

Finally, Grover's political leadership hammered away in support of the DPI's technical autonomy. Taking the DPI, "the only agency that didn't have its own policy shop" in 1981 (as one former employee said), to one that trumpeted its competence was no small undertaking. In his first months of office, he undertook an audit of the state's mid-level educational service agencies as a way to pump up his request that they be consolidated. (He had sent a letter to the senate and some assembly members to this effect *before* he was sworn in!) (Grover 1981a, 1981b). Grover got his request. Two years later, when he was asking for increased state support for local schools (a perpetual request), Grover had the DPI crunch school finance numbers—numbers to which only the DPI had access—to show the inequities of the property tax between districts. The report was well done and widely cited (Wisconsin Department of Public Instruction 1983). In fact, it was cited in a study that Governor Thompson's aides used to justify his property tax cut proposal in the early 1990s (Rossmiller 1990).[15] Grover was not hesitant to bring in experts to support his policy initiatives. In the two-year debate over state standards and competency-based testing, he brought in a professor from UCLA to explain the proposals. "I personally guarantee that you will enjoy Mr. Popham's presentation," Grover wrote to Representative Ed Jackamonis and other legislators (Grover 1981c). By the mid-1980s, legislators of both parties were routinely asking Grover's DPI for analyses of educational problems. Indeed, complaints about the "excessive data collection by the Department" started to appear—just as they had in Georgia (Moen 1983 [see the reply in Grover 1983d]).

To some extent, Grover was successful at convincing others that his department was technically competent. After Senator Clifford Kreuger received a letter from a university professor attacking Grover's plans for competency-based testing, he replied, "My initial attitude toward this proposal [competency-based testing] was favorable. A major reason for this was the support given it by Dr. Bert Grover, Superintendent-elect. I was impressed by the fact that Dr. Grover is being advised by Dr. Bowles, who . . . is reputedly without peer in matters of educational policy making" (Kreuger 1981). Nevertheless, the DPI's technical autonomy would be weakened by professionalization in the legislature. Grover complained to me that by the 1990s the Legislative Fiscal Bureau, the Legislative Audit Bureau, and the Legislative Council (all policy analysts for the Wisconsin Legislature) had displaced the DPI's role in providing information.

In conclusion, Grover was successful at bringing responsibility into his department—made easier, perhaps, by the Wisconsin Department of Public Instruction's relatively few responsibilities to begin with—but the DPI's political and technical autonomy foundered when the political regime changed. When he lost his gubernatorial support, he was able to maintain the DPI, but he was continually challenged to hold his own. When Grover left, Governor Thompson made his move to gut the DPI, as explored in chapter 7. The universal consensus among my Wisconsin interviewees was that the governor was out to make sure that there would never be another Grover.

Conclusion

Public agency leaders are perhaps more constrained in their activities than leaders in private organizations. But those constraints—legally public decision making, strong job protections for civil servants, inexpert political oversight—also give leaders opportunities to act autonomously in ways that would be far more difficult if their agencies ran like private organizations. Public decision making allows leaders to adopt a public strategy to introduce new ideas to the policy agenda, or to defend old ones, in a way that hits legislators and governors where it counts: their constituents. Strong job protection means that agency leaders have a reservoir of technical expertise that is unrivaled by legislators, the public, and stakeholder organizations, despite the stasis that this encourages in organizational culture. The benefits of both of these characteristics are amplified by the inexpert oversight by legislators and governors, who may have to rely on the agency for information, even as they critique its performance.

Some generalizations emerge from these cases. First, insider leadership appears best when an agency has other external support to act. For Ohio, this was a state supreme court decision, but some crisis might also empower an agency to make unusual demands on other political actors (the federal Department of Homeland Security may offer one example, but see Kettl 2007). Second, political leadership was effective when it was practiced routinely, so that an agency leader knew who the agency's supporters were and what political bargains were in the agency's interest to make. It was also effective when political supporters were *in* government as opposed to stakeholders outside of government. Third, although public leadership always indicated some weakness on the part of the agency, such leadership could work if the agency leader also courted the support of other political principals. That is, it worked if the agency leader did not run "against government" or at least against its politicians. Although such action may bolster an agency's support among some stakeholders, the agency relies on neutral or positive action by governors and legislators to support autonomous choices it makes.

Several common strands emerge from all three kinds of leadership. First, the plans and politics of the governor and legislative majorities are crucial in building support, although, as Schrenko's experience shows, it is possible although difficult without them. Second, effective leadership is contingent upon tireless energy and a bit of ruthlessness. John Goff was an able leader, but his own tenure ended because he came up short on these. Third, the base of support that leaders build for their agencies must be just broader than the base of support for any other actor. Both Schrenko and Grover used this to their advantage when they short-circuited complaints from teachers' groups and school districts. In addition, the leaders' prior experience often gave them a leg up on governors or legislators when arguing for increased responsibilities or defending autonomy. Clearly, Grover's time in the legislature was an asset in his work with them.

In general, my expectations for the effects of leadership were met—in the short term. Public leadership was successful in causing headaches in other branches and wresting more autonomy and responsibility in Wisconsin and Georgia. In Ohio, however, it only kept the agency about even. Inside leadership did consolidate responsibilities in Ohio, and political leadership built responsibilities in Wisconsin and Georgia.

The surprise was in the long-term effects. In both Wisconsin and Georgia, years of public leadership led to strong reactions from the governor's office. In both states, the governor attempted to eviscerate the education agency in favor of a gubernatorial- controlled department. Georgia's Roy Barnes succeeded; Wisconsin's Tommy Thompson won in the legislature but lost in court. Even in Ohio, where Sanders was a close confidant of the governor, his public leadership gave George Voinovich an opening to push through changes to the state school board after Ted Sanders left. Public leadership, although it may be an excellent way to exercise independence in the short run, also appears to be an excellent way to excite jealously in the state's highest elected office in the long run. This was particularly true in Wisconsin and Georgia, where both superintendents are constitutionally independent of the governor.

Political leadership, curiously, also allowed agencies a great deal of technical autonomy. This appears to be so because Grover and Rogers built political alliances explicitly using the agency's monopoly on data. When talking to me, Grover as much as admitted this—he complained mightily that legislative data-crunching agencies had taken the ball out of the DPI's court. Because political leadership depends on political alliances, it hampers long-term political autonomy when the political environment shifts. The hits that both agencies took demonstrated this.

Inside leadership appears to generate the most benefit for agencies in search of a new scope. Although both Franklin Walter and John Goff had sour endings to their tenures in office, ODE emerged at least as responsible and, especially in Goff's case, more technically autonomous than at the start of their terms. After Goff's tenure, ODE may have been more politically autonomous because Goff was able to extricate the department from the high-profile fights with public opinion under Sanders. The state school board, even with gubernatorial-chosen members, rebuffed an attempt by the incoming governor to pick Goff's successor. In Walter's case, Governor Voinovich had to deal graciously with him and made every effort to respect Walter's educational expertise and interest group bargains.

Undoubtedly, leaders have something of their own style, and many factors other than stakeholder acceptance, public resonance, and political viability influence the leadership strategy that an agency leader can adopt. Personality, demeanor, and fiscal climate, for example, may prevent some agency leaders from pursuing a full-fledged public or political campaign for their preferred policies. Nevertheless, all of the state superintendents I studied were able to borrow tactics from different leadership strategies.

Even Linda Schrenko, who had no opportunity for personal, insider leadership, came to rely on a few highly placed, long-term department employees who *had* contacts and could supplement her bombastic style and strategy, according to an interviewee who worked at the department at that time. The most successful state superintendents did indeed borrow from all three strategies.

7

Making New Friends

Institutional Turnover

Something is wrong when, as an educator, the further away from
the children you get, the more money you make. . . . That's why I
am asking you to help Superintendent Schrenko and me perform
radical surgery on the education bureaucracy in this state. This
budget cuts $30 million out of the education bureaucracy and puts
it into the classroom.

—Georgia Governor Zell Miller, 1995 State of the State Address

At one time, governors were not very active in education. An education bureaucrat in Wisconsin told me, "In the '70s, if we could get the
governor to mention the word 'education' in his state-of-the-state we
were exhilarated." Now, of course, governors use the word all the time.
The 1980s and 1990s saw the rise and, some might argue, dominance
of "education governors" such as Zell Miller.[1] Although some governors
had been involved in changing state education policy in the 1960s and
1970s, the 1983 *Nation at Risk* report gave governors a national platform and national talking points. Arkansas Governor Bill Clinton first
gained national prominence at the "Education Summit" in 1990; many
other governors (Lamar Alexander, Tennessee; George W. Bush, Texas;
and Roy Romer, Colorado) became education governors of one sort
or another in the 1990s.[2] Although many of the education observers
with whom I spoke were skeptical of their governors' true interest in
education, the governors in my cases devoted a great deal of staff time
to the subject. Governors in Ohio, Georgia, and Wisconsin often saw
their respective departments of education as stumbling blocks to change.
Education departments, through their superintendents, were unable to
fend off gubernatorial advances, except when resorting to arguments
emphasizing their technical or political autonomy. These governors'

141

increasing interest in education compounded the splintered accountability that already characterized education departments.

Governors are one of the most potent exogenous influences on an agency's scope. Although they have no legislative power to set the scope for an agency, they can command the attention of legislators and the public for new programs or for new limits on agency activity through speeches and photo ops. More formally, governors may have appointment powers for the state superintendents or board members. In the 1990s, governors often sought direct appointment of superintendents—including in Wisconsin and Ohio. An agency's political autonomy is restricted when its leadership is appointed by a governor, which is exactly what governors have in mind. Appointment is also an indirect way for governors to redirect an agency's scope. If a pro-state-standards superintendent is appointed, then it is far more likely that the agency will pursue policy along those lines.

Because governors are single persons, they have unique advantages as political principals. Unlike the legislature, agency personnel cannot play off one legislator against another or one party against another. Similarly, governors are the first source for state budgets, and so a favorable mention by the governor in her or his initial budget draft can make negotiations with the legislature easier. Agencies that fail to work with the governor up front may find that their scope is reduced simply through gubernatorial omission. Agencies must be especially attentive to these chief executives, as governors are very visible political principals.

Agencies do have a fundamental advantage over governors, however: they are not bound by elections. They have expertise and an existing budget prior to governors arriving in the capital. Scholars have shown that what an agency does remains about the same regardless of new political leadership, although an agency's vigor responds quickly to new political signals (Wood and Waterman 1991, 1993). Agencies may be protected by institutional arrangements. In both Georgia and Wisconsin, state superintendents are independent constitutional offices. In Ohio, the existence of the office is constitutional, but the duties of the office are defined purely by statute. (The state board must also exist, but law defines its membership.) These splintering arrangements help preserve agency autonomy because there is guaranteed to be an agency leader who is not directly dependent on the governor for the post.

The competition between institutional agency independence and gubernatorial power leads to a conditional hypothesis. The governor *could* be a difficult principal to control, as there may not be the same long-term benefits for being on good terms with the governor as there are with legislators. Institutional independence of agencies, the (usually) regular turnover of governors, and crowded gubernatorial agendas may allow agencies the freedom to act autonomously and whisper new programs into the ears of governors. Unless the governor has a keen interest in education, that is. Then an agency will have to draw on its technical expertise and other political autonomy to protect its scope. The expectation is that *the effect of gubernatorial turnover on an agency will be contingent upon the governor's interest in education relative to other activities of the administration.*

This chapter portrays three different situations in which departments of education encountered the governor. First I show how education department staff can go from a governor's confidants to his enemies when department leadership overreaches the limits of its autonomy. The best example of this is the drastic change in GADOE's stature from the 1980s to the 1990s. Second, a department can tussle with a governor over the appropriate use of his or her power in education, can compromise, and then can lose a little political autonomy in return for an increase in fiscal autonomy from the legislature (with a gubernatorial advocate) and a great increase in departmental responsibilities. Ohio's department of education may have been the "fourth branch of government" in the 1980s, according to Superintendent Franklin Walter, but the governor quickly moved to reshape it in the early 1990s. Finally, a department can lose scope if it becomes too identified with the governor's political opposition. As Wisconsin's case demonstrates, Governor Tommy Thompson was able to temporarily gut the department because it had become too identified with particular interest groups and was weakened by a change in its elected leadership. The department's political autonomy derived from the state's constitution, however, saved the department, although it lost much of the scope and residual autonomy that it had built up in the 1980s.

Gubernatorial Over-reaching with a Strong Department

Georgia's department of education enjoyed a cozy relationship with the governor's office for most of its history. Part of the relationship was from the strong state government built after the Civil War, part was the elite, one-party monopoly that the Democrats enjoyed, and part was a natural by-product of a sixty-one-year hiatus of competitive state superintendent elections.[3] This comfortable link allowed GADOE to act with a great deal of autonomy. The governor was rarely a check on the department, and department personnel frequently drafted education plans for the governor. In the 1990s, however, the arrival of a bona fide elected state superintendent who adopted a public leadership strategy clashed with a new governor who had a keen interest in detailed education policy, which temporarily curtailed the department's autonomy and scope.

The contrast between the 1980s—and the decades before—and the 1990s is stark. In the 1980s, Governor Joe Frank Harris continued the state's tradition of appointing a superintendent to fill the newly vacant post. Following Superintendent Charles McDaniel's death, Harris appointed Werner Rogers, who had already worked closely with the governor on QBE. Ties between Harris and GADOE ran even deeper than usual: a chief assistant superintendent, Bill Gambill, was related by marriage to the governor (Taking charge of school reform, Harris in-law Bill Gambill is hard worker 1985). Rogers had to run for office in 1986 against two contenders, but he felt so secure in his post that he skipped the first debate, sending Gambill to fill in (Rogers to miss first debate in school chief's race 1986). Rogers was right; he won handily. He won again in 1990 with no competition.

Rogers's department had tremendous success with the Quality Basic Education Act, discussed at greater length elsewhere. Rogers and Gambill worked extensively on the details of the act and were able to maintain the program in the face of strenuous complaints about assessment (see chapter 6) and record keeping. GADOE's extensive scope under QBE was able to keep a lid on these complaints about Rogers and the department through the early 1990s. Teachers and districts simply did not have an alternate route to policy in Georgia—GADOE did it all.

But QBE spawned two enemies of GADOE that would be Rogers's downfall and that eventually stymied the department. First, QBE hardened opposition to Rogers in the field. The restiveness was such that Governor Zell Miller specifically promised an overhaul of the department of education to reduce mandates, to be led by Rogers, in his first state-of-the-state address in 1991.[4] Second, there were those who thought they could do QBE better. Senator Roy Barnes, who would later become governor, was one of these. Although he was rarely a named cosponsor of education bills in the Senate, he formed definite ideas about expanding the reach of state government while on the Senate and House Education Committees.

Rogers's opponents in the field included Linda Schrenko, a classroom teacher, principal, and counselor of twenty years. In her 1994 run for superintendent, she crystallized opposition to QBE by airing hostile criticism of GADOE that had been simmering since 1985. She alleged that there was one administrator for every six students (a claim exaggerated by two orders of magnitude), and that the state placed too many restrictions on local school districts, including dictating the choice of textbooks (White 1994a). Although Rogers correctly questioned her numbers on the size of the bureaucracy, he could not counter the core criticism. Despite holding the superintendency for just over eight years, he had only recently moved to shrink the department.[5]

Schrenko's outspokenness did not stop with her upset victory over Rogers, although she won by 13,335 votes out of 1.4 million votes cast. In her first term she pulled Georgia out of the Council of Chief State School Officers, bashed the national Parent-Teachers Association, and publicly aired her difficulties with the state board of education (Jacobson 1999). Nevertheless, Schrenko was able to work with Governor Zell Miller (see chapter 6). Miller appeared more interested in the HOPE Scholarship for higher education than in primary and secondary schools. In general, he let Schrenko work as she wished within that department. He even accommodated her difficulties with the board by instructing all of them to resign (Cumming 1999c). Although the longtime department employees I interviewed were disgusted with Schrenko's internal leadership style, GADOE continued to operate autonomously with the same scope as it had under Rogers. Indeed, Schrenko was able to increase the department's emphasis on reading programs, and, for three years running, obtained more money from the state budget than her department requested (Cumming 1998b).[6]

All might have been well had Miller not left office after two terms. Roy Barnes, a twenty-two-year state legislator, was elected in 1998 on a platform that included sweeping changes to education. Although less brusque in manner than Schrenko, Barnes's keen interest in the details of primary and secondary education set him on a collision course with GADOE.

Watching Superintendent Schrenko from the state house of representatives for four years convinced Barnes that his best hope for change was replacing an elected Schrenko with an appointed superintendent (Salzer 1999b).[7] This went nowhere; his failure was not surprising, given that similar constitutional amendments had failed under the watch of Superintendent Rogers—and had failed then with *Rogers* campaigning for them!

His second option was to create an independent agency to take all of GADOE's assessment responsibilities, leaving the department to cut checks, oversee curriculum lists, and assist school districts struggling to pass assessments. This Barnes began within six months of taking office as governor. The Governor's Education Reform Study Commission took aim at major elements of GADOE's autonomy and scope. It decided that school district aid was unequal but also drafted a plan to remedy the inequality, an activity that had been within the scope of GADOE since the early days of the twentieth century. But a second commission task struck deeply at GADOE and at Superintendent Schrenko in particular.

Barnes's commission decided that GADOE had done a poor job assessing student's learning, despite the department's long attention to student performance under QBE. It recommended that the governor create the Office of Educational Accountability (OEA), which would be "independent," although attached to the governor's office. In his 2001 budget, Governor Barnes alleged that the department was under the "influence" of interest groups and therefore reporting faulty performance data to protect the educational establishment (Georgia Office of Planning and Budget 2000, 183; the document proposed that "the [Office of Educational Accountability] will be an independent agency to avoid any suggestion of influence by any educational entity or interest group"). This was only a formal statement of what Barnes had campaigned on and what he had accused Superintendent Schrenko of covering up: Georgia's students were near the bottom on national-test comparisons. Despite fifteen years of QBE, the governor called public education Georgia's "Achilles' heel." Superintendent Schrenko struck back vigorously. She went on the road touting the improvements in test scores on her watch and the department's competence and initiatives to improve the state's testing regimen (Salzer 1999b).

The OEA was supposed to begin collecting baseline data on student assessment in 2002–03 and then grade schools for performance in 2004–05. Although the OEA would grade the schools, the governor recommended that the legislature provide funds to GADOE for twenty school improvement teams to help schools bring up their scores. (This division of labor could be seen to help shield the governor from retribution in school districts: while the office under his oversight would grade schools, the OEA could always argue that GADOE was not adequately helping districts) (Georgia Office of Planning and Budget 2000, 183, 2001, 195).

Barnes also did his best to stifle Schrenko using a traditional gubernatorial prerogative, his appointment power. He replaced all but four of the state board members (one, J. T. Williams, he reappointed. Williams was a frequent critic of Schrenko's and the only board member who refused to resign for Governor Miller; see Cumming 1999c). Barnes also appointed an "obnoxious" chair who would deliberately ignore departmental testimony at meetings, according to one interviewee. Barnes appeared to be successful: At about the same time, Schrenko stopped going to state board meetings (Salzer, Warren, and Torpy 2006).

Although Barnes convinced the legislature to pass every element of his education program, no element was particularly original. Barnes's solution to poor accountability at GADOE was to fund the completion of a new criterion-based exam that Schrenko's department had almost ready by the time Barnes came to office. Barnes complained that Georgia's curriculum was not rigorous enough, but he praised GADOE's overhaul of QBE's standards in 1997—*before* he came into office (Georgia Office of Planning and Budget 2000, 184–85). Barnes's recommendation to grade all schools and provide for penalties in disguise for poorly performing schools was not new. Schrenko had already suggested it (Cumming 1998c).

Indeed, the chief difference between the two appeared to be who could claim credit for accountability. Superintendent Schrenko complained as such: "The biggest difference between Roy and I is centralization. Roy pretty much wants to run everything. . . . He just doesn't want me to do it," an assessment that many of my interviewees confirmed (Salzer 1999b). "He was called King Roy for a reason," recalled one.

Who won? If broad scope reinforces departmental autonomy despite heightened gubernatorial interest, then the department should be able to withstand attacks on both scope and autonomy. This is exactly what happened in Georgia. There is no doubt that Barnes was extremely interested in primary and secondary school accountability. Even Wisconsin Governor Tommy Thompson did not spend as much of his state-of-the-state messages at the height of his similar takeover attempt of the DPI, as Barnes did (see text that follows). Barnes *was* successful in the short run; a non-GADOE office did begin work on overseeing educational accountability in Georgia.

But Barnes had trespassed on another's ground. Even the *Atlanta Journal-Constitution*, a longtime Schrenko basher, conceded that Barnes had gone too far (Education battlefield 2000). In addition to weakening GADOE, Barnes had eliminated tenure for new teachers, introduced teacher performance pay to be determined by his new OEA, and generally alienated teacher groups when he assailed the quality of Georgia education. Schrenko, who had few friends inside the government, in her party, or in her department, did appear to hold a high moral ground for teachers. Even her foes whom I interviewed acknowledged that Schrenko had better traction on teacher issues than Barnes had. When asked to explain Barnes's primary-election loss in 2002, one Georgia legislator told me, "It was the teachers who defeated Barnes" (see Salzer 2000a).

Given the politicized environment that GADOE had to work in—no love was lost between Schrenko and Barnes—it had no expansion in autonomy under Barnes. Superintendent Schrenko had to use every report that GADOE issued to emphasize her department's technical competence (Salzer 1999c). Incidentally, Schrenko tried to run against Barnes in 2002, but she lost, also in a primary. The new state superintendent, Kathy Cox, was universally lauded by department officials, teachers' associations, and legislators with whom I talked.

With both Barnes and Schrenko out of the picture, GADOE regained *all* of the scope narrowed under Barnes as the OEA was rolled back, according to longtime department personnel. The quick reversion of scope to GADOE indicates that Barnes's changes were paper-thin. He had his commission, but it called for reforms that GADOE was already making. Had Schrenko run for another term as superintendent and won, perhaps the OEA would have had a longer life; as it was, Barnes's successor had no cause to push his reforms. With Schrenko gone, GADOE's reputation for integrity could return unhampered. Schrenko had worked tirelessly to preserve GADOE's autonomy, and though she failed in the short term, she exposed the shallowness of the governor's authority. The department was constrained because of the governor's interests, but its long-term autonomy and broad scope helped convince legislators, teachers groups, and eventually voters that children's education should remain with GADOE, and GADOE won.

Gubernatorial Attack and Compromise

Before his election as governor in 1990, George V. Voinovich was mayor of Cleveland, Ohio, a city with a troubled school district. Not only did the district have academic problems, but it also had severe financial troubles created by poor budgeting and poor scores. Partly to keep the district afloat, Voinovich worked with some of the city's top business leaders to make them stakeholders in the financial and academic performance of the Cleveland School District. Voinovich thought he was successful (Voinovich 1992a; Maher 1991).

His experience with the education community—as a political and a business figure rather than as an educator or a school administrator—colored his work with ODE. From the start he was suspicious of the department and worked to change it and its supervisor, the state board of education. He thought that the state board was too unresponsive to his education agenda (Durfee-Hidalgo 1990).

The state board, of course, did not see it that way. In a commissioned history of the board, members recounted how political boards had caused problems in the early part of the century and believed that the board—large though it was with eleven members—was responsible for improving state standards without needing the governor's ear (Ohio State Board of Education 1989).

By the end of Voinovich's two terms, eight out of nineteen state school board members were appointed by the governor. A department insider could still boast to me in 2003, "Ohio has been able to anticipate the Bush agenda very successfully. Since 1987 [Ohio's adoption of state tests], we've been a rigorous example for NCLB," regardless of the state board. This department employee went on to credit the department's technical work and its thorough "budget background." Clearly, ODE made it through this institutional storm without much deviation from its existing policy direction, but how?

ODE's autonomy prior to Voinovich was real. Voinovich's predecessor, Ohio Democrat Richard Celeste, had some interest in education, but he was generally content to follow ODE's lead. On occasion, he borrowed topics from Franklin Walter for his own speeches (marginalia in Celeste's handwriting in Walter 1987a). He was supportive of Superintendent Walter's push to improve learning opportunities for at-risk children. He was an attendee of several state-board-sponsored meetings after being invited by Walter (Walter 1986; Walter 1987b). Celeste was also concerned about the speed at which the department was developing state standards, to which Walter felt compelled to reply as follows:

> We are moving as quickly as possible to implement the new statewide testing mandate. Recognizing . . . the potential litigation in this area, we are working with many groups to identify problem areas and sound responses prior to implementation. It would appear that the time lines in the law are relative, and we assure [you] that Ohio's program will be exemplary. (Walter 1987c)

Although Celeste had his own fights with the school board and created a legislatively stacked Commission on Education Improvement, the tone of Walter's weekly letters indicates that Walter, the board, and ODE felt independent of the governor, and the governor likewise kept them on a long leash (Budget fight with Celeste 1987; Celeste "slaps" state board of education 1989).

As Walter's letter in the previous quote indicates, he believed, with justification, that the design of Ohio's testing program was fully within the purview of the department. Walter had a tremendous advantage over Celeste. He had a purely elected state board, and, as one longtime bureaucrat recollected, "Walter was a master of playing the [state board]. He made sure to have contact with each board member every week." Later-superintendent John Goff seconded this and complained that Walter had it easy: "He had eleven members. I had nineteen."

But Walter's "insider" leadership caused him problems when the state board and the governor became less acquiescent. In 1990, the state board president, Paul Brickner, called Walter the "Saddam Hussein of Ohio education" (State journal: Demanding answers; counterattack 1991). Brickner later accused Walter of obfuscating facts and abetting fraud in Ashtabula County, writing to the governor, "The Board is entirely dependent on the state Superintendent, Franklin Walter, and his Ohio Department of Education for information" (Brickner 1991). While a credit to Walter's phenomenal influence on education policy, Brickner also signaled the end of Walter's dominance of the board. Although Walter would not confirm this to me, some reported rumors were that Walter retired in part because of the trouble with Brickner (The Brickner affair 1991).

This trouble coincided with Voinovich's assumption of the governor's office in 1991. When Walter was able to keep the institutional clout of the board behind him, he could leverage his statement that ODE was the "fourth branch of government. We were totally independent." But when his persuasiveness began to weaken and the board got away, he was unable to argue to Voinovich that the people of Ohio were behind him. Walter's letters to Voinovich were terser than those to Celeste, and he resigned soon after Voinovich came into office. As it so happened, Voinovich also removed the state board president, Brickner, around the same time (based on the charge that he was a federal employee and therefore ineligible to serve on the state school board).[8]

Soon after his election, Governor Voinovich called for an audit that indicated the weakening of ODE's institutional autonomy and the ascendancy of the business community as a significant interest group in Ohio education. The governor had expressed his unhappiness with ODE repeatedly on the campaign trail, arguing that ODE should generate more research for state curriculum standards and provide technical assistance to local school districts. Although ODE was singled out for a special report, Voinovich had created a blue-ribbon commission to study each state government agency (Durfee-Hidalgo 1990; Maher 1991, 13, 22).

The audit was produced by the Governor's Task Force on Education, a group comprised of executives from B. F. Goodrich, Goodyear, Proctor & Gamble, and TRW, all large, Ohio-based companies. This report damaged the department's reputation and provided the governor with a political excuse to seek greater gubernatorial interference with the department and the state board.

In particular, the report revealed that the department was run almost solely by the state superintendent. It found that, "when in doubt, Department staff consult the Superintendent, even on as minor an issue as delaying the start of a new hire by a few days" (Governor's Task Force on Education 1991, 25). The state board was ineffective:

"Few educators . . . had read the State Board of Education's published educational goals, and fewer still coordinated their long-term goals with those of the Board" (40). Communication within the department was rare, as "many lower-level Department people report hearing news of other divisions 'in the newspaper' " (47).

Although the governor tried to soften the blow by complimenting Walter on his operation of ODE over the past decade, the damage to the organization's autonomy was done, and the governor was able to push an education policy council independent of the department and to agitate for board appointment powers.[9]

The Governor's Education Management (GEM) Council was to provide "a vehicle for state-level policy input from Ohio's business community," and, according to the governor, to reorganize the department of education (Droste 1991b). Its fifteen members initially included only four (formal) educators: the president of the Ohio Federation of Teachers, the president of the Columbus Education Association, the chancellor of the state university system, and the state superintendent. The GEM Council was an influential sounding board for the governor, as its members suggested changes to the state testing system, conducted joint studies with ODE on business involvement in education, and provided advice to keep State Superintendent Ted Sanders when he appeared ready to leave in 1995 (Voinovich 1991b).[10]

Walter's retirement in 1991 created an opening for the governor to push for appointment powers. Voinovich wrote to Walter proposing that the governor should appoint the state superintendent:

> Given the pending change in governance, as well as the priority that I have placed on education, it is extremely important that I play a significant role in the selection of the new Superintendent. Most importantly, the next Superintendent must have the support and confidence of the Governor if this individual is to succeed. . . . We need to create a new governance structure to ensure greater accountability. (Voinovich 1991b)

An internal memo further recommended that the governor make the state board "an offer they cannot refuse" by publicizing his interest in appointing Walter's successor (Cosgrove 1991; see also Voinovich 1991a).

The state board, seeing the writing on the wall, allowed Voinovich to submit a nomination for Ted Sanders and for him to sit in on the interviews. It eventually ratified the governor's choice. (Sanders's only serious contender was William Phillis, an assistant superintendent under

Walter, who was widely supported by district superintendents but was a "loose cannon" according to the governor's education aide [Droste 1991a].)

Sanders was a solid choice from the governor's point of view. He shared many of the governor's views and was inclined to push "outcomes-based" education, a style of education that the governor believed was analogous to success and failure in business. Sanders did reorganize the department to address the failings noted by the audit, and he was a very competent promoter of the department's technical abilities. Even a cursory reading of Sanders's weekly memos to the governor gives the impression of a competent department—or at least that Sanders thought so.

If Sanders was an effective spokesman for the governor's education program, then he also gave Voinovich a reason to be less suspicious of ODE. Although several of my interviewees claimed that the outcomes-based education crisis—discussed in chapter 6—had driven ODE into a "bunker mentality" (a phrase used by more than one interviewee), ODE's performance under pressure helped convince the governor that the department was useful to his education agenda. He was especially interested in using the department's links to districts to impress upon local superintendents and local business that the ninth-grade proficiency test should be taken seriously for graduation and employment (Voinovich 1992b, 1993a).[11] By the end of the governor's term, ODE was undertaking a joint study with the Ohio Business Roundtable to produce *Knowledge and Know How: Meeting Ohio's Skill Gap Challenge*—a document that was widely recognized as well done, even though some groups took issue with its conclusions.

Sanders's mistakes on outcomes-based education opened the door for the department to show its own colors independently of the superintendent. Although the outcomes-based imbroglio and difficulties with the board helped prompt Sanders to take the presidency of Southern Illinois University, it also tempered Governor Voinovich's direct involvement with ODE (Wehling 1995). Although he again stated that it was "absolutely critical" that he be involved in choosing Sanders's replacement, he supported the longtime assistant superintendent, John Goff (Voinovich 1995a). Although Goff often had been on the road with Sanders, Governor Voinovich no longer had a state superintendent so closely tied to his education program (nor one whose appointment was so clearly the work of the governor). Yet the governor and Sanders did realize that passing over Goff would "send a message to the department that the Board does not support the direction the department (and the Governor) are heading" (Palagyi 1995). Goff got the job.

By the mid-1990s, Voinovich had come to appreciate the abilities of the department, but he was no closer to the state board. One newspaper's editorial board catalogued the state board's ills: "The board opposes the governor on equity funding; they're anti-school choice and anti-vouchers and anti-anything-else that threatens the status quo. The board even fought Ohio's proficiency tests. . . . Opponents argue that an elected state board represent 'all the people,' but fact is it mostly represents the entrenched system" (Let George do it 1995). The governor's biggest feud with the board was its opposition to appealing *DeRolph*, which the state lost in the first round. This only served to strengthen the governor's perception that the board served the "entrenched system" (Chalfant 1995).

Voinovich was able to insert language to abolish the elected board in the 1995 budget after several years of trying. The House of Representatives stripped this language out of the budget in April, prompting a stern rebuke from the governor. He sent his missive to state newspapers, noting that he was "extremely disappointed" with the House. He said he would remind legislators' constituents that the board opposed appealing *DeRolph*, which would result in "billions of dollars in additional taxes." The governor's staff worked into the summer on a compromise, and in June, the legislature gave the governor the authority to appoint eight members of the board. This gave him the ability to have his representatives in close contact with the department without having to be intimately involved (Voinovich 1995b). Unlike the initial proposal in April, allowing the governor to appoint part of the board came with "little fanfare . . . media coverage of the whole episode was minimal" (Palagyi 1995). At the same time, the governor sought to clarify what powers the board had in relation to the state superintendent. After his experience with Ted Sanders, the governor sought an increase in the autonomy of the superintendent and the department from the board.

Although reconstituting the state board did not generate much media attention, the move did gain the governor—and ODE—a persistent critic, Diana Fessler. Fessler later complained that groupthink dominated the board, she thought, because of his appointees (Fessler 1996). Eventually she left the board and became a Republican state representative, where she continued to be a troublemaker from ODE's point of view. One Democratic lobbyist with whom I spoke noted that Fessler was a reliable ally whenever he needed someone to "stir things up in the Republican caucus." Despite Fessler's complaints, few others found the board so critical for education. State Senator Cooper Snyder told the governor that even though the board had "not supported you consistently . . . that has been irrelevant. . . . Such things as proficiency tests, technology, equity funding, etc. have been accomplished with or without the State Board" (Snyder 1995).

Though John Goff was not nearly as visible as Sanders had been, he was able to enhance Ohio's testing system and continued to pursue the business-ODE links that Sanders had forged. With Goff's appointment, however, the governor became much more hands off—he now had appointment power to the state board—and communication between Goff and the governor became more formal. Goff, who had been a longtime employee at ODE even before he was an assistant superintendent, was left to pursue the department's own program, with an expanded set of responsibilities and with generally full support of the governor. Outside groups complained that ODE was an independent, standoffish agency, but it had to be: under Goff's tenure, the department expanded and refined its testing capabilities, continued to oversee financially delinquent school districts with varying degrees of success, and was the perennial defendant in the state's inconclusive ten-year school finance case.

In Ohio, the state department of education and its board are defined in statute, giving the governor an opportunity to push for changes that were not possible in, say, Wisconsin, where the department has some constitutional authority. But after Voinovich found an ally in the department, he was much more amenable to leaving the department alone. He compromised, and found that the department could be a useful counterweight to the many educational groups that the governor lumped into "the system." Thus while ODE suffered initial setbacks and experienced some loss of electoral independence, it was still able to gain responsibilities to define standards and accountability, and it was given significant leeway by the governor's office to pursue them.

Politics and Bureaucrats

While my expectation was that *gubernatorial* turnover would reduce the autonomy of an agency if a new governor were very interested in education, this expectation needs modification in the case of Wisconsin. Governor Thompson was governor from 1987 until 2001—Wisconsin's longest-serving governor—and the superintendent changed twice in that time. Therefore, in this section, I look at how a turnover of the *agency* chief impacts autonomy and scope.

Shortly after John Benson replaced Herbert Grover as state superintendent, Governor Tommy Thompson announced that his vision of education had no DPI. He spent fully 15 percent of his biennial budget address in February 1995 explaining how his new department of education would give "power back to the parents—the teachers—and the taxpayers of Wisconsin." In a not-so-veiled criticism of State Superintendent John Benson and his department, Thompson said, "This new Department will be a new voice of leadership committed to education reform, committed to meeting the demands of the twenty-first century . . . [and] not a voice for the education establishment" (Thompson 1995, 77).

Thompson's assault consisted of an attack on all three forms of the DPI's autonomy: political, technical, and fiscal.

First, Thompson's proposed changes weakened the department's political autonomy. Because the Wisconsin constitution partly sheltered the DPI, Thompson's plan had to leave at least John Benson's office. But he did his best to reduce Benson's role to simply reporting on the state of education, and no more. Although Thompson's plan appeared to preserve the constitutional separation between the governor and the superintendent, the proposed department of education would clearly serve the policy program of the governor.

Second, the DPI—as in the DPI remaining under Benson—would lose all of its technical expertise to the new department of education. Assuming that many of the same people who would have staffed the governor's department came from the DPI, technical autonomy would not have suffered much. Despite the change in control at the top, technical *expertise* would remain.

Fiscally, Thompson's budget left only $393,000 for John Benson's office versus $2.8 billion in general-purpose revenues for Thompson's department. He further weakened the "education establishment" vision of Wisconsin school funding by recategorizing school aids as simply another form of state-local shared revenue, payable through the department of revenue. This change would help break the special status of school aid funds and help the governor realize his stronger-than-ever desire to run the state's education program—to deeply cut property taxes. In many of his addresses to the legislature, he spent an equal or greater amount of time talking about property taxes and the pathologies of their link to school funding than he did about education proper.

The Wisconsin DPI had slowly built its responsibilities through the 1980s under the leadership of Superintendent Grover. In his official communication with the Wisconsin Legislature in the 1980s, Governor Thompson, though rarely referring to the department by name, frequently indicated his support for some program with reference to Superintendent Grover, as in, "I join Bert Grover in proposing the school improvement fund" (Thompson 1989, 47). How did the DPI, which had low levels of autonomy and scope to begin with, come to endure a frontal assault on all three aspects of its autonomy—political, technical, *and* fiscal?

"Bert Grover," was the two-word answer most of my interviewees gave. "Grover was a strong leader. So strong that Thompson's takeover was basically to ensure there would never be another Grover," one lobbyist remembered. In fact, John Benson himself suggested this as the number-one reason for the governor's actions in my interview with him.

There is no doubt that the time Grover spent chafing under Tommy Thompson had hardened the governor's dislike of the department. Their fights were so well known that newspaper headlines identified Grover as a "foe." But Grover's opposition in the past had never stopped Thompson from proposing—and enacting—controversial education plans. Exhibit A was the Milwaukee Parental Choice Program, which allowed poor students to attend private schools. Grover was an ardent and a public opponent of the program but could not stop the program. One editorialist opined, "If Bert Grover's booming voice was still in residence at DPI, Thompson might move more carefully, but he would still move. The Capitol betting line is that Benson is toast" (Still 1995).

Deeper factors also permitted the DPI to lose autonomy. These include factors that I identified in chapter 2: leadership, reliance on interest groups, and perceptions of poor internal management. Governor Thompson's interest in education—beyond reducing the property tax— also dramatically increased after the success of the school choice proposal in Milwaukee, which roughly coincided with the end of Grover's term. Figure 7.1 shows the number of words related to PK–12 education; a

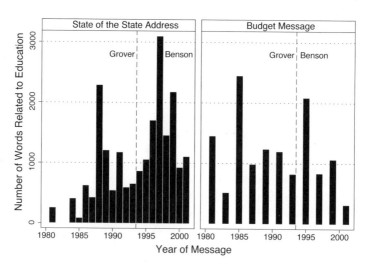

Figure 7.1. Frequency of Education as a Topic in Wisconsin Gubernatorial Messages.

simple difference-of-means test confirms that the mean before and after
Benson came to office is significantly different ($p < 0.05$).[12] Electoral
turnover at the agency and in the state Senate gave the governor an
opportunity to change the "initial conditions" for Benson.

First, Benson's attempt to move from insider leadership to public
leadership drew the governor's ire. It is true that Grover's "volcano of
emotion" had angered the governor in the past, but Grover was an
old legislator who still had friends in the Capitol. Benson, who had no
favors to call in, ended his brief dispensation of grace from the governor
when he tried to duplicate Grover's public leadership.

The governor had hopes that Benson would be more amenable
than his predecessor. Thompson had refused to make an endorsement for
Grover's successor, despite a string of teachers' union-sponsored television
commercials boosting Benson (though Thompson had no love for the
union) (Dehli 1993). A meeting between Benson and the governor's
staff on April 13, 1993, one week after Benson was elected, promised
conciliation. The governor was willing to work with Benson and meet
with him "bi-monthly or whenever," if Benson promised that " 'I will
not publicly bash the governor.' " Thompson also wanted Benson to
"fix up DPI" (Fonfara 1993).

For his part, Benson was optimistic as well. He grew up "six miles
away" from Thompson, and their families knew each other well, he said.
Benson was careful to keep the governor's office abreast of his activities
in the first few months. The DPI's purported lack of responsiveness was
a key component of Thompson's complaints about the department in
the waning years of Grover's terms, so Benson held an all-department
retreat in July 1993, when he discussed reorganizing the DPI to be more
responsive to teachers and other taxpayers (Dorsher 1993c). Benson
made sure to solicit the governor's input too: he wrote that he would
"appreciate any thoughts you have about our planning process and/or
the restructuring efforts in general" (Benson 1993).[13]

Unfortunately for Benson, he made a number of public pronounce-
ments in his first year of office to convince Thompson that his heart was
in the wrong place. Two of Thompson's centerpiece education programs
were the school choice programs in Milwaukee and a new, state-wide
charter school program. Both Benson and Grover were adamantly opposed
to the Milwaukee voucher program. In late 1994, the DPI produced a
report titled "Private School Vouchers: An Idea Whose Time Has Not
Come," which claimed that the program would segregate students on
ethnic, economic, and religious lines (Simms 1995). The product was
somewhat ironic, given that the state's voucher program *had* come and
had been operational for five years. Benson himself argued that the
program "does not deal directly or substantially with the challenges

faced by the Milwaukee public schools." He called for more "practical" programs (Dehli 1993).

The state's nascent charter school program came in for milder treatment. Department officials originally called the charter school program "unworkable" and complained that the charter law had been drafted without their input (note the lack of scope—such would never have happened in Georgia) (Kelley 1993). After a few months, Benson quietly shifted his position and held meetings with skeptical school district officials who had applied for charters to reassure them that the DPI would abide by the charter law (Howie 1994).

Further, Superintendent Benson lowered the passing score on the high school equivalence degree, the General Educational Development (GED) test. Through the administrative rule process, Benson had the passing score lowered from 250 to 230 out of 400. The passing cut point had been raised in 1988, a move Benson called a mistake. Predictably, he and the department came under heavy fire for lowering education standards, to which Benson replied "the high schools are doing just fine" (Mayers 1994).

In each case, Benson chose a public position clearly at odds with Thompson's. Despite the warning to not "bash the governor," Benson managed to bash all of the same programs that Grover had—the Milwaukee voucher program, the charter school program, and high state standards.

A second cause of loss was the department's long reliance on interest groups. Superintendent Grover had *strong* backing from many interest groups, and he had *good* backing from most of the rest of them. One longtime education lobbyist noted that Benson could not keep the interest groups together like Grover had: "Benson didn't know what he wanted to do. He couldn't put four points together for a speech. . . . For better or worse, when [Grover] wanted to do something, he'd come in here [my office] arms flailing, and loud, but he could bring all the players to the table."

John Benson, however, *was* clearly identified with the state's largest teachers' union, the Wisconsin Education Association Coalition. Many of my Wisconsin interviewees said something to the effect that "Benson was in the pocket of the union." Benson's campaign for the superintendency certainly lent credence to that view: WEAC spent $174,525, mostly on television commercials, to help elect him—almost equal to the $203,477 Benson spent himself. (His opponent, Linda Cross, spent $218,496; see School superintendent contest set cost record 1993.) One interviewee argued that the fight to take the DPI's power was actually a proxy war between WEAC and Thompson, but said, "You can't fight someone who holds all the cards."

Benson also walked into the role by strongly supporting WEAC's position on the state's mediation-arbitration law (usually called "Med-Arb"). Governor Thompson successfully rewrote the law to substantially limit the bargaining power of the teachers' union. In Thompson's version, called the qualified economic offer (QEO), if a school district offers a contract that meets certain financial criteria (pay and benefits must be higher than those offered in the previous contracts), then the union may either accept the district's offer or abide by the existing contract (Watchke 1998). Not only did this policy coup on Thompson's part help split the education establishment (school boards found the QEO useful to maintain budgets), but Thompson also considered this a signal achievement. Not surprisingly, WEAC found this distasteful, and it continues to vilify this particular law (Beilke 2001).[14] Because Thompson placed great weight on this particular policy change, and because Benson supported the union's side, he was easily cast as a "mouthpiece" for the teachers' union.

Even the one policy change clearly within the scope of the DPI, teacher certification, appeared to put the department in the unions' camp. As I argued in chapter 5, the DPI had to rely on interest groups to prop up its autonomy. The licensure reforms under Benson are an excellent example. Benson appointed a work group to create standards and later to draft the specifics of the program. The number of teachers' union representatives in the group, ten, exceeded even the number of DPI employees in the group. Administrator certification was added late to the teacher certification rules, angering representatives of other education groups, and it was WEAC that went on the road to promote the new rules.

In every case, the DPI appeared to favor the teachers' union—and even though Benson frequently denied this influence, the appearance of collusion was certainly strong. Governor Thompson's long animosity toward the union was able to find an easy target in Benson. The strength that might have been derived from interest group support stood the DPI in very poor stead.[15]

The third factor weakening the DPI was the allegation of poor internal management. This made the agency an easy target for reorganization. Not only did Benson call for an audit after his election, but former superintendent Grover appeared to have given a valuable testing contract to a company in which he had an interest without asking for bids.

John Benson asked for an audit the week he was elected to the state superintendency. He told the Joint Audit Committee that he "wanted to go into the agency with a clean slate" (Dorsher 1993a). John Benson had worked under Grover for almost ten years in the 1980s. Though he later said that "there was never a doubt" that Grover was a competent administrator, calling for an audit of an agency he knew intimately certainly implied that there were problems at the DPI (Dorsher 1993b). For his part, Grover was incensed by the audit. To the press, Grover only said that asking for the audit was an "unusual request" (Dorsher 1993b). In my interview much later, however, he mocked Benson: "Well, that makes it look like old Grover was mismanaging DPI. I didn't even replace furniture in my office that Barbara Thompson [Grover's predecessor] had left. . . . Benson thought he was going to run the place in a more respectable manner than me. Sniff. Benson was going to be more grown-up."

When the results of the audit came in, Benson quickly agreed with the report—but before consulting with his department. The audit found that the number of supervisors at the DPI had risen 45 percent since 1983, even as overall staff had fallen 8 percent. In December 1993, Benson told the press and the Joint Legislative Audit Committee that not only did he agree with the audit's generally negative findings but that he would cut twenty-eight supervisory positions in the department (State school chief to cut jobs 1993). An uproar inside of the DPI forced Benson to circulate an internal memo within a month saying that no one would lose a job due to the cuts. He suggested that either new positions would be created for "cut" employees, or that employees would be shifted to other departments. He also apologized for making comments about cutting jobs without informing staff first (Benson apologizes; vows no layoffs 1993). In addition, the DPI "reorganization" apparently only required "major shifts in thinking" as it actually happened, according to a staff member (Dorsher 1993d). Benson's actions could only reinforce the governor's perception that he would not be a useful participant addressing problems in education that the governor had identified. Such backtracking and lack of communication inside the department did little to build confidence in the agency's ability to administer the state's education programs.

Finally, Bert Grover himself had made several politically damaging missteps at the end of his term regarding the state's test contract. In 1992, the DPI awarded a five-year, $4.5 million, no-bid contract to American College Testing (ACT) to process the state's standardized tests. ACT subcontracted some of the work to a company called National Computer Systems (NCS). Grover had personal ties to both: he had accepted an honorarium from ACT for a speech in 1991, and he sat on NCS' advisory board. Although the state department of administration (DOA) found no violations of law, the appearance of a conflict of interest was strong. Grover said, "I did everything according to Hoyle," but the DOA did say that Grover had no reason to bypass standard contracting rules (Grover denies influence peddling 1993). The DOA required the DPI to put out a call for bids, and ACT's bid was $200,000 higher than the firm that eventually won (McDade 1993; Firm with Grover tie loses state contract 1993). Grover did Benson no favors by ending his tenure under a cloud.

The combination of a governor with an abiding interest in changing education policy, the turnover in DPI leadership, and the state superintendent's self-inflicted wounds gave the governor an opening for an assault on the DPI's scope and autonomy. The governor's changes flew through the state legislature. Even after the state supreme court declared the action unconstitutional through a grammatically gymnastic interpretation of Article X, which created the office of the state superintendent, Thompson had little further to do with the DPI. His lieutenant governor chaired the commission to redesign state standards—replacing work that the DPI had done earlier (Walters and Heinen 1996; Hall 1997). Said one lobbyist after Benson's successor, Elizabeth Burmaster, arrived: "Grover was weakened, Benson neutered, and Burmaster is irrelevant."

Conclusion

Governors, even when they are institutionally separate from the state's education apparatus, are now unlikely to leave education alone. When President Bill Clinton lectured members of Congress that politics should be left "at the schoolhouse door," he was assuredly not advocating leaving politicians at the schoolhouse door (Clinton 1997). He had been a governor, after all, and he had played a major role in promoting gubernatorial involvement in education through the National Governors' Association.

Indeed, in each case presented here, a governor's strong interest in education led to credible attacks on agency autonomy, to say nothing of scope. In each case, the governor was temporarily successful. Turnover in the governor's office (and in Wisconsin, the superintendent) revealed the strength or weakness of each education agency's autonomy and links to other politicians and groups. New governors tested agency ties as they sought to push education in new directions.

In Ohio and Georgia, which had departments of education with wide latitudes of autonomy and a broad scope of responsibilities, the governor-inflicted setback was temporary. Both state agencies had expended their resources in the past building up autonomy and scope for such an occasion. When new governors arrived who thought they could improve on their agencies' work, they were unable to match the agencies' abilities. In Georgia, some sources even credited the governor's meddling with GADOE as a cause for his electoral loss to Georgia's first successful state-wide Republican gubernatorial candidate since Reconstruction.

In Wisconsin, the education agency had less autonomy and a smaller scope. It was also very dependent on the personal abilities of a former state superintendent. This weakness was exacerbated when the agency chief left and a new superintendent tried to fill his shoes. In the absence of Herbert Grover, the DPI made an easy target. The agency was widely seen as being tied to particular interest groups, so it was unable to provide an "unbiased" report on education. These one-sided links limited the department's autonomy and made it far easier for the governor to circumscribe the agency's scope. The governor was able to find sufficient outsiders to perform some of the department's functions.

Even in Wisconsin, the DPI kept its political autonomy by dint of its constitutional status. The state supreme court decided that the DPI could not simply be reduced to a "supervisory" role, as the Thompson administration argued. The DPI should design and administer programs, thereby granting the agency some measure of legal protection for its autonomy and scope.

The governor, as a single individual, may have significant short-term power until the next election. Yet an agency's institutional position and existing scope built over time can trump the overtures of a governor.

Part 3

8

The View from the Dome

Legislative Salience

I don't want my government making too many laws.

—Georgia legislator, on education

Bureaucracies do not function in a vacuum. Although critics might argue that agencies are not responsive enough to the public (that is, not participatory enough), agency leaders can ill afford to ignore other branches of government—especially if the other branches of government are paying attention (Peters 2001). In this chapter, I show how legislators' interest came and went over and how that interest interacted with state education agencies' scope and autonomy. This chapter demonstrates the *effects* of agency autonomy on legislators' behavior.

Bureaucrats in all three state education departments were keenly aware of how legislators viewed their departments. Wisconsin Superintendent Bert Grover, a former legislator himself, was perhaps the best able to persuade legislators to take up an issue, although the DPI's weak position meant he had to expend an inordinate amount of energy pounding on doors in the Capitol two blocks away. Georgia Superintendent Linda Schrenko became the "Republican that both parties learned to hate" because of her poor relations with Republicans and the majority Democrats in the statehouse (Salzer 2006; Salzer, Warren and Torpy 2006). When I asked, Ohio agency officials could rattle off the department's enemies in the General Assembly—led by former state school board member Diana Fessler—as well as its friends.

As I set out in chapter 2, the legislature is one of three major exogenous challengers to the autonomy and the scope of an agency. The risks to the agency are highest if education is salient to constituents and therefore salient to legislators. High salience, unchecked by a strong department, may lead legislators to write legislation directing the agency to do things it would rather not do, or that it would prefer to do in a different way.

Scholars have argued that this drives legislative intervention, especially in topics that are in the public eye and are relatively simple (Ringquist, Worsham, and Eisner 2003). But measuring the salience of a topic for legislators is a quixotic task. Although such diverse scholars as Kingdon (2003), Drezner (2000), Majone (1989), and Hall (1986) have emphasized the role of ideas in prompting new policy, none of them has a good way to quantify how important an idea is to policy makers. If an easy measure did exist, then one would run the risk of uncovering stated preferences, which might or might not be the same as true preferences.

This chapter presents one method to uncover the revealed preferences of legislators through their committee memberships. Although equating committee membership with the relevance of an idea is undoubtedly a tenuous link, it is an improvement over the current dearth of measurement techniques. Further, state committee systems are fluid, unlike the U.S. Congress'. These two facts make states an excellent place to test how preferences are formed.

This chapter proceeds in three parts. The first part defines salience and shows how it fits with the book's theoretical argument. The second part explains how the salience of education in state legislatures is measured over time. And the third part, using the success of education bills in the legislature, shows how salience moderates autonomy and scope over time.

Salience, Autonomy, and Scope

Salience means the relevance of a policy topic or an area to legislators. For example, in the early 1980s, Ohio experienced a rapid loss of manufacturing jobs, revenue, and property taxes. Combined with the state's strict limits on school revenue, many school districts could not meet costs, causing some to file for bankruptcy and end the school year early. This situation created a flurry of bills that included prohibiting districts from declaring bankruptcy, shortening the school year to save costs, and declaring that any school bond issue proposed by a district be declared "passed," despite violations of Ohio's constitutional limitations. In Georgia, the allegedly heavy paperwork requirements of the Quality Basic Education Act prompted legislators to introduce bills in the early 1990s trying to roll back aspects of QBE. In Wisconsin, school choice bills, pro and con, gained prominence in the mid-1990s as the state added charter schools and expanded the state-funded Milwaukee private-school voucher program to parochial schools.

Salience

In each case, some education issues became prominent for a legislative session or two and then disappeared. When Ohio's economic situation improved in the 1980s, school finance bills became scarce until the *DeRolph* finance cases. QBE bills became rare after Superintendent Werner Rogers, one of QBE's architects, lost his position to Linda Schrenko. Although school choice continues to grow in Wisconsin, the issue does not have the legislative prominence it did in the 1990s. Selected topics appear in Table 8.1 (next page). Legislative salience is a significant explanatory variable for agency scope.

How do ideas gain prominence with legislators? National reports such as the 1983 *Nation at Risk* are often credited with standards-based reform in the mid-1980s (e.g., Smith and O'Day 1991). As shown by perusing legislative yearbooks, many legislators on education committees have come from teaching backgrounds, giving them a natural affinity for education. Because local education systems are one of a state's largest expenditures, legislators often seek to change how the state collects and distributes these revenues. The wide variety of causes makes it difficult to pinpoint *why* an issue becomes important.[1]

One might conceive of two effects of legislative salience on agency scope. If legislators are responding positively to an autonomous agency, then they may be more willing to take the agency's point of view and do what agency personnel suggest to extend scope. If legislators respond negatively—whether because the agency has little autonomy or because the agency over-reached its autonomy—then the agency will have to work harder to ensure that legislation is to the agency's liking. These differential effects affect the expectations, which will be noted later.

Regardless, increased salience creates the risk of additional attention by legislators to agency activities. Legislators' diverse motives for introducing and marking up legislation rarely include giving another person, or agency, credit for a program. In fact, as Mayhew (1974) noted long ago, this runs opposite to what members of Congress and, by extension, state legislators do. If the salience of education is high, inducing more legislative interest, then legislators should seek to direct the agency to change programs, create new ones, and eliminate others. Although none of these necessarily *reduces* the scope of an agency, such impositions impinge on its autonomy in the short term, as explained in chapter 2. In the long term, these impositions by legislators serve to increase an

Table 8.1. Number of Education Bills Introduced with Selected Subjects, 1983–2001

Subject	'83	'85	'87	'89	'91	'93	'95	'97	'99	'01
Departmental Operations and Staffing	9	13	21	24	27	21	34	14	6	11
Teacher Certification and Requirements	14	21	33	49	28	18	25	28	16	10
Curriculum Standards	6	5	10	12	16	17	12	8	8	7
Testing and Assessment	0	3	5	10	14	13	22	10	14	10
School Finance	10	34	49	53	56	58	73	48	15	8
Crime and Discipline	7	8	10	19	17	28	26	24	28	11
Public and Private School Choice	1	4	6	12	7	16	15	16	7	9
Property Tax Relief	10	10	16	17	12	16	5	6	11	3

Source: Compiled and coded by the author from legislative journals (includes Ohio, Georgia, and Wisconsin).

agency's scope, which leaves the door open for more autonomy.[2] The first expectation for this chapter is that a*s the legislative salience of state-level education increases, the more likely it will be that legislators will seek to reduce the autonomy of a state educational agency.*

Literature on Congress provides at least two rough ways to estimate the preferences of legislators for certain issues: committee service and bill cosponsorship. (Bill cosponsorship is addressed in the next section.)

Equating committee service with a topic's legislative salience is a difficult translation. Not only do many committees handle multiple topics (e.g., Defense and Veterans Affairs, Health and Welfare, Tourism and Economic Development), but some are also power committees on which ambitious legislators would naturally seek to serve (e.g., Rules or Finance). Nevertheless, using committee selection as a proxy for salience, as developed later in this chapter, has the advantage of being a rough estimation of revealed preference based on actual behavior.[3] Using the method described in Appendix B, I use the likelihood that a legislator *serves* on a committee and the likelihood that that legislator *leaves* the committee after a given number of terms in the legislature as proxies for legislative salience. When education is more salient, a legislator should be more likely to serve on the education committee and less likely to leave it.

Across time and cases, however, the hypothesized link between legislative salience and autonomy will be contingent upon how autonomous the agency is at the beginning of the legislative session. The education committee should be less desirable to legislators if the department of education is autonomous, simply because the agency can make many policy decisions on its own. That is, a "popular" education committee is an indicator of a less autonomous agency, in that there are more policy areas where legislators can direct the education agency's activity.

The likelihood of exit should work in reverse. Because only legislators who are already on a committee can exit it, higher autonomy should *not* deter committee membership, because committee members gain some intrinsic value from serving (again holding salience constant). Legislators on the committee are likely to have a better understanding of how the agency works and have relationships with department personnel. For more autonomous agencies, legislators' motivations should be more clearly held: they should be willing allies who support an agency's request for increased scope, be determined critics who seek to limit an agency's new actions, or be intrinsically interested in education, independent of an agency's activity. This link should strengthen as tenure increases.[4]

From the evidence presented in the earlier chapters, I expect that, given the same level of salience, Wisconsin legislators would see the greatest value in committee service because the DPI appears to have the least autonomy of the three states. Georgia legislators should have the least interest in serving on the committee, and Ohio somewhere in between.

Autonomy and Scope

Previous chapters have given qualitative descriptions of an agency's scope. For example, the Wisconsin DPI lost autonomy and scope because of budget cuts in the mid-1990s due to a backlash against a former state superintendent; Ohio's department gained scope because of a school finance court case; and Georgia's autonomy was largely untouched, despite personality conflicts between the state board and the superintendent. Legislative production—the number of bills and the duration of bills in the legislature—offers the possibility for concrete, quantitative measures of scope and autonomy.

The vast difference between the number of bills introduced and those passed has presented a puzzle to scholars: if the likelihood of passage, or even consideration, is so low, then why bother in the first place? Clearly the salience to the public of an issue is one source of ideas. A small base of research suggests that bills introduced also serve as indicators to constituents of positions they hold—even if they never vote on them (Talbert and Potoski 2002; Canon 1999, 191–99; Mayhew 1974). Bill introduction also reflects the subject expertise and seniority of a legislator (Schiller 1995). Further, *cosponsoring* bills may serve as an indicator of the ideological breadth of support in the legislative chamber (Kessler and Krehbiel 1996), a reflection of extrapartisan issue alliances (Talbert and Potoski 2002), or a result of the institutional position within the legislature (e.g., a committee chair will introduce more) (Schiller 1995; Sinclair 1989; see also Wawro 2000).

In each case, introducing a bill requires careful consideration on the part of the sponsor. Unlike roll-call votes, where legislators may dodge responsibility for specific elements of the bill, especially in the case of omnibus bills, sponsors can be pinned on every detail in legislation they propose (Burden 2007). Said one legislator about cosponsoring, "I had to first think what the people back home would think, and if it would help them, or [whether it] was something they weren't interested in" (quoted in Talbert and Potoski 2002, 872).

At this stage, legislators have the most control over agency activity: legislation can permit *discretion*, but the agency will have relatively little autonomy in newly delegated activities. (Recall that agency autonomy is cyclic: the activity of this legislative session will affect agency autonomy for the next session—but this session's activity is affected by the *current* level of agency autonomy.) I expect that wide-scope agencies will also have the greatest number of bills targeted at them. A second expectation for this chapter is that *the greater the scope of an agency, the greater the legislative production related to that agency, conditional on the salience of the agency's policy area.*

In the following sections of this chapter, I use two dependent variables to measure legislative production. The first is bill introduction and the second is the speed at which bills are reported from committee.

When legislators introduce bills, they indicate that some issue is salient to themselves or their constituents. Moreover, they demonstrate faith that *state* action is relevant to some policy area—if local control of education is truly ascendant, then there is little cause to introduce bills at the state level. As legislators introduce more bills, they set and perhaps expand the scope of the agency. This number should be conditioned on the salience of education: as salience increases, more bills should also be introduced. The barrier to introducing bills is very low, and the bills introduced are the best expression of what scope legislators believe an agency should have. Further, agencies with more scope already should be likely targets for additional tasks.

The second part of legislative production is bill passage. But there are limitations on this measure. Many roadblocks may hinder bills, including scheduling, partisan pressures, and coalition building, and all of these are unrelated to the salience of education or to the autonomy of an agency. Of the 2,104 bills I coded that were assigned to committees in all three states in twenty years, only 757 made it out of committee. Of these bills, 321 passed both houses, and the sitting governor signed 266. Just 12.6 percent of education bills made it through the entire process.[5] As such, I consider the effects of agency autonomy on bill reports from committee as the best first measure. Although bills leaving committee may be delayed for many reasons not related to their content—scheduling, partisan goals, election cycles, and protracted budget negotiations, for example—I perform a parallel estimation with the caveat that agency autonomy would have less influence on the floor than it might in committee.

How does an agency's autonomy affect bills? Agencies do not introduce bills, even if their fingerprints are on them, but their autonomy can speed or slow their departure from committee onto the floor.[6] That is, I assume that an agency can independently decide *which* bills to support and oppose, and it can direct its lobbying resources accordingly. One might argue that a positive view of the agency should speed bills out of committee, but my agency interviewees were generally leery of legislative meddling—even if the meddlers were friends of the agency. Therefore, I expect that as an agency's autonomy increases, bills will take longer to leave committee, as department personnel try to cajole legislators to alter a bill to the department's liking.

Salience also has a role. While higher salience should increase the number of bills introduced, it should also mean that more legislators have an interest in some bill, thereby lengthening the time it takes to get out of committee. A third expectation is that *conditional on legislative salience, the greater the autonomy of an agency, the slower the rate of legislative production.*

Given the findings of the previous chapters, I expect Georgia to have the highest number of bills introduced regarding education and Wisconsin the least. Further, Wisconsin's education bills, on the whole, should take less time to leave committee, because the agency will have less clout in slowing down the legislative process to ensure that a bill is to the agency's liking. Georgia should have the longest times in committee.

The Salience of Education in the Legislature

Before estimating the effects of legislative production, I need to show how legislative preferences for education committees have changed over time. I explore two ways to generate an estimate of committee preference: the likelihood of *serving* on an education committee and the likelihood of *exiting* an education committee on which one is currently serving.

Likelihood of Service

To estimate legislative preferences, I recorded changes in all committees from 1983–1984 to 2001–2002. The relative desirability of the education committee should indicate education's salience. Obviously the salience of any given topic is not the sole cause of service on a committee, and some committees are administrative or have fingers in all bills (such as finance or budget committees). For topical committees, such as education, I expect that committee service should be affected by three groups of influences. The first set includes legislators' individual characteristics: the legislator's tenure in the legislature, service on the same committee in the previous session, and party. A second group includes state-level characteristics that apply to all legislators: which party has majority status, the existence of divided government, and a new governor. A third set, which concerns education specifically, includes the frequency with which a governor mentions education in his or her state-of-the-state addresses, a change in the state superintendent, and the relative size of the education agency's budget. I discuss each of these in turn. Further statistical details and control variables appear in Appendix B.

CORRELATES OF SERVICE

The individual characteristics of legislators can capture some of the intrinsic motivations for legislators to serve on a committee. The most prominent of these is the length of service in the same legislative chamber. I expect that the longer a legislator serves in her or his House chamber, the *less* likely she or he is to serve on the education committee. Because education is not a power committee, legislators are likely to seek better committees, especially as they become more experienced in the legislature. Likewise, I expect that longer terms in the legislature should correlate with a *higher* likelihood of exiting the education committee—more experienced legislators should appear on budget and appropriations committees.

When estimating the likelihood of exit, I also include the number of terms a legislator has served on the education committee. After controlling for legislators' total tenure, I expect that members with fewer terms of service will be *more* likely to exit than those with more terms. Since I control for the overall loss of experience due to overall tenure, I expect that legislators who have a greater interest in its work are more likely to stay over the long term. More terms on the committee indicate greater interest. Members using the committee simply as a stepping stone should leave earlier in their careers.

If a legislator serves on a committee in one session, then there is a good chance that she or he would serve on the same committee again. I created a binary variable to indicate prior service. (This measure is implied in the committee tenure variable for the exit analysis.)

The effect of party membership is less clear. Because all committees have to be staffed, there should be little difference in a "global" likelihood of service or likelihood of exit simply based on partisanship. Nevertheless, as shown in earlier chapters, because Republicans have tended to support state oversight against the claims of (usually Democratic) teachers' associations, Republicans should be more likely to serve on education committees over time. The effect should be slight, because members of both parties must serve on committees, however, there should be greater continuity for Republican members.

All legislators are affected by a second set of influences, regardless of individual motivations. The first is majority party status. Because majority parties are over-represented on more important committees, more seats are available for members to move into. I do not expect this to be a strong influence, but belonging to the majority party should increase the temptation to exit an education committee for a more prestigious one.

Divided government presents the opportunity for less oversight because of increased conflict between the different parties that control government. Therefore, the existence of divided government should prompt an increase in the likelihood of serving on an education committee—there might be a perceived need to counter the other branch's or the other house's proposals. Exit should be unaffected.

One of the U.S. president's strongest powers is public persuasion (Kernell 2006). By analogy, one would expect that the more a governor talks about education in his or her public address, the more desirable a seat on the education committee should be. I coded state-of-the-state addresses because these are the most public forum for a governor to express his or her legislative platform. The effect on exit is unclear. Presumably, legislators on the committee already have preferences of their own that are not likely to be swayed by a governor, at least not by his or her speech making.

A new governor presents opportunities for legislators to take advantage of a less experienced chief executive. Legislators may seek to remain on their respective committees, especially if they are unsure about the new chief executive. By remaining on the committee, they may be able to shape the course of education under new leadership.

A similar change in the state superintendency is the first educational factor that might influence committee service. In Georgia and Wisconsin, the state superintendent is the constitutional equal of the governor, although this has never been observed in practice, according to my interviewees. If the state superintendent is the key player the framers of state constitutions assumed, then a change in the superintendent should have the same effects on service and exit that a change in the governor would. A change creates a temporary leadership vacuum, and legislators may see an advantage to serving on the education committee in this case. Legislators already serving might stay to guide the new superintendent.

Finally, I include the size of the education agency's general-purpose revenue budget relative to the state's total general-purpose revenue as a measure of scope. As will be explained more fully in the following chapter, the use of state-source funds is a better measure of legislative preferences than overall revenues, which contain earmarked federal funds. I expect that as the state agency's share of the budget increases, there will be more interest in the committee and less incentive to exit the committee. (An alternative is the percentage of change in the education agency's budget from last session, but there is little reason to believe that a change in budget would suddenly induce a legislator to join or leave a committee, unless the change is drastic. Therefore, I simply use this percentage measure.)

RESULTS

Results from the first analysis (full results are in Appendix B) suggest that committee service on education committees was endogenous to individual legislators—that is, there was something particular about education that drew legislators to that particular committee (there may also be district-level influences not captured by these data). The only two influences that had strong effects on education committee membership were, as expected, previous service and legislative tenure. Both effects were strong: previous education committee service predicted future service ($b = 2.60$, $p < 0.01$), and the longer a member had served in the legislature, the less likely she or he was to serve on the education committee ($b = -0.26$, $p < 0.01$). However salient education is, most legislators tend to gravitate toward more powerful committees over time, and education is not one of those.

Neither party nor majority party status had any significant effect on the likelihood of education service. Since party had no statistically significant effect, it is not surprising that the presence of divided government had no effect either. Again, party should be a significant factor for committees, such as Rules or Finance.

Further, neither a change in governor nor superintendent had an effect on likelihood of service. This is not surprising, given that the election cycle between governors (and superintendents in Wisconsin and Georgia) is different, and legislators rarely run with a governor and certainly not with a superintendent. Yet the lack of effect from the change in the superintendent provides weak evidence that agency autonomy is at work. If a new agency chief has no effect on legislative preferences, then legislators are saying, in effect, that the agency is what the agency is, regardless of its leadership.

Curiously, the emphasis on education by the governor had little effect. Although I did not expect that legislators would take the governor's legislative prescriptions whole, this finding suggests that, at least for serious education legislators, the governor does not provide cues for important policy committees.

More interesting, however, is the difference between the states. If committee service is approximately inversely related to agency autonomy, then, as shown in Figure 8.1, the Wisconsin DPI would be the least autonomous. The figure shows the 25th, 50th, and 75th percentile predicted probability that an individual legislator will serve on an education committee. Wisconsin legislators are the most likely to seek education service; even Wisconsin's low points are about equal to the others' high points. Note that some legislators are *very* likely to serve on the education committee, as shown by the 75th-percentile line.

Ohio and Georgia show a smaller range of difference in the likelihood of service, although legislators in both states are less likely to serve on education committees than their counterparts in Wisconsin, all other things being equal. Georgia's data do show that median legislators (the middle line) were more likely to serve on the committee toward the end of Superintendent Werner Rogers's terms in office (the early 1990s). At this time, the GADOE was under heightened scrutiny for burdensome paperwork resulting from the Quality Basic Education Act's process and district standards. Ohio legislators showed a slightly lower probability of service during the state's experiments with outcomes-based education

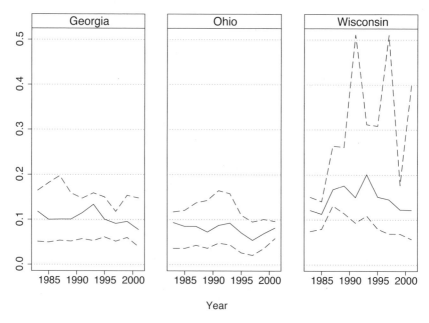

Figure 8.1. Predicted Probability of Education Committee Service, 1983–2002.

and Governor Voinovich's successful attempt to appoint state board members (note the bump between 1990 and 1995).

Likelihood of Exit

Perhaps a more revealing measure of salience is the probability that members of a committee will leave that committee. This analysis uses the same set of explanatory variables as the previous one. Members leaving a committee indicate that they see better use of their service elsewhere.[7] A statistical explanation appears in Appendix B.

As expected, legislators with more terms *in the legislature* are more likely to leave the education committee ($b = 0.22$, $p < 0.01$), but legislators with more terms *on the education committee* are less likely to leave ($b = -0.29$, $p < 0.05$). This confirms the expectation that education is not a powerful committee, but it also provides support for the expectation that legislators who stay on the committee longer are more likely to stay, perhaps due to intrinsic interest or expertise in the topic.

Surprisingly, party has a strong (but small) effect on the likelihood of exit ($b = 0.07$, $p < 0.10$). Members are more likely to leave as the proportion of Republican legislators increases. Both parties had strong, if competing, ideas about education in this time span, but Republicans may have migrated to other committees more in line with the party's broader interests.

Divided government has no effect on the likelihood of leaving a committee. Neither does a change in superintendent, the governor's emphasis on education, or the size of the agency's budget. *Remaining* on the committee is unaffected by these if education is a salient issue rather than a partisan issue or simply a gubernatorial interest.

Again, with the exception of Republican seat share, committee exit appears to be driven by factors endogenous to the legislator herself or himself.

Figure 8.2 (next page) shows the estimated likelihood that an *individual* legislator leaves the education committee in a given session. The overall trends show that, as expected, Georgia legislators are the least likely to leave the education committee once they are on it, especially median legislators (the middle line). Ohio legislators, in general, were less likely to leave the committee—at least until the 1990s, when the department was embroiled in the controversy over outcomes-based education and the *DeRolph* school finance case. In the late 1990s, Ohio legislators were more likely to leave the education committee than Wisconsin legislators.

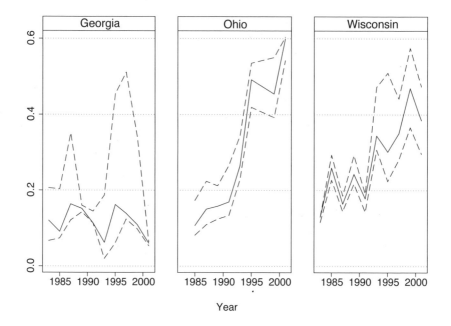

Figure 8.2. Predicted Probability of Leaving the Education Committee, 1983–2002.

Legislative Production

Whatever the preferences of legislators, agency autonomy and scope are unlikely to change until legislators' preferences generate real legislation. This section explores whether salience has an effect on bill introduction. To test these hypotheses, I compiled legislative histories for all education bills introduced in Georgia, Ohio, and Wisconsin between 1981 and 2001, inclusive.[8]

Bill Counts

Which factors might influence legislators to introduce education-related bills? Greater numbers of bills should indicate a greater willingness to countenance state action and higher legislative salience, thus improving an agency's scope. Table 8.2 shows the total number of bills introduced in each session that relate to education. Georgia legislators introduced double the number of bills of either Ohio or Wisconsin—even though both Ohio and Wisconsin have essentially year-round legislatures and Georgia does not. Yet the same pattern observed in previous chapters continues here: Georgia shows evidence that legislators recognize that their education agency has broader scope than legislators in the other two states do for their respective agencies.

The following section lists the variables that I expect will influence bill introduction. These data are grouped by legislative session, rather than by legislator, in these analyses.

CORRELATES OF BILL INTRODUCTION

I expect that a reduction in an education agency's budget will produce a smaller number of bills. A larger budget indicates greater scope, and if that scope does lead to more opportunities for an agency to claim autonomy, then a *reduction* in that budget should reduce the attempts by legislators to direct an agency's behavior through legislation. This does not detract from the claim that more bills are a result of broader scope and more autonomy, only that a reduction in an agency's budget should depress the number of bills introduced. This variable is measured as the percentage of change from the previous biennial budget.

Partisan correlates should include the governor's party, the partisan competition of the legislature, and the partisan composition of those introducing bills. If Democrats are less likely to favor state action in education in defense of local control and district-level collective

Table 8.2. Number of Bills Introduced Relating to Education

Session	Georgia	Ohio	Wisconsin
1983	65	42	21
1985	73	82	24
1987	102	105	22
1989	145	78	55
1991	120	119	44
1993	148	83	71
1995	209	94	30
1997	152	61	25
1999	131	21	20
2001	64	22	20
Mean	121	70	33

Note: Data compiled by the author are from legislative journals.

bargaining, then more Democrats in the legislature and a Democratic governor should result in fewer bills. I expect that fewer Democrats would introduce bills.

Further, I expect that the existence of divided government and changes to or away from divided government will have a material effect on legislative output. Divided government should increase the number of bills introduced, because the likelihood of any particular bill passing both houses and being signed by the governor is much less. Therefore, there is an incentive to introduce more to counter the effects of the other party's policy preferences. How a *change* in divided government will affect bill production is unclear. It may depress production, as higher-priority policy items are brought to the fore as a new majority status allows opportunity; or, it may depress production, because a switch to divided government means that new committee members are less experienced with the needs of education. Otherwise, a change may actually increase production for the same reasons that divided government might: distrust of another branch. Regardless, I expect that this change in status will be significant.

As I explained earlier regarding committee service and exit, I expect that changes in the state superintendent and governor introduce a temporary leadership vacuum, which should encourage legislators to introduce a wider variety of bills as the new administration creates a concrete policy platform. That is, a change should lead to a greater number of bills introduced.

I add the median probability of service and likelihood of exit that I estimated in the previous section.[9] These capture the salience of education to the legislature. I have also included a more direct measure of salience, the number of federal laws related to elementary and secondary education that passed Congress. I expect that a greater likelihood of education committee service will increase the number of bills and a lower likelihood of exit to prompt a similar increase in the number of bills. Similarly, if more federal laws indicated a national "mood" for education bills, then an increase in this number should prompt more bills. A detailed statistical table appears in Appendix B.

RESULTS

The results of the analysis provide good evidence that greater agency scope discourages legislative interference in agency affairs, while the salience of education, the presence of divided government, and greater numbers of Republicans in the legislature are all associated with increasing numbers of education bills.

When the state education agency receives a budget boost, the number of bills introduced relating to education decreases—about one bill fewer for every additional percentage increase in the budget (b = −0.02, $p < 0.01$). This finding supports my contention that given the faith legislators place in state action, agencies with more scope will be subject to relatively fewer bills.

The salience of education, on the other hand, had the expected effect of increasing the number of bills (b = 11.54, $p < 0.01$). A change from the lowest value for the likelihood of committee service (5 percent) to the highest (20 percent) generated with an increase of sixty-eight bills. This is no small increase, but just over two fifths of the average number of education-related bills introduced in an Ohio legislative session. Similarly, as the likelihood of leaving an education committee increased, the number of bills declined (b = −1.43, $p < 0.05$; this predicts a decrease of twenty bills between the extreme observed values). The department of education personnel I interviewed were often suspicious of "education legislators," because they often had ideas department leadership did not think were sound. These twin findings indicate that the suspicion was reasonable. This interpretation is also supported by the effect that changes in the budget have on bill introduction. Although an increasing number of bill introductions might increase the likelihood that an agency's autonomous actions could be codified into scope, agency personnel would have to lobby that much more to shape the bills to their liking.

A larger Republican percentage also correlates with a higher number of bills (b = 0.02, $p < 0.05$)—a strong finding, given that one case, Georgia, had a majority of Democrats in the legislature through the entire time span. This is consistent with my story that Republicans should be more amenable to state action in education, in general, against the claims of local teachers' unions or associations.[10] The governor's party has no statistical effect.

In the second chapter, I postulated that divided government would make it more likely that an agency's autonomous actions would be incorporated into its scope. In terms of the number of bills introduced, divided government indeed has a positive effect on the number of bills introduced (b = 0.41, $p < 0.05$). This finding is somewhat at odds with the federal divided government literature, which suggests that legislative production goes down (Edwards, Barrett and Peake 1997; Binder 1999).[11] A *change* from the last legislative session to or from divided government also increases the number of bills introduced (b = 0.42, $p < 0.10$). One explanation for this pair of findings is that education is an issue that neither Republicans nor Democrats have a natural advantage with the electorate at the state level. Thus both parties continue to seek the mantle of "party of education." These opportunities are greatest when a party wins unified control and wishes to fulfill campaign promises, or when a party can showcase its differences under divided government. A continuous period of unified government would lessen the need to capture attention with education, as electoral prospects would appear to be more secure in unified government.

A change in the governor mildly depresses the number of bills, contrary to my expectations (b = −0.36, $p < 0.01$). Legislators may be seeking direction from a new administration, and major policy bills do originate in the governor's office. In Ohio, for example, Governor Voinovich's decision to push for gubernatorial appointment generated several bill introductions, although the idea originated out of the governor's office. In Wisconsin, elements of the state's standards were introduced "at the request of Governor Tommy G. Thompson," and, as shown in the chapter on leadership turnover, able governors are able to push for changes to education agencies that the agencies themselves may not desire. A change in superintendent has no effect on the number of bills introduced, which, as earlier, indicates that legislators have some sense that agency autonomy is independent of its chief.

Time to Report and to Pass

A final area in which salience and agency autonomy may play directly is in the selection effect for bills reaching the floor.[12] In this section, I show how these concepts influence the number of days it takes for education bills to leave committee. I only look at *leaving* committee because a host of other issues on the floor—partisan dynamics, floor rules, scheduling, or earlier or later in the session, for example—would make it difficult to link the time a bill spends in the legislature to education-related issues. Further, bills in committee have a much greater chance of being discussed, and committees routinely mark up bills. It is in committee that an agency's technical expertise (and interest group complaints) would be the most important. After all, once a bill reaches the floor, the debate and vote, if any, are far more public than committee work. (For completeness, I also estimate the time it takes a bill to pass both houses. Many factors unrelated to the content of the bill may slow bills after they leave committee, so any findings from this estimation should *understate* the effect.) Statistical details appear in Appendix B.

Recall that I expect the bill to take more time to leave committee and to pass when an agency has greater autonomy. Given the evidence of previous chapters, this would mean Georgia bills should take the most calendar days to leave committee and Wisconsin bills the least.[13]

CORRELATES OF TIME IN COMMITTEE

As with the previous analyses, I expect that a change in superintendent will cause bills to take *less* time to leave committee, because the preferences of the new superintendent are unclear both to legislators and department lobbyists. Department lobbyists should be less able to convince legislators of the department's position in this temporary leadership vacuum. Such a shortening might be more pronounced if education committee legislators had adversarial relations with the department (and thus saw an easy opportunity to curtail the department's autonomy), but even if the relevant legislators had a good working relationship with the department, legislators seek to claim credit for themselves rather than others. The easiest time to do this is when there is a change in departmental leadership. (A change in the governor should have a similar effect.)

I offer two examples of department lobbying to illustrate this. The first is Georgia Superintendent Werner Rogers's observation that he had to haul in the department's two best legislative supporters to ensure that they did not write and pass legislation to which the GADOE might object. If the apparently most autonomous department found it necessary to check on legislation—thus prolonging its life in committee—then surely less autonomous departments would also. The second example I give suggests this. One of my Wisconsin interviewees recalled that Superintendent Grover's staff was able to keep him and the department's lobbyists "singing out of the same hymnal" in the legislature. He then criticized Grover's successor, John Benson, for having to backtrack on public statements and failing to respond to legislative requests before bills made it onto the floor.

I also expect the department's relative share of the state budget to influence the passage time. The larger the department's budget, the slower bills should be to be reported from committee. A larger budget is an indicator of scope, which leads to opportunities for autonomy.

I do not expect a significant difference to emerge based on the partisan composition of the legislature or based on the party of the governor as such. There is no reason to believe that one party or the other would speed bills out of committee—unless that party is the majority party. If a bill sponsor is of the majority party, then the bill should spend less time in committee than one introduced by the opposition party. Divided government should slow down bills for a corollary reason, although the effect in these analyses should be muted because, to reduce complexity, I do not include a bill's referral committee in the House other than that it introduced it.

Finally, I expect that as education is more salient for the bill sponsor as measured by the likelihood of committee service, a bill should be reported more quickly. The same should happen as the bill sponsor's tenure on the education committee increases.[14] Not only do these indicate a legislator's facility with education, which counteracts some of the education department's autonomy, but a longer tenure also means that a member will have more experience with other members of the committee.

RESULTS

In line with the theory about the interaction between legislators and an agency's autonomy, greater salience leads to threatened autonomy. The salience of education to the introducing legislator has a strong effect on shortening the time bills remain in committee (b = 0.86, $p < 0.01$). Even if the legislators are friendly to the agency—my department interviewees could name their friends in the legislature—new legislation always presents the threat of new restrictions on the agency. This appears to support the position that legislators have a naturally adversarial relationship with an agency. This finding also suggests that agencies will have a more difficult time shaping legislation with expert legislators. The tenure on the committee, however, had no statistical effect, indicating that "expert" legislators do not necessarily speed or stall legislation when a policy area is highly salient.

Agency lobbyists would also do well to build cross-party alliances, as I suggested in chapter 5: if a member of the majority party introduced a bill, then it is 207 percent more likely to be reported the next day than if a member of the minority party introduced the bill (b = 1.12, $p < 0.01$). The effect of party is *very* strong in the committee system, even though party has no statistically significant effect elsewhere. If party control of the legislature changes, then a rational agency lobbyist would not want to have to start over.

Legislators do appear to take advantage of new education department leadership. A bill is 23 percent more likely to be reported the next day (provided it has not yet been reported) under a new state superintendent than a bill introduced when there has been no change in the superintendent (b = 0.21, $p < 0.05$). This estimation also provides evidence that an agency's scope slows bill reporting (b = −0.02, $p < 0.10$). Taken together, these findings suggest that agency leadership and agency scope do play a role in keeping bills in committee when they are not to an agency's liking.

A change in governor had no statistical effect on a bill's exit from committee. At least in the narrow confines of education legislation, this finding belies the common belief that the constitutional equality of these offices is a legal fiction—the superintendent's office has greater weight.

Curiously, divided government sped up bill reporting (b = 0.38, $p < 0.05$). This may be because legislators do not have to consult with their counterparts in the other chamber when marking up a bill. This is only speculative, however. The observations for this analysis are only drawn from one house. The practical effect of this exclusion is that bills passed by the other chamber, perhaps controlled by another party, are not considered.

As expected, neither the distribution of party membership nor the party of the governor had any effect on the time between introduction and reporting.

This chapter has considered bills in committee. Certainly most activity on bills appears there, but a bill surviving the committee markup process does little to change the law. This final analysis considers the effect of autonomy on the time it takes to send a bill to the governor—that is, how long did a bill take to pass both houses of the legislature in identical form? As I mentioned earlier, these bills are subject to many other considerations than simply agency autonomy, so these results should be interpreted with caution. Statistical details appear in Appendix B.

Unlike the earlier analyses, partisanship was a key factor in bill passage rates. When states had Republican governors, bills took 37 percent longer to pass than when Democrats sat in that office (b = −0.46, $p < 0.05$). A larger number of Republican legislators, on the other hand, marginally sped up a bill's passage (approximately 1 percent faster; b = 0.01, $p < 0.10$). This result suggests that governors were more active once bills had a serious chance of passing. If their lobbying follows a similar logic to. that of departments of education (that is, lobbying results in lengthening the time spent in the legislature), then this provides suggestive evidence that Republican governors were more likely to interfere with state departments of education generally. This interpretation supports the findings of previous chapters: two of the governors most antagonistic to some part of the state department of education, Thompson and Voinovich, were Republicans. With the exception of Georgia Governor Roy Barnes, all other Democratic governors were supportive of their departments of education.

In sum, department autonomy appears to have the expected effect in each of these states. Figure 8.3 shows the predicted duration of the time education bills remain in committee. Bills in Ohio are the slowest to leave committee, in part a tribute to that state's high-caliber department of education. Both Wisconsin and, interestingly, Georgia's bills take the least time to leave. Wisconsin's was expected, as the department has little reputation in the legislature. Georgia's appearance here may indicate some of the difference in legislative procedures (for example, Georgia bills tend to be single-subject ones, unlike those in either Ohio or Wisconsin, with a compressed legislative schedule).[15]

Conclusion

Legislators are the arbiters of state government. Legislators amplified the complaints of teachers and superintendents in Georgia over QBE's paperwork requirements. They called upon the Ohio department to redesign its school funding formula. One year, they permitted the DPI's budget to be cut in half, and another year they agreed with the governor that the DPI should not exist. Legislators can be champions of the state agency—one, Cal Potter of Wisconsin, was named to an assistant superintendency after his tenure in the legislature—or, a thorn in the side, as former Ohio state board member Diana Fessler became.

Bureaucracy appears to protect itself, however. As scholars have shown, legislatures rarely set the policy agenda. Instead, they respond to the decisions, statements, and desires of other leaders, because they are at a tremendous information disadvantage (Edwards and Wood 1999; Edwards 1989). These findings have generated significant research that

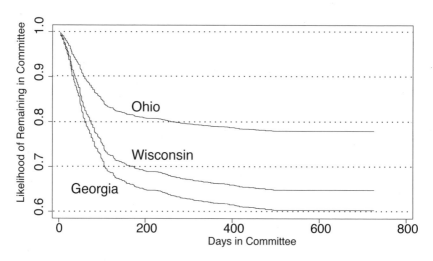

Figure 8.3. Predicted Time That Education Bills Remain in Committee, by State, 1983–2002.

seeks to understand how legislators can serve as the overseers that framers of state constitutions intended them to be (Ringquist, Worsham, and Eisner 2003; Calvert, McCubbins, and Weingast 1989).

If, as others assert, salience is the mechanism by which legislators decide to introduce legislation and hold oversight hearings, then greater salience should be bad news for agency autonomy (but not necessarily scope) (Bawn 1997). In this chapter, I used two ways to measure salience: how likely a legislator is to serve on an education committee and how likely a legislator is to leave that committee. I tied salience to bill introduction and to the speed with which education bills reached the chamber floor. As salience increased, legislators would introduce more bills, and those bills would reach the floor faster. In fact, salience only served to shorten committee work.

This chapter indicates that salience is of small import to an agency's *scope*. Bills are no more likely to be introduced when education is salient than when it is not—although empirically, *which* bills are introduced is clearly driven by current events. Even though the topics change, all of these could be considered major legislation affecting an agency's scope. Said another way, agencies face uniform pressures from the legislature over time, although different parts of agencies feel pressure at different times.

Salience does work against agency autonomy, however. Bills that are introduced when education is more salient are quick to leave committee, which shortens the time that agency lobbyists would have to reshape bills to align with their preferences (or halt them). This conforms to my expectation that expert legislators are more able to generate policy independent of agency lobbyists. Stable leadership and broad scope mitigate these effects. As Ringquist, Worsham, and Eisner (2003) note, agencies with strong leaders will be less affected by the whims of salience. The findings here confirm this.

In sum, education agencies are able to channel state legislators' desires to claim credit for legislation into activities that education agencies find useful for their own purposes. Legislators were most likely to grant expanded scope to the Georgia Department of Education, given its solid autonomy and able handling of administration. Wisconsin's DPI had the least given to it. Yet bills—whether passed or just introduced—only indicate what an agency *should* do. How important these activities are is revealed only in dollars. The final empirical chapter extends the analysis to state budgets in search of autonomy and scope.

9

Budgeting for Success

We used to do our budget separately and then send it over to the
governor. But now that we've got a friendly governor, we don't
even bother. We pretty much let him do it all in-house.

—High-level education department official

However much some governors fulminate, some interest groups protest,
and some superintendents preach, an agency only has money for those
things in the budget. This chapter first shows that state departments
of education vary in their fiscal autonomy through the appearance of
nonincremental budget increases. Then it demonstrates how agencies
successfully transform their budget requests into budget appropriations.
Both tasks are a tall order: interpersonal conflicts can explain some budget
decisions as much as agency needs or available state funds. More than
one Wisconsin observer credited DPI's budget troubles in the early 1990s
to a personal vendetta between the governor and the DPI. Similarly,
Georgia in the late 1990s found Governor "King Roy" Barnes facing
off against Superintendent Linda "That Woman" Schrenko—in which
GADOE received funds in excess of its budget requests, despite visceral
disagreements between the department's dually-elected chiefs.

Despite these unique situations, fiscal autonomy is not the result of
happenstance. As I have argued throughout, autonomy is built through the
competent execution of tasks that it already has, a vigorous advocacy of
new programs, the careful management of selected interest groups, and an
awareness of institutional barriers. Autonomy, specifically fiscal autonomy,
appears when agencies can request and receive more financial resources
than one would predict in normal times. If successful, fiscal autonomy
will translate into new funds, thereby increasing an agency's scope.

Yet simply having a large change in one's agency budget is an
incomplete picture of fiscal autonomy. If an agency consistently has
increases in its budget, but it consistently requests far more money
than the legislature appropriates, then the meaning of fiscal autonomy is

189

weakened. Simply put, an agency has to convince legislators and governors that the budget requests it makes are a legitimate representation of the scope that agency leaders deem important for education policy in the state. To the extent that the agency can do this, its requests for money should come close to being met, and in very good years, exceeded. This is the subject of the second part of this chapter.

In short, this chapter explores one concrete *result* of agency action.

Part of the ability to capture greater budgets comes from an agency's scope. Scope is partly revealed by the size of the agency's state-source budget per capita, shown one year at a time in Figure 9-1.[1] A bigger budget should result in legislators and governors giving greater deference to an agency's requests. A larger budget translates roughly into the agency serving a large clientele. As Pierson (1994) has noted, targeted cuts for identifiable groups rarely allow politicians much breathing room. Agencies can develop a strong interest in the programs and clients they serve—which translates into a government "interest group" that can alert members that there will be an impending negative change should there be cuts. One of the most frequent defenses that my interviewees gave for

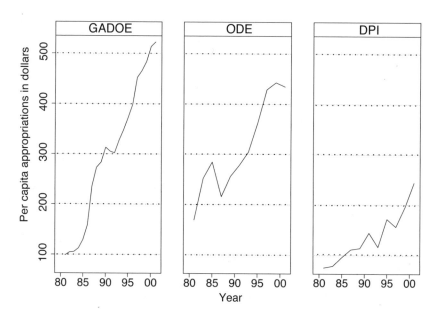

Figure 9.1. Per Capita Appropriations for State Education Agencies, Excluding School Foundation Supports.

their work at the state was a variation on, "It's all about the kids, after all." And if agencies do not pick up the baton, then the proliferation of special-interest groups may do it for them (see chapter 5). A bigger budget will involve more of these groups, therefore, cuts to an agency's budget will impose greater risks to legislators and governors.

But the risk must be unspoken and understood by all to be effective. Some state agencies that have tried to invoke this risk explicitly have little credibility, merely because their budgets are small. The Colorado Department of Education is an example. The introduction to its fiscal year 2000 budget listed fourteen interest groups that it consulted in drafting the department's budget to demonstrate the broad support the department had—but the department had a budget of only $302 million. Compared to ODE's almost $5 billion budget (excluding school foundation support), the Colorado Department of Education has little chance of convincing legislators that changes to its budget will actually cause much consternation on the part of Colorado education interest groups (Colorado Department of Education 1998, ii; Ohio Office of Budget and Management 1979, E-103–E-109). The first part of this chapter seeks to explain how much an agency requests. If scope parallels autonomy, and agencies that *do* more are more readily believed, then one would expect Georgia and Ohio to have more fiscal autonomy than Wisconsin.

Practical and Symbolic Budget Politics

It would be an understatement to say that state budgeting has undergone anything less than a metamorphosis between 1980 and 2000. At the beginning of the period, documents were cumbersome, numbers were often approximate, and predictions were simplistic. At the end, computer technology had transformed both the format and detail of state budgets. For example, in the 1979 budget request document, the Ohio legislature was doing obeisance to the governor's Office of Budget and Management for "letting them have budget documents so early in the budget process," with hand-corrected photocopies of agency budget requests (1979, ii). At the end of the period, Ohio won awards from the Government Finance Officers Association for a high-caliber budget document presentation.

State budgets formally start with agencies submitting requests for the governor's inclusion in the executive budget. In some states, these requests are made publicly and explicitly; in others, they are referenced in the governor's budget; and in others still, they disappear into the troves of executive branch files. Some states do not keep agency budgets in order to preserve the "fiction" that there is no disagreement within the executive branch (Clarke 1997, 305, fn. 4).

The governor then incorporates these suggestions into an executive budget, which is sent to the legislature. A legislative finance committee then uses the governor's budget as a starting point for the committee's bargaining. In states with line-item vetoes, such as Wisconsin, the legislature must also place items strategically to avoid creative vetoes, although at least some researchers have found that line-item vetoes have little effect on overall spending.[2]

Both Ohio and Wisconsin have biennial budgets, but budget repair bills in the interim are common. Some have argued that biennial budgets improve the efficiency of the budgeting process, however, the omnibus nature of these budgets has induced legislators to cram the bill with many nonfiscal items.[3] Georgia has an annual budget.

Budget requests and appropriations are the best empirical measure of the revealed preferences of agency chiefs, legislators, and governors. Of course, the preferences in budget requests may be distorted by the dissimulation in which bureaucrats engage to ensure that their agency receives a budget acceptable to them (Niskanen 1975; Sharkansky 1968). This is not to impugn them: both Brehm and Gates (1997) and Bowling, Cho, and Wright (2004) use detailed surveys to show that bureaucrats are not invidiously budget maximizing. Nevertheless, even these surveys show that a hefty majority of bureaucrats—even those who say their preference is for no increase—still request budget increases, regardless of the financial situation of their agencies.

From the agency's perspective, budget requests may symbolize four kinds of preferences. First, agency leaders may use budgets to promote favored programs. In the 1980s, the DPI consistently requested large increases in school foundation funding. Superintendent Grover made increasing state funding a major priority—in his introductory budget letter every biennium, he highlighted the variability of school spending across Wisconsin's school districts. To bolster this request, the DPI compiled a statistical analysis of the "disequalizing factors" in the Wisconsin funding system (Wisconsin Department of Public Instruction 1983). Grover made frequent reference to this document in his quest to raise the fraction of state school funding to two thirds.

Second, scholars have also noted that agencies may use requests to signal that certain programs are disfavored (Krause 1994; Sharkansky 1968). To use another DPI example, the department consistently opposed Governor Tommy Thompson's school voucher program both in public, in administration (by interpreting the law to give as little funding as possible to voucher schools), and in the budget. In the DPI's 1991 budget request, the department asked that the voucher program be repealed. It repeated this request in 1993 and 1995. After Thompson's high-profile crusade against the department, the DPI stopped critiquing the program in the budget, but it was sufficiently obvious that it found the program distasteful (Harp 1995; Wisconsin Department of Public Instruction 1990, 1992, 1994).

Next, budget requests reflect budget directors' calculation of uncertainty. Krause (1996) has shown that in years where agency budgets had large fluctuations, the Securities and Exchange Commission requested more funds than would be normally expected. Although budgets are normally slightly overstated to account for expected reductions, uncertainty prompts extra padding. No official I interviewed, of course, admitted to this, but the education agencies often requested additional staff for tasks that they currently performed. While the legislature sometimes granted the request, the agencies' arguments in the text of the requests referenced a lack of staff (as in the epigraph for chapter 2).

Finally, agency requests may simply be a reflection of the budget-maximizing behavior noted by Niskanen (1975). In this situation, agencies simply request as much as they can, every year. Such behavior is more likely in situations where agency managers believe that the current political climate is inhospitable (which also probably leads to great fluctuations in agency requests) (Bowling and Wright 1998; Bowling, Cho, and Wright 2004).

Budgeting Requests

An agency's scope is a direct function of the size of its budget. An agency that seeks to increase its budget is necessarily seeking to increase its scope, and I expect that more autonomous agencies will be more successful in securing these scope increases. This section describes agency budget requests.

I use only state-source funds throughout this chapter. Some large state programs are heavily funded by the federal government (especially for low-income assistance), and states have little control over how they spend federal monies. For education, this has historically included some fund for free- and reduced-lunch programs, teacher development, and handicapped education, among other things. But because I am examining how education agencies interact with state legislators, federal funds would cloud the analysis. (State department officials *do* lobby legislators to "pull down" federal dollars, but these conversations are outside the scope of this chapter.)

What nonidiosyncratic reasons explain budget requests? Previous literature suggests that budget requests are shaped by budget uncertainty, partisanship, divided government, and the previous budget. Statistical details of the analysis appear in Appendix B.

Correlates of Budget Requests

Budget uncertainty provides the first part of the explanation. Scholars suggest that organizations seek to reduce uncertainty, and requesting a larger-than-necessary budget helps ensure that core programs are not cut (e.g., March 1999; Pfeffer and Salancik 1978; Thompson 1967; Selznick 1948). That is, they are willing to risk overpadding their budgets in return for a desired base level of funding—after elected officials cut the budget. Using differences between current- and past-budget dollar values, I create a measure of uncertainty. I expect that education agencies will adjust their requests to match what budget officers perceive as the year's budget climate. They should request more funds in times of uncertainty to make up for greater potential losses.

Second, the partisanship in the governor's office and the legislature may affect budget requests. Because budget requests indicate favored policies, and political parties tend to favor different policies, the party control of the state legislature should influence requests. Republicans tend to be associated with slower growth in government (Alt and Lowry 2000; McAtee, Yackee, and Lowery 2003). Voters also punish Republican incumbents for spending increases, unlike Democratic incumbents (Lowry, Alt, and Ferree 1998). Agencies should be more likely to request funds in friendlier environments. Therefore, increases in budget *requests* should be inversely related to the share of Republicans in the legislature and to a Republican governor.

In his own right, a new governor should push a new agenda rather than anything that agencies requested in the closing days of his predecessor. Both Ohio Governors Celeste and Voinovich did this explicitly by ignoring the budget requests made under former Governors Rhodes and Celeste, respectively, and even failed to present them for comparison's sake in the executive budget. Yet agencies might be willing to try a bigger request than usual: a new governor may not have firm ideas about concrete programs and certainly not dollars, and a bigger request (on the margin) at the start of a term might improve the agency's chances later on. Therefore, I expect that a new governor would prompt agencies to increase their requests, whatever their level of autonomy or the size of their scope.

Third, divided government will make it difficult for agencies to decide on an appropriate budget request. Alt and Lowry (2000) show that a change from divided to unified government speeds up a shift in the overall state budget toward a party's preferred target—whether positive or negative. Divided government itself implies different visions of a government's scope (and therefore an agency's scope as well); an agency should seek to exploit these competing platforms and request more funds than under unified government. If budget requests are, in fact, partly symbolic expressions of what agencies believe should be their scope, then agencies should selectively emphasize parts of their request. The omnibus nature of budgets may allow agency lobbyists to convince legislators to support the whole package. This process should happen more easily under divided government than under government controlled by a single political party. Given the uncertainty that surrounds divided government, agencies should request more in hopes of exploiting that uncertainty.

Fourth, the previous budget should be the best predictor of this budget, and it is included as a control variable. This is a factor either due to incrementalism or simply because governmental agencies are created in response to recurring policy issues, and so unless an agency is terminated, its scope is likely to remain close to what it was (see Dezhbakhsh, Tohamy, and Aranson 2003; Jones, True, and Baumgartner 1997; Wildavsky 1992; Berry 1990). Larger relative budgets should be associated with smaller percentage-change requests.

Because it is difficult to argue that the budgets of education agencies follow a different process than other state agencies, I use ninety-one state agencies across the three states for comparison. The following section explores education budgets specifically. The explained variable is a ratio of the one department's budget change to all departments' changes.

Results

The results of the analysis (tables appear in Appendix B) show that in times of uncertainty, agencies request more, as expected (b = 0.13, $p < 0.01$). (As the next section shows, this padding is often an accurate reading of the political environment.) Partisanship and divided government also prompted agencies to request funds as predicted.

Although the previous chapter showed that partisanship had no impact on bill introduction, it weighs heavily on budget appropriations. Changes to agencies' budget requests are likely to be far smaller in budget cycles with Republican governors in these states than not (b = −0.39, $p < 0.01$). An increasingly Republican lower house, however, has a small positive effect (b = 0.04, $p < 0.01$). These findings support the expectation that agencies respond to party composition (recall that these are *requests* and not appropriations) by recasting their budgets to fit different policy expectations of different parties.

Agencies also appear to exploit the uncertainty that ensues in divided government, as expected. The existence of divided government increased agency budget requests almost the same amount as Republican governors decreased them (b = 0.418, $p < 0.01$). This finding should be taken with some caution, however: Between 1877 and 2002, Georgia always had unified government, so the variation in this explanatory variable is smaller than might be expected. Note that this *understates* the effect. Nevertheless, the strength of this finding reinforces the argument that agencies can shape others' preferences: If agencies are bold enough to ask for large increases in politically uncertain waters, then they are likely to feel confident that they can convince political principals of the need for expansions of scope. Changes in divided government, however, had no statistically significant effect.

Predictors of Budget Success

Agencies, then, are able predictors of uncertainty, but how well do their budgets actually fare? Do agencies receive the amounts they request? The answers to these questions reflect how well an agency can shape the preferences of its political principals. If there are wild variations in the residual—that is, an agency really has no idea how much funding it will receive—then its fiscal autonomy is weak. It has little influence on the actual appropriation. On the other hand, if an agency's requests are close to the actual appropriation, then legislators and the governor have acquiesced to the agency's policy vision: the agency has greater fiscal autonomy. This section focuses on education agencies specifically.

To begin, I use a "budgetary residual," the difference between the actual and requested amount as a percentage of the previous budget cycle's appropriation (a positive value indicates that the agency received more money than it asked for).[4]

Figure 9.2 shows the budget residuals in relation to the previous budget's appropriation, revealing that the residual is generally negative for education agencies. State education agencies request more money than the legislature and governor allow. This in itself does not necessarily mean that there is no fiscal autonomy; it does show, however, that agencies request more money than they expect to receive.

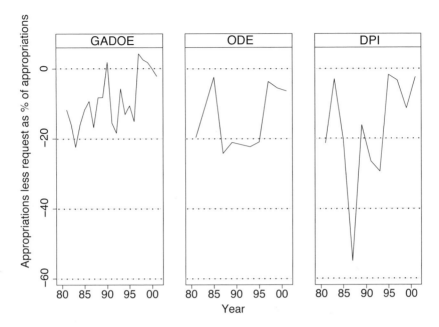

Figure 9.2. Budget Residuals for State Education Agencies as a Percentage of Total Agency Appropriations.

Note that these gaps are the greatest for Wisconsin and the least for Georgia, consistent with the findings of the previous section. Georgia has the greatest level of fiscal autonomy, while Wisconsin has the least. Ohio again appears in the middle.

Superintendent Grover's DPI asked for as much as 54 percent more money than the governor and legislature actually appropriated, and it was not until after he left in 1993 that the DPI appears to return to a more normal residual (the median Wisconsin residual for all agencies in this time period was –4.68 percent). Although Grover did improve the standing of the DPI to such a position that the governor wished to rid himself of the agency, it appears that much of his bluster went unfulfilled in terms of actual appropriations. This pattern suggests that Wisconsin's department may have used a padding strategy because of its politically difficult situation.

The Ohio Department of Education residual shows that the agency routinely asked for 20 percent more funds than were appropriated (at least until John Goff became superintendent). This is probably an example of the agency using budget padding to guarantee that favored programs received funding.

Finally, this descriptive data suggest that Georgia department officials simply asked for the money for the programs they wished to be funded, and legislators and governors agreed without the agency having to resort regularly to padding or maximizing.

The analysis that follows uses the absolute value of the residual; although a positive or negative residual has substantive implications for the agency, I am analyzing how *closely* an agency can come to its actual request—I expect that *the difference between agency requests and actual appropriations will be relatively smaller for more fiscally autonomous agencies and relatively greater for less fiscally autonomous agencies.*

Budget Residuals

What explains these differences? I expect that many of the same factors that explain the size of the budget request also contribute to the success of state agencies in procuring the funds that they request. These include partisanship, changes in the governor, divided government, and the relative size of the agency's budget. Statistical details appear in Appendix B.

Correlates of Budget Residuals

First, following from the expectations in the previous section, I expect that agency requests should be influenced by changes in government partisanship. It is difficult to argue that either Democrats or Republicans are more likely to appropriate more money at the state level (Alt and Lowry 2000). Democrats and Republicans do, however, have reputations for spending on different programs. In the states here, Democrats were seen as the friend of many governmental agencies *as agencies*, as shown by the epigraph at the beginning of this chapter—the governor in question was a Democrat. Therefore, it is likely that greater Democratic control of legislatures and control of the governorship would spur agencies to request more funds as they sought to protect and expand favored programs (one of the uses of the budget process). Therefore, as overall levels of appropriations remain more stable than unstable for state agencies, budget residuals should increase with more Democratic governments. Agencies will seek to capitalize on the potential for increase, even though this increase is not likely to be as large as the agency requests.

Second, the arrival of a new governor should prompt agencies to capitalize on the *governor's* uncertainty in her or his new office. This is a simple extension of the finding in the previous section. If an agency appears to be a spendthrift in the first budget, then its reputation will be damaged in future budgets. But if an agency can credibly argue that it actually needs the existing, new, or extra funds that it is requesting—funds that the previous governor just would not grant—then it may have a better chance in future budgets and may give the governor an opportunity to claim credit for new programs. If agencies can accomplish this feat, then I expect that budget residuals would be smaller because they will have an information advantage over the governor. They should request more, but not too much more, in order to cement into scope their previously autonomous actions.

Third, split control of the legislature should lead to increased agency budget requests to hedge against interbranch rivalry and uncertain policy expectations (Epstein and O'Halloran 1999; Bowling, Cho, and Wright 2004). Agencies request more in cycles with divided government to protect against cuts, as shown in the previous section. If the agency's assumption—that divided government will lead to cuts—is true, then the residual should be narrower.

The last substantive measure is the relative size of an agency's budget to the total state general-purpose budget. A larger budget indicates more scope, which should, in turn, lead to more opportunity for autonomous action and therefore fiscal autonomy. Thus a larger budget should lead to more requests to solidify autonomy into scope. If the process works as described in previous chapters, then a fiscally autonomous agency should have a smaller residual. It should be more successful in gaining its request, whatever the political environment.

Results

The results of the analysis indicate that party, new governors, divided government, and relative size substantially affect an agency's budget success.

As with agencies' requests, gubernatorial party politics plays a major role in agencies' accuracy. Agencies are least accurate under Republican governors. There is a 54 percent increase in the size of the residual between Democratic and Republican governors (b = 54.60, $p <$ 0.01). This appears to support the expectation that Democrats will be more accepting of agencies' requests. The partisan composition of the legislature has minimal effects on an agency's accuracy, a finding that highlights the tensions that emerge with governors. Education agencies, as shown earlier, are vulnerable to these high-profile fights because they have nominally independent executives.

This finding parallels the experience of my interviewees. In Wisconsin, Republicans were staunch opponents of the DPI's activities and its boosterism of the teachers' union. Even in 2005, the Republican who ran for state superintendent, Gregg Underheim, ran on a platform of scaling back the agency. Consequently, the DPI has fared worse in conservative governmental settings. For Ohio education, however, this result runs counter to experience: although Governor Celeste, a liberal Democrat, was a strong proponent of teacher pay, he was not as enthusiastic about other parts of ODE's program—and certainly not as enthusiastic as Superintendent Walter. Governor Voinovich, a moderate, was suspicious of the leadership of ODE, but he pumped state money into a broad array of the agency's programs. After Voinovich was able to appoint part of the state school board and both of Ohio's legislative chambers became Republican, the agency's budget requests became closer to actual appropriations. Part of an (untested) explanation lies in the probability that different agencies fare better or worse in different ideological climes.

In line with my expectation, discussed earlier, agency budget officers appear to be more realistic (or conservative) when a new governor is installed. In both Ohio and Georgia, a new governor prompted significantly smaller gaps between the desired amount and the amount actually appropriated ($b = -6.88$, $p < 0.01$). Agencies appear to be acting cautiously to ensure a good reputation to build future scope and autonomy (or to be working more closely with a new governor's office, as with the agency of this chapter's epigraph).[5]

I argued earlier that divided government drives agencies to hedge their bets when they request additional funds under divided government. This proved to be statistically and substantively true ($b = -23.77$, $p < 0.01$). Tentatively, agencies appear to benefit from divided government, in that the actual budgeted amount is likely to be very close to the agency's requests. Given the findings earlier in the book regarding leadership, it would seem that divided government makes it simpler for agency leaders to play different party leaders off against each other to arrive at a desired budget, with all other things being equal.

Finally, the size of an agency's budget is also a good predictor of accuracy. Larger budgets lead to smaller percentage gaps between the request and the actual appropriation ($b = -5.60$, $p < 0.01$), although an agency's magnitude is clearly secondary to other influences. This suggests that an agency's scope is an important component of solidifying autonomy into a new scope—those agencies with more scope are able to secure even more.

Conclusion

This chapter has presented evidence for the fiscal autonomy of state agencies. It confirms that Georgia's department of education had the most fiscal autonomy, followed by Ohio's department. The Wisconsin Department of Public Instruction had the least. But all state education agencies—and all agencies in these states generally—were able to request sizable increases, even in politically difficult times. For state agencies, that means trying to make a budget request in a unified government of conservative legislators and governors. This is evidence of independent, fiscal autonomy. This chapter also suggested which independent factors might influence this autonomy for any agency. All three education agencies made good use of whatever level of fiscal autonomy they had. The effects were muted in Wisconsin, due to very unfavorable political circumstances for the DPI, but both Ohio's and Georgia's education departments showed marked increases in funding over the period—far in excess of the inflation rate. This dramatic increase over time suggests that they have made good use of their fiscal autonomy to solidify their scope, as expected.

10

Conclusions and Implications

For to everyone who has, more will be given, and he will have an abundance: But from the one that has not, even that which he has shall be taken away.

—Matthew 25:29

State departments of education have substantial sway over education policy in the states. Even as the No Child Left Behind Act purports to increase federal involvement, critics have charged that state departments have thwarted the intent of the law by lowering requirements to be labeled "proficient" on state exams.[1] In my work, all three states were, at one time or another, accorded significant leeway in suggesting, drafting, or implementing educational law. While the amount of autonomy and the breadth of scope that were allowed each department varied over time and by conditions, evidence of independent action appeared even in these departments' darkest moments. In this chapter, I first highlight some broad conclusions from my empirical work and then suggest implications for state education departments and executive-agency relations. Finally, I explore the positive implications for democracy.

This project began by asking whether state departments of education were able to shape the preferences of their political principals. How autonomous are they? Practically, I ask whether and how well state education agencies—rather than legislators or governors or even the courts—should be able to reshape state policy, perhaps to align it with federal expectations. I find that both are happening.

Existing theories of political bureaucratic decision making were an excellent starting point, but I found that they were too tied to conditions that prevail at the federal level. Empirically, I found that state agencies in general often operate with much more latitude than the term *discretion*, so often used in the literature, would allow. Autonomy is a better description of agencies' characteristic decision-making power. Discretion relies on three elements being present in a policy area: principals, whether legislators or executives, have a known policy preference; principals may appoint an agent with a known policy preference; principals have resources, interest, and information to oversee agents' activities. None of these seemed to fit the evidence uncovered in this project.

First, in state education policy, state legislators and governors have low levels of information in general and must rely on state agency interpretations. This was apparent in Georgia, where GADOE wrote the state's Quality Basic Education Act with the imprimatur of the governor. In Ohio, Governor Voinovich asked Superintendent Ted Sanders to create an education-standards platform for him to support. Even in Wisconsin, where legislators have regularly bypassed the DPI for ideas, Superintendent Grover was able to work his name into several of Governor Tommy Thompson's state of the state addresses—an honor bestowed on no other state official besides the lieutenant governor.

Second, in state education, the appointment power is rarely given to the governor, and even more rarely to the legislature. In all but nine states (see chapter 1), the state superintendent is either directly elected by the people or appointed by a state board, which is often elected by the people. Thus the appointment power is lost. Not only does this prevent "principals" from hemming in a recalcitrant agency a priori, but the agency can pursue a path widely divergent from whichever preferences the legislature or governor may have had.

Third, state legislatures have not had the resources to monitor the activity of state agencies to the same extent as the U.S. Congress might have. This is particularly true in Georgia, where the short legislative session (three months a year) precludes any day-to-day oversight. Balla and Wright (2001) argue that interest groups may fill this role; but, as I argued in chapter 5, state education agencies can "manage" interest groups, therefore, interest group oversight is suspect. This appeared in Ohio, particularly when every major interest group opposed the department's linking of school finance to school performance. The department's view was still privileged. In Wisconsin, the legislature has better resources than many states, but the DPI still provides the data and often the analysis to the state's research bureau.

Since discretion did not fit the data well, I proposed an autonomy-scope cycle. As an agency gains more things to do, and the better it does them, the more ability it should have to decide how best to do those activities. This cycle is moderated by institutional characteristics, such as how the agency is structured; endogenous factors, including leadership style and interest group coalitions; and the exogenous factors of legislative salience, electoral turnover, and legal actions. This model appears to better fit the data as agents inform political principals on feasible policy and the limits of practical enforcement.

Empirically, state departments were able to shape the preferences of their political principals. In all three of my cases—even in Wisconsin, the weakest of these agencies—state departments of education advocated for some form of competency or achievement testing for students and sometimes for teachers. In every case, they got it, often in the very form that they originally proposed.

In Georgia, GADOE proposed annual student assessment exams for all grades except seventh, ninth, eleventh, and twelfth. This request was scaled back in the Quality Basic Education Act, but GADOE, not the legislature, pushed for multigrade assessment.

In Ohio, ODE drafted multiple, comprehensive state standards to put teeth into the state's ninth-grade graduation exam. Despite public missteps on Outcomes-Based Education, ODE persevered and implemented even tougher student accountability standards. Further, when ODE became embroiled in the state's long-running school finance case, legislators and the state's justices were forced to turn to ODE for information and analysis, despite the strong opposition of the state's education interest groups.

In Wisconsin, the DPI urged a major overhaul of teacher licensure, emphasizing more course taking and peer review by teachers. The DPI was successful, in spite of a hostile political climate. This was true even though the agency was among the least successful in securing state budgets for any of its favored programs, as shown in chapter 9. Although the teacher program was not funded at the DPI's desired level, the program was still made to the agency's liking.

In each state, the department of education was the "first mover" to propose a concrete, specific policy. Only later did legislators and governors begin to provide their preferences to bureaucrats. Even then, as shown in chapter 8, agencies with a broad scope can delay bills in legislative committees, presumably to alter them to be more suitable.

Therefore, for states and in education policy, when political principals have little to no technical expertise, knowledge, or realistic expectations about policy outputs, state agencies *can* shape the preferences of their political principals.

Implications

State bureaucrats are expected to do much heavy lifting when implementing new federal policies, whether those policies are the voting reforms of the 1960s, the welfare reform of the 1990s, or the rollout of prescription drug coverage for the low-income elderly of the early 2000s. But if these federal policies are given to state agencies without a track record of success, even the responsibilities they do have will probably be given to another agency or to a blue-ribbon commission. Agencies must use their scope lest it be taken away. Here I explore some implications.

State education departments may be able to strengthen their hand in bargaining for policy with a few of the findings of this project. The first possibility, and probably the most remote, is to change the means by which a state superintendent is selected. This first option is most likely to yield visible results in the short term. Second, agencies can head off interest group conflict by bringing together disparate interest groups at select stages of the policy process. Third, careful management of a governor's and an agency leader's leadership can improve an agency's chances to gain autonomy and scope.

Constitutional Structure and Appointment

Building autonomy and scope in a department relies heavily on the ability of the agency's leader to advertise the agency in all the right places. And that leader's effectiveness is conditioned by the department's institutional situation. The arguments supporting the various methods (see chapter 1) of appointment, election, and removal of state chiefs have not changed much in the last 200 years. The best summary of these is found in Keesecker (1951). These costs and benefits circulated around governors' offices in both Ohio and Wisconsin when the governors were miffed at the departments' activities and were seeking to seize their departments' reins (see chapter 7).

From my work, Ohio's board-appointed state chiefs were best able to play on their department's strengths. Even though Superintendent Ted Sanders was the virtual pick of Governor Voinovich, neither Franklin Walter before him nor John Goff and Susan Tave Zelman after him had the imprimatur of the governor. When groups outside of the department railed against the department for various reasons, they knew that the superintendent could not be brought down through normal political channels. Instead, policy arguments had to be made on empirical, rather than emotive, grounds. The Ohio Federation of Teachers tried emotion in the school finance case and failed badly (see chapter 5).

Board-appointed chiefs may be the most technically competent and politically insulated, but their advantages with regard to the political environment at large may be liabilities within the formal apparatus. John Goff, who used his political insulation to his and his department's benefit, was not very politically astute himself. In retrospect, he admitted that he had not spent enough time shoring up his support among members of the state board. The result for him was the loss of his job. Nevertheless, the board picked a successor very similar in aims to Goff—the maintenance of a tough accountability regime for both students and teachers.

An elected state chief (as in Georgia and Wisconsin), on the other hand, may be very sensitive to public political pressure. Although this does allow the department to "go public," the department may *have* to court the public. This was certainly Wisconsin Superintendent Grover's predicament when Tommy Thompson became governor. Although Georgia's superintendent historically has not had to consider either running for office or partisan appeals, Superintendent Linda Schrenko showed the power of forcing both. But these strong-arm tactics became the only way she was able to advance her goals at GADOE, particularly after Governor Roy Barnes, who had distinct ideas of his own, was elected.

Although the major institutional effect I studied was the role of appointment or election, one might suspect that state boards of education play some meaningful role in an agency's quest for increased scope. The vast majority of states, as was shown in Table 1.1, use state boards in some capacity. Indeed, part of the rationale for studying Wisconsin as a case was that it has no state board.

Yet in neither of my cases did the state board play an active role in either the department's day-to-day operations or in providing guidance for forays into autonomy. This is not to say that state boards of education in these states were inconsequential. In Ohio and Georgia, they are instrumental in drafting a budget for their respective departments, and they do headline new educational initiatives. The boards *did* serve as the conscience, or, in less charitable terms, as the speed bumps, for the department. Yet in neither of these cases did the state school board provide specific guidance for the significant educational programs of the 1980s and 1990s *before* the state superintendent and his department had plotted a course for action. One member of the Georgia state board told me that the board was only *supposed* to set a broad vision for education. It would leave all specific policy to GADOE's staff. That observation was supported by my research.

In Ohio, Superintendent Franklin Walter, not the board, was the force behind ODE's policy agenda. At least this much was supported by the external review conducted at the request of the governor's office:

the state board was remote from everyday educators (Governor's Task Force on Education 1991, 40). The board eventually grew restless with Walter and likely contributed to his decision to resign. But it was because the board no longer agreed *with him* as to the direction of Ohio education that *he* decided to leave. (The board could have fired him at any time, but it did not.)

Later, Governor Voinovich lamented that the state board was not responsive enough to what he wanted on his education agenda—or, rather, what he had told Superintendent Sanders should be on the agenda. His solution was to reconfigure the board to include gubernatorial appointees. Even so, a top legislator lectured the governor on why he should leave the state board entirely elected. "Such things as proficiency tests, technology, equity funding, etc. have been accomplished with or without the State Board," wrote Senator Cooper Snyder (Snyder 1995). From Snyder's point of view, the board only provided political headaches for the governor and was not a force for policy change.

In Georgia, the board helps set the broad outlines of policy and has served as the governor's voice in state education. The board can serve as a political counterweight to the state superintendents. Yet even here GADOE proved that it often could go ahead without the board's approval for major projects: the state's controversial kindergarten assessment program of the 1980s was approved by its state board *after* GADOE had designed the test (see chapter 5). During the tumultuous terms of Superintendent Schrenko, board members often interrupted the department's presentations, and late in her term, Schrenko stopped going to meetings altogether. All the while the department continued to press on with its internal reorganization and redesign of assessment tests.

In neither state was the board able to prevent the department from doing something significant, although it is true that both boards proved to be difficult for the department to handle. Although some preliminary work indicated that appointed boards and chiefs might marginally improve policy continuity and thus the educational performance of students in the state (Manna and Guthrie 2008), boards of education in this study served as restraining influences on the department rather than as substantive policy guides. This is perhaps partly a result of the case selection. (Kansas' state board, for example, has made headlines for the curriculum it requires for the evolution/creation debate). Future research should address this question further. If state boards should serve as leaders of education policy, then why was it that these boards were reactive rather than directive? Or, do they serve merely as sounding boards for ideas for education departments? If so, then why are governors so eager to appoint their members?

Endogenous: Interest Groups

Interest groups can also provide strength for departments seeking autonomy and scope if departments are careful to incorporate them into select parts of the policy process and incorporate normally competing interest groups into the department's activities.

Interest groups are useful for departments to ensure "buy-in" in the field for new policies. The Wisconsin DPI used this to good effect with the state's teacher licensure changes. The department enlisted the help of WEAC early in the redesign to ensure that the organization would support it; then, when the rules were enacted, the DPI had WEAC conduct seminars around the state to convince teachers that they could successfully meet the new licensure requirements. Unfortunately, the DPI used the teachers' union too heavily. Other state interest groups (representing other parts of the educational system) and the governor were able to peg the DPI as tied to WEAC. WEAC's support was probably crucial for the DPI's teacher licensure policy change, but by not incorporating other groups as visibly, the DPI lost the ability to expand its autonomy.

Georgia's department of education was able to incorporate interest groups to further its autonomy and scope in the mid-1980s. At that time, the department was implementing QBE, including what proved to be a controversial kindergarten assessment test. Although the state's education interest groups were nearly unanimously opposed to having an exam, they were only able to force GADOE to retool the exam. In revising the test, GADOE provided seats on an advisory committee to many of the dissenting interest groups. The influence of their advice was limited, however, by the test's tight design deadline and by the department's decision to use the same assessment firm *prior* to receiving any advice from the advisory board. The department did adopt their biggest concern, at least in name, that the kindergarten test be "developmentally appropriate." GADOE maintained that the exam was within its scope by acknowledging the dismay of the state's early-education and teacher-advocacy interest groups and offering a wide range of groups an opportunity for input. GADOE preserved its autonomy by carefully delimiting the time, manner, and place where those interest groups could offer input, and it allowed them input only after the major outlines of the testing policy were fixed.

Exogenous: Executive-Agency Relations

The implications of this study for executive-agency relations are marked. Lacking the appointment power for education has been deeply troubling to "education governors." Governors have tried to inject a personal representative into the state education apparatus not only in Wisconsin and Ohio. They often argue that the public holds them accountable for education, so they need a direct hand in shaping education—this was Ohio Governor Strickland's contention in the epigraph to the first chapter of this book. Only nine states allow the governor to appoint the state superintendent directly. Without the appointment power, governors, legislators, and agency personnel must adopt a careful logic of accommodation for the state's education program to function.

For the agency and for the governor, the temptation to "go public" is greater without the appointment power. Although some styles of leadership, particularly insider leadership (see chapter 6), may reduce the need to use either the governor's or the superintendent's office as a bully pulpit, the lack of a formal, legal means of communication and policy selection greatly increases the temptation to avoid working together.

In Georgia, Superintendent Linda Schrenko early on pursued a confrontational, public leadership style that she honed over her eight years in office. Although Governor Zell Miller was content to work with her, Governor Roy Barnes was not. Schrenko's public leadership did not win her friends, and it tipped off Barnes that he would have to pursue an aggressive strategy to move education policy in a different way than the department desired. Neither he nor Schrenko made any attempt to work together, and both went public with their education plans: Barnes, by calling for an independent Office of Educational Accountability, and Schrenko, by vilifying Barnes as incompetent. Because neither had a legal claim on the other, both got part of what they wanted—the most inefficient outcome possible. Barnes got an independent office with some of GADOE's former responsibilities, but Schrenko's GADOE was given more money by the legislature than Barnes proposed. Some longtime observers credited Barnes's defeat at the polls after only one term to his public high-handedness with Schrenko. Notably, all of the responsibilities taken by Barnes's education office were returned to GADOE.

In Ohio, Superintendent Ted Sanders used his office as a bully pulpit only after his department's initial OBE standards proposal was in serious trouble. Sanders used going public to shore up support and to regain the confidence of the governor. Governor Voinovich was not pleased to work with ODE after Sanders's missteps. Voinovich then successfully gained appointment power over part of the state board (his second choice, but in his view better than the status quo). Although Voinovich was supportive of Sanders at the start, the poor communications between the two and the governor's nonexistent leash on the superintendent undermined stable executive-agency relations.

Both of these cases demonstrate the inherent weaknesses of going public. Although the lack of the appointment power frees education agencies of relying on gubernatorial support, running full speed around normal legislative channels may undermine an agency's ability to expand its autonomy and preserve its scope.

Good relations with the governor are not necessary if the agency has a high degree of autonomy and broad scope—that is, if legislators can be brought on board. An agency's autonomy can propel its preferred policy without the governor, or without the legislature, but it is very unlikely that the hostile opposition (rather than disinterest) from both will stand it in good stead. John Benson of Wisconsin discovered that having few friends in the legislature and a governor opposed to the department can hollow out a department. As both chapters 8 and 9 have shown, an agency's autonomy is a strong predictor of success in cases of divided government (the normal course of affairs in Wisconsin), but an agency has to be respected by both sides. The DPI was not.

In addition to preserving good relations with key legislators, an agency can help build a broad legislative coalition by being careful not to cater to a few interest groups. That is, an education agency should build ties not only to the state's teacher associations but also to its school board associations, trade groups, and business interests. Such breadth helps insulate a department from oscillations in political power. Wisconsin's DPI was so clearly identified with Democratic interest groups such as WEAC that Republican majorities and urban Democrats, who were supportive of the state's school choice program, had little incentive to trust the department. In Georgia, GADOE has been able to weather a sea change in partisan power over the last twenty years, partly because the interest groups with whom the department regularly works are spread across the political spectrum. Legislators know that GADOE takes its job seriously and seeks to create policy that is minimally acceptable to all parties. Thus working with GADOE will not automatically tar a state legislator in the next election.

Therefore, education agencies can be most effective if they pursue a logic of accommodation with governors, legislators, and interest groups—not to be captured by any of them, but to keep an open dialog with all of them.

Beyond Education

State activities in standard setting and teacher development proved prescient of the federal 2001 No Child Left Behind (NCLB) Act.[2] I have shown how three state education agencies fared against prevailing winds while implementing teachers' professional development, standards and assessment, and, to a lesser extent, school finance. Given their track record, Georgia and Ohio should perform the best in implementing NCLB's requirements. How well does this autonomy-scope cycle transfer? Should states like those here meet the expectations of the federal government in other policies?

All agencies have some elements of autonomy and scope. Even in other major state bureaucracies without constitutional officers, agency leadership is just as important. Agencies build scope across leaders, though leaders can aid in the building; and agencies' behavior from one administration to the next tends to be stable, but autonomy and scope will be most visible in those agencies that take on major policy projects, often leading to federal legislation. I will present two examples where high autonomy and broad scope may lead to the successful adoption of an agency's preferences.

First, as health care costs continue to rise, especially for low-income and elderly populations, many states have looked for ways to cut costs. States such as California, Massachusetts, Tennessee, and Wisconsin have toyed with creating state-wide insurance pools.[3] Given the breadth of most state health departments, these agencies should have a broad enough scope to have at least a middling level of autonomy. They have the same huge budget that education does. And, like education, elements of the policy transfer easily to campaign slogans such as "Health care for all." But the details are no less complex. Here again, an autonomous state agency that has already handled medical claims should be a major contributor to the draft of the legislation. Indeed, the Wisconsin Assembly Medicaid Reform Committee called on the Department of Health and Family Services for a three-month-long "intro to Medicaid and Medicare" in 2004 (personal interview). In the process, legislators sought the opinion of department personnel on how they might save funds without unduly compromising the services the state provided to vulnerable populations. If such insurance becomes federal, then state agencies that are already handling insurance claims will be in good stead to use their technical autonomy and program scope to acclimate the new federal program to their state.

State environmental agencies are a second candidate. These agencies have been well studied at the federal level, particularly in studies of bureaucratic enforcement (see, e.g., Canes-Wrone 2003; Balla and Wright 2001; Bressers and Rosenbaum 2000; Tobin 1992). The fluidity of federal environmental enforcement, however, should put state environmental agencies in a good position to use their technical knowledge to inform state policy (Wood and Waterman 1993). The expertise required for understanding hydrogeology, ozone diffusion, and power-plant emissions should ensure that these agencies have technical autonomy. Leveraging this autonomy may help them convince legislators to expand their scope. Such agencies should be just as affected by the exogenous factors I have identified: legislative turnover, salience, and (perhaps especially) legal actions. But the endogenous factors of agency leadership and interest group coalition building are just as vital. Indeed, there are probably more interest groups in the environmental field than in education. Finally, the gubernatorial appointment of executive agencies is not universal, even for nonconstitutional bureaucracies. In Wisconsin, the Department of Natural Resources (DNR) faced the same struggle as the DPI did over who would appoint its leader, except that it was over whether the governor or the Natural Resources Board had the right. One Wisconsin lobbyist I interviewed noted the similarity: "Should DPI be an independent agency? This is the same thing as with the DNR. Yeah, probably. But if you run into a situation with a long-term governor like Tommy where you can't get along, you don't get anything done."[4]

Autonomy, Scope, and Democracy

Highly autonomous agencies could pose problems for participatory democracy. Reporters for the mass media rarely cover bureaucracy with as much zest as they cover elected politicians, even though most voters learn about their government through the news media. Bureaucracies may be able to operate free of press scrutiny for a time, yet in none of the cases I studied did education agencies get a free pass. Even in Ted Sanders's case with OBE, when the governor felt blindsided by the controversy, ODE came in for rough treatment in the press, and it had to retreat from its original program. Georgia's experience with the kindergarten exam also illustrated the quick response to the uproar by legislators and the public over its policy choices. Autonomous agencies still trip fire alarms.

This apparent freedom from scrutiny might bode ill for democracy if agencies sought to *exclude* participation—something no agency I studied attempted. Instead, agency leaders sought to bring together "appropriate" players to shape policy. These may have been brought in after the fact, but they were still brought in at some stage of the policy process. Agencies' deliberate inclusion of relevant stakeholders contrasts markedly with legislators who frequently do not have sufficient information to make thorough judgments about public policy. They may be much more reliant on others for information. Legislators have an excellent excuse though. They are adept at learning, but they are faced with countless other issues. The best representatives are general practitioners—able to understand most policy discussion but specialists in none of them. Governmental agencies, on the other hand, are responsive to complaints by affected segments of the public, suggesting that highly autonomous agencies, with a broad scope of power, may improve the quality of democratic discourse.

An efficient system of representation is characterized by meaningful input from constituents, clear lines of responsibility, and prompt responses from government. David Truman described citizen input to the American legislative process as "a crude device, a shotgun technique" (Truman 1951, 389). Although state legislators are closer to their constituents than federal legislators, the separation is still wide, particularly when considering policy details. Further, while legislators seek to claim credit for legislation of interest to constituents, they are equally adept at avoiding traceability for potentially unpopular actions (Mayhew 1974; Arnold 1990). This is particularly true when the clients of the policy are easily identified (Pierson 1994). As such, unpopular policy decisions are difficult for voters to consider at the ballot box, even setting aside the inherent difficulty of distilling the hundreds of policy positions a legislator may hold into one vote.[5] Further, as chapters 8 and 9 have shown, autonomy has a strong effect under divided government, when legislative representation is least coherent.

Governmental agencies, on the other hand, can neither avoid making difficult policy decisions nor deflect criticism for unpopular stands. Greasing the representative process are interest groups that, whatever their value to the department, do alert concerned members of the public to an agency's actions. Even though accountability might be splintered among many different groups—the legislature, the governor, the state board, federal agencies, stakeholders, and the public—each of these outside actors can raise an alarm. There might be *more* opportunities for the public to hear about a renegade agency with splintered accountability than there would be with a single political principal.

In Georgia, GADOE could at no time avoid being targeted as the perpetrator of the "standards box" of the 1980s, loathed by school personnel throughout the state, despite the overwhelming legislative support for the Quality Basic Education Act. Superintendent Rogers responded by repeatedly promising studies of the ways in which the department could reduce mandates. And GADOE was forced to reconsider its kindergarten assessment test due to uproar from early-education advocates, parents, and teachers. How much the department valued outside input is open to question, but it is clear that the department felt compelled to respond quickly to its constituents, whether parents, teachers, or administrators.

In Ohio, the department of education in the early 1990s responded quickly and vociferously to criticism of its curriculum standards. Sanders sought the feedback of educators, but he also went on the road to build the support and hear the complaints of parents. After Sanders left, ODE became embroiled in the *DeRolph* school funding lawsuit, yet its school finance division tried to respond to redesign the formula to mitigate the more pressing complaints of the plaintiffs.

In Wisconsin, Superintendent Herbert Grover vigorously sought public support on the road, in newspapers, and by mail. As noted in chapter 6, Grover's public leadership was due, in part, to the department's poor condition relative to the governor and legislature. But his loud-and-out-there leadership included responding to virtually every letter that came to his office, often explaining his philosophical attachment to some policy and usually noting that he would consider the person's suggestions. Of course, such a claim could be considered boilerplate text. But given that Grover claimed that "I read all my mail" personally, he at least knew his constituents' opinions firsthand.

Of course, legislators *could* possess the same technical knowledge and courage to confront every issue in the face of angry constituents, but the likelihood of doing so, and to continue to be elected, is small. Legislative incentives prevent this.

Therefore, the quality of public discussion of policy is enhanced when agencies are autonomous and commune regularly with many legislators and interest groups—bureaucrats know public desires; legislators empower agencies; and everyone knows who is accountable.

Appendix A

Historical Appendix

Table A.1. List of Chief State School Officers

Georgia	
John Lewis	1870–1872
Gustavus John Orr	1872–1887
James Schley Hook	1888–1891
S. D. Bradwell	1891–1895
Gustavus Richard Glenn	1895–1903
William B. Merritt	1903–1907
Jere M. Pound	1907–1910
Marion L. Brittain	1910–1922
Marvin M. Parks	1922–1923
Nathaniel H. Ballard	1923–1925
Fort Elmo Land	1925–1927
Mell R. Duggan	1927–1933
M. D. Collins	1933–1958
Claude Purcell	1958–1965
Jack Nix	1966–1977
Charles McDaniel	1977–1986
Werner Rogers	1986–1994
Linda Schrenko	1995–2002
Kathy Cox	2002–

Ohio	
Samuel Lewis	1837–1840
(Office abolished, 1840)	
Hiram H. Barney	1854–1857
Anson Smyth	1857–1863
Emerson E. White	1863–1866
John A. Norris	1866–1869
William D. Henkle	1869–1871
Thomas W. Harvey	1871–1875
Charles S. Smart	1875–1878
J. J. Burns	1878–1881
D. F. DeWolf	1881–1884
Leroy D. Brown	1884–1887

continued on next page

Table A.1. *(continued)*

Ohio

Eli T. Tappan	1887–1888
John Hancock	1888–1891
Charles C. Miller	1891–1892
Oscar T. Corson	1892–1898
L. D. Bonebrake	1898–1904
Edmund A. Jones	1904–1909
John W. Zeller	1909–1911
Frank W. Miller	1911–1916
F. B. Pearson	1916–1920
Vernon M. Riegel	1920–1927
J. L. Clifton	1927–1931
B. O. Skinner	1931–1935
E. L. Bowsher	1935–1937
E. N. Deitrich	1937–1941
Kenneth C. Ray	1941–1945
Clyde Hissong	1945–1953
R. M. Eyman	1953–1957
Edward E. Holt	1957–1966
Martin W. Essex	1966–1977
Franklin B. Walter	1977–1991
Theodore Sanders	1991–1995
John Goff	1995–1998
Susan Tave Zelman	1999–2008
Deborah S. Delisle	2008–

Wisconsin

Eleazer Root	1849–1852
Azel P. Ladd	1852–1854
Hiram A. Wright	1854–1855
A. Constantine Barry	1855–1858
Lyman C. Draper	1858–1860
Josiah L. Pickard	1860–1864
John G. McMynn	1864–1868
Alexander J. Craig	1868–1870
Samuel Fallows	1870–1874
Edward Searing	1874–1878
William Clarke Whitford	1878–1882
Robert Graham	1882–1887
Jesse B. Thayer	1887–1891
Oliver Elwin Wells	1891–1895
John Q. Emery	1895–1899

Lorenzo D. Harvey	1899–1903
Charles P. Cary	1903–1921
John Callahan	1921–1949
George Earl Watson	1949–1961
Angus B. Rothwell	1961–1966
William C. Kahl	1966–1973
Barbara Thompson	1973–1981
Herbert J. Grover	1981–1993
Lee Dreyfus	1993
John T. Benson	1993–2001
Elizabeth Burmaster	2001–2009
Tony Evers	2009–

Appendix B

Statistical Appendix

This appendix includes an explanation of the statistical methods used in chapters 8 and 9. Summary statistics for all variables appear in the final section of the appendix.

Committee Service

Scholars have been able to use legislators' requests to serve on particular committees in the U.S. Congress because the parties have kept records of these requests (Groseclose and Stewart 1998). At least these states do not maintain such records. Therefore, I estimated legislative preferences based on observed committee service in each legislative session from 1983–1984 to 2001–2002 (ten sessions).[1]

The great variety of committees in the states also presents a problem for isolating the "education" committee. In the U.S. Congress, legislators benefit from fairly stable committees. Indeed, by 1825, both the House of Representatives and the Senate had largely given up special select committees in favor of persistent, standing committees (Canon and Stewart 2001, 172). This does not hold true in the states. Wisconsin is an extreme case. Between 1979 and 2002, the assembly had 139 identifiably different committees; the Senate had 112. Often these committees were combinations of previous committees. For example, in 1979, the Senate had the Agriculture, Labor and Local Affairs Committee; in 1985, agriculture was paired with health and human services, and labor was matched with business, veterans' affairs, and insurance. This does not include various special committees. Even in more stable states, such as Georgia and Ohio, committees still disappeared from one session and reemerged later connected to a different committee.

To compensate for this, I coded all committees with education as one of its topics as an "education" committee. In the lower house, this usually resulted in one and, rarely, two committees being so coded. In the upper houses, where the membership is smaller, education often finds a home with many different unrelated topics. Although using combination committees clouds the analysis, any substantive results should indicate an especially strong effect given this blunt instrument.

In addition to the variables of interest noted in chapter 8, I included five control variables: the legislator's chamber, the session, indicator variables for Georgia and Ohio, and the size of the education committees. A large committee should correlate with a higher likelihood of service, but only because more seats are available. As such, it is a control variable. The analysis is clustered by the legislator.

To calculate committee service, I estimated a random-effects, cross-sectional logistic regression with the data grouped by each of the 1,253 legislators. This method allows each legislator to have both a different base likelihood (coefficient) for committee service and each of these covariates to have a different effect on each legislator, producing estimates that use more information from the available data. The explained variable is service on an education committee in a given session. The results for the likelihood of service are presented in Table B.1. For the likelihood of exit, I also used a cross-sectional logistic regression with the data grouped by each of the 414 legislators who served on education committees. These results appear in Table B.2 (page 224).

Bill Counts

In addition to the variables noted in chapter 8, I also include indicator variables for Georgia and Ohio (Wisconsin is the omitted category) and the chamber where bills are introduced. I perform a negative binomial regression to predict the number of bills in each session. The results appear in Table B.3 (page 225).

Time to Leave Committee

To analyze how long bills remain in committee, I used a duration analysis. Duration analyses such as this are somewhat rare in the literature and are best known in medical studies. Politically, Shipan and Shannon (2003) show how legislative experience, legal experience, and divided government can delay Supreme Court nominations. Others have used these analyses to argue that when members of Congress take positions on bills is a strategic choice based on conditions at home and other members' timing choices (Box-Steffensmeier, Arnold, and Zorn 1997). These models are useful to predict the time between a clear entry and a clear exit. Bills in committee fit this description: they have a clear

Table B.1. All Legislators' Likelihood of Serving on an Education
Committee, 1983–2002

	Legislator Variables		
Sessions in office	−0.259	***	(0.026)
Previously served on committee	2.597	***	(0.154)
Member of majority party	0.032		(0.160)
Party membership (1 is R)	0.090		(0.191)
	Session Variables		
Divided government exists	0.347		(0.227)
Percentage of chamber Republican	−0.012		(0.011)
Change in governor	0.057		(0.122)
Change in superintendent	−0.044		(0.157)
Percent of state-of-state devoted to education	0.063		(0.476)
Percent of state budget to education agency	−0.023		(0.017)
	Control Variables		
Size of committee	0.061	***	(0.014)
Chamber (1 is upper)	1.580	***	(0.318)
Biennium (1 is 1983–84)	0.024		(0.041)
Georgia legislator	−0.994	**	(0.415)
Ohio legislator	−0.265		(0.367)
Constant	−0.193		(0.880)
Log likelihood	−1,784.570		
χ^2	410.100	***	
N	4,951		
Groups	1,253		

Standard errors are in parentheses. *** $p < 0.01$, ** $p < 0.05$, * $p < 0.10$

assignment date and a definite date when they are reported. All bills die
at the end of the session if nothing has been done to move them.

Again, control variables are included for the bill's chamber, Ohio,
and Georgia.

Results for the Cox hazard estimation appear in Table B.4 (page
226).[2] Table B.5 (page 227) repeats this analysis using the total time a
bill spends in the legislature as the explained variable.

Table B.2. Likelihood of a Legislator Exiting the Education Committee, 1983–2002

	Legislator Variables		
Previous sessions in legislature	0.219	***	(0.057)
Previous sessions on education committee	–0.294	**	(0.119)
Member of majority party	–0.286		(0.275)
Party membership (1 is R)	–0.183		(0.274)
	Session Variables		
Divided government exists	–0.169		(0.536)
Percentage of chamber that is Republican	–0.072	*	(0.040)
Change in governor	–0.352		(0.308)
Change in superintendent	–0.066		(0.401)
Percent of state addresses referring to education	–1.235		(1.261)
Percent of state budget to education agency	–0.052		(0.044)
	Control Variables		
Size of committee	0.022		(0.034)
Chamber (1 is upper)	2.957	***	(0.844)
Session (1 is 1983–84)	0.104		(0.142)
Georgia legislator	–1.404		(1.038)
Ohio legislator	–0.622		(1.013)
Constant	–2.932		(2.934)
Log likelihood	–202.670		
χ^2	53.020	***	
N	414		
Groups	167		

Standard errors are in parentheses. *** $p < 0.01$, ** $p < 0.05$, * $p < 0.10$

Table B.3. Negative Binomial Regression Estimating the Number of Education Bills in a Session, 1983–2002

	Aggregate Legislator Variables		
50th-percentile probability of service	11.541	***	(3.856)
50th-percentile probability of leaving committee	−1.430	**	(1.865)
Majority party seat share	0.155		(0.360)
	Session Variables		
Change in divided government	0.424	*	(0.219)
Divided government exists	0.413	**	(0.207)
Percent of chamber that is Republican	0.017	**	(0.009)
Governor's party (1 is R)	−0.004		(0.229)
Change in governor	−0.358	***	(0.131)
Change in superintendent	−0.042		(0.156)
Percent change in education agency appropriation	−0.022	***	(0.008)
	Control Variables		
Number of federal education laws passed	−0.004		(0.013)
Chamber (1 is upper)	−0.760	***	(0.106)
Georgia bill	2.216	***	(0.351)
Ohio bill	1.493	***	(0.276)
Constant	0.951		(0.791)
Log likelihood	−215.131		
χ^2	93.85	***	
N	57		
Pseudo R^2	0.18		

Standard errors are in parentheses. *** $p < 0.01$, ** $p < 0.05$, * $p < 0.10$

Table B.4. Education Bills' Time to be Reported from Committee, 1983–2002

	Sponsor Variables		
Previous terms on education committee	0.037		(0.052)
Education committee service probability	0.864	***	(0.155)
Member of majority party	1.124	***	(0.101)
	Session Variables		
Divided government exists	0.377	**	(0.191)
Change in divided government status	0.291		(0.205)
Percent of chamber that is Republican	0.004		(0.005)
Governor's party (1 is R)	−0.103		(0.171)
Change in governor	0.117		(0.086)
Change in superintendent	0.209	**	(0.099)
Percent of state budget to education agency	−0.021	*	(0.012)
	Control Variables		
Number of federal education laws passed	−0.022	*	(0.012)
Georgia bill	0.394		(0.274)
Ohio bill	−0.764	***	(0.239)
Log likelihood	−5,489.024		
χ^2	241.36	***	
N	2,104		
Bills leaving committee	757		

Standard errors are in parentheses. *** $p < 0.01$, ** $p < 0.05$, * $p < 0.10$

Table B.5. Education Bills' Time to be Passed by Both Houses,
1983–2002

	Sponsor Variables		
Previous terms on education committee	0.002		(0.085)
Education committee service probability	0.438	*	(0.246)
Member of majority party	1.248	***	(0.167)
	Session Variables		
Divided government exists	0.152		(0.278)
Change in divided government status	0.214		(0.310)
Percent of chamber that is Republican	0.016	**	(0.008)
Governor's party (1 is R)	−0.520	**	(0.241)
Change in governor	0.081		(0.136)
Change in superintendent	0.360	**	(0.155)
Percent of state budget to education agency	−0.014		(0.019)
	Control Variables		
Number of federal education laws passed	0.008		(0.018)
Introducing chamber (1 = Senate)	0.171		(0.124)
Georgia bill	0.130		(0.399)
Ohio bill	−0.472		(0.362)
Log likelihood	−2,334.717		
χ^2	89.89	***	
N	2,077		
Bills passing both houses	321		

Standard errors are in parentheses. *** $p < 0.01$, ** $p < 0.05$, * $p < 0.10$

Budget Uncertainty

In chapter 9, I discuss how agency autonomy and scope relate to the state budget. Following Krause (1996), I calculated an agency-specific measure of uncertainty as the natural logarithm of the absolute value of the difference between the current cycle's appropriation and the previous cycle's. Although this value is unknowable to budget directors at the time they draft their budgets, it represents the "feel" of the political climate. The figure is logged to linearize the highly different absolute sizes of agency budgets. A high value indicates greater uncertainty. Agencies should request more funds in times of uncertainty to cover for greater potential losses. I also include indicator variables for Georgia and Ohio (with Wisconsin being the omitted variable).

Using only state education agencies for the analysis would pose a methodological challenge. Georgia operates on an annual budget, but both Ohio and Wisconsin budget biennially. This produces just ten observations for agencies in those two states. (In Ohio, budget requests for two biennia are not recorded due to a change in the administration's political party, which leaves just eight observations.) Therefore, I compiled budget data for most state agencies. I excluded constitutional agencies—the governor's office, the legislature, and the courts—because there was virtually no deviation between their budget requests and appropriations, sometimes by law. I also omit short-term panels, boards, and commissions that each state had from time to time (e.g., the 1996 Olympic Safety Commission in Georgia), and those agencies for whom state funds served only to shore up shortfalls from federal or other earmarked funds. This left ninety-one state agencies.

The explained variable in this section is the percentage change in an agency's budget request as a ratio of the standard deviation of all agencies' budget percentage changes. A ratio of 1 means that the agency's requested percent change from its last budget was equal to a "normal" request for that state in that budget cycle. Agencies' budget change requests ranged anywhere from a decrease in a budget request of 4.03 times this standard deviation, to no change, to a 5.75-fold increase, relative to the standard deviation. The mean request was 0.78 of the standard deviation percent change.

The rationale for this measure is both to control for the very different size of state budgets in Georgia, Ohio, and Wisconsin and because of the nature of the budget documents. In Wisconsin, budget requests are explicitly set in terms of the last budget—to the extent that it is difficult to figure out how much money is actually being requested without other supporting documents. Georgia agencies also used relative amounts for several of the years I used.

An ordinary least-squares regression that predicts the standardized percentage change in appropriations from the previous budget appears in Table B.6.

Budget Residuals

Budget residuals measure the difference between the requested budget and the actual budget appropriated. For control measures, I include budget uncertainty as defined for the previous analysis. As uncertainty increases, agencies should request more, but there is no reason to believe

Table B.6. Factors Affecting the Percentage Change in All State Agency Budget Requests

	Explanatory Variables		
Budgetary uncertainty	0.127	***	(0.019)
Governor's party (1 is R)	−0.391	***	(0.119)
Change in governor	−0.060		(0.062)
Pct. Republican upper house	0.012		(0.010)
Pct. Republican lower house	0.041	***	(0.009)
Divided government	0.418	***	(0.117)
Change in divided government	0.144		(0.142)
	Control Variables		
Pct. of overall state budget, prior year	−0.301	***	(0.058)
Indicator for Georgia	1.870	***	(0.378)
Indicator for Ohio	−0.308	*	(0.179)
Year count (1981 is 1)	−0.134	***	(0.020)
Constant	−2.084	***	(0.439)
R^2	0.13		
F (11, 90)	14.36	***	
N	1,078		
Number of groups	91		

Standard errors are in parentheses. *** $p < 0.01$, ** $p < 0.05$, * $p < 0.10$

that uncertainty will lead necessarily to bigger or smaller actual appropriations. Instead, the residual should track uncertainty. I also include
indicator variables for Georgia and Ohio.

Budget levels in this year's budget are highly likely to be related
to last year's budget. In Wisconsin, budgets are explicitly so: this biennium's budget is expressed in terms of changes to the last biennium's.[3]
To compensate for this situation, I predicted budget success using an
autoregressive, conditional heteroskedastic regression.[4] Such a model
incorporates the possibility that the variance in budgets between years
is correlated. Table B.7 presents the results.

Table B.7. Absolute Budget Residuals for All State Agencies as a Percentage of Prior Appropriations, 1982–2002

	Explanatory Variables		
Governor's party (1 is R)	54.605	***	(0.970)
Pct. Republican upper house	−2.114	***	(0.062)
Pct. Republican lower house	1.796	***	(0.056)
Change in governor	−6.881	***	(0.735)
Divided government	−23.767	***	(0.862)
Agency budget as pct. of last state budget	−5.596	***	(0.427)
	Control Variables		
Budgetary uncertainty	1.154	***	(0.147)
Indicator for Ohio	89.751	***	(1.352)
Indicator for Georgia	28.758	***	(1.054)
Constant	−11.673	***	(1.240)
ARCH Lag (1)	8.626	***	(0.177)
Constant	113.364	***	(19.885)
Log likelihood	−5,703.127		
χ^2	16,325.65	***	
N	1,008		

Standard errors are in parentheses. *** $p < 0.01$, ** $p < 0.05$, * $p < 0.10$

Summary Statistics

The tables that follow are summary statistics for the noted tables.

Table B.8. Summary Statistics for Table B.1

Variable	Mean	Std. Dev.	Min.	Max.
	Explained Variable			
Committee service	0.256	0.436	0.000	1.000
	Explanatory Variables			
Sessions in office	4.421	3.471	1.000	22.000
Biennium	6.512	2.880	1.000	11.000
Chamber	0.238	0.425	0.000	1.000
Majority party member	0.644	0.479	0.000	1.000
Change in governor	0.301	0.458	0.000	1.000
Change in superintendent	0.174	0.379	0.000	1.000
Pct. share of state budget	38.670	7.533	24.377	52.485
Share of state-of-state to education	0.233	0.143	0.037	1.000
Previous education committee service	0.207	0.405	0.000	1.000
Party (1 = R)	0.387	0.487	0.000	1.000
Pct. chamber Republican	38.405	15.123	8.929	63.637
Divided government exists	0.365	0.481	0.000	1.000
Georgia indicator	0.475	0.499	0.000	1.000
Ohio indicator	0.260	0.439	0.000	1.000

Table B.9. Summary Statistics for Table B.2

Variable	Mean	Std. Dev.	Min.	Max.
	Explained Variable			
Committee exit	0.258	0.438	0.000	1.000
	Explanatory Variables			
Session in office	3.304	2.405	1.000	14.000
Sessions on education committee	1.715	1.146	1.000	8.000
Biennium	6.935	2.643	2.000	11.000
Chamber	0.171	0.377	0.000	1.000
Majority party member	0.606	0.489	0.000	1.000
Change in governor	0.285	0.452	0.000	1.000
Change in superintendent	0.181	0.386	0.000	1.000
Pct. share of state budget	39.483	8.257	24.377	52.486
Share of state-of-state to education	0.233	0.134	0.037	0.501
Party (1 = R)	0.430	0.496	0.000	1.000
Pct. chamber Republican	41.644	11.906	8.929	63.637
Divided government exists	0.478	0.500	0.000	1.000
Georgia indicator	0.364	0.482	0.000	1.000
Ohio indicator	0.271	0.445	0.000	1.000

Table B.10. Summary Statistics for Table B.3

Variable	Mean	Std. Dev.	Min.	Max.
	Explained Variable			
Number of bills	38.561	29.504	5.000	107.000
	Explanatory Variables			
Chamber	0.491	0.504	0.000	1.000
Governor's party (1 = R)	0.526	0.504	0.000	1.000
Pct. share of state budget	38.282	8.385	24.377	52.485
Pct. chamber Republican	41.666	15.061	8.929	63.637
Divided government exists	0.439	0.501	0.000	1.000
Change in divided government	−0.035	0.325	−1.000	1.000
Georgia indicator	0.351	0.481	0.000	1.000
Ohio indicator	0.298	0.461	0.000	1.000
Median prob. committee service	0.111	0.034	0.054	0.201
Median prob. committee exit	0.228	0.141	0.060	0.599
Change in governor	0.281	0.453	0.000	1.000
Change in superintendent	0.175	0.384	0.000	1.000

Table B.11. Summary Statistics for Tables B.4 and B.5

Variable	Mean	Std. Dev.	Min.	Max.
		Explained Variable		
Bill's time to leave committee, in days	46.781	69.335	0.000	491.000
Bill's time to pass both houses, in days	55.026	70.383	0.000	476.000
		Explanatory Variables		
Governor's party (1 is R)	0.321	0.466	0.000	1.000
Percent of state budget to education agency	37.006	7.249	24.377	52.486
Majority party member	0.685	0.464	0.000	1.000
Pct. chamber Republican	37.286	14.390	8.929	63.637
Divided government exists	0.342	0.474	0.000	1.000
Change in divided government	0.062	0.241	0.000	1.000
Number of federal education laws passed	5.576	4.316	0.000	17.000
Georgia indicator	0.548	0.498	0.000	1.000
Ohio indicator	0.327	0.469	0.000	1.000
Previous terms on education committee	0.194	0.673	0.000	8.000
Education committee service probability	0.247	0.227	0.001	0.859
Change in governor	0.239	0.427	0.000	1.000
Change in superintendent	0.179	0.383	0.000	1.000

Table B.12. Summary Statistics for Table B.6

Variable	Mean	Std. Dev.	Min.	Max.
		Explained Variable		
Pct. change in agency request	2.242	160.794	3,196.092	1,021.972
		Explanatory Variables		
Budgetary uncertainty	8.228	2.477	1.609	16.022
Governor's party (1 is R)	0.348	0.477	0.000	1.000
Change in governor	0.188	0.391	0.000	1.000
Pct. Republican upper house	36.952	16.823	8.928	63.636
Pct. Republican lower house	36.889	15.824	13.889	60.606
Divided government	0.258	0.437	0.000	1.000
Pct. of overall state budget	0.267	0.717	0.000	7.190
Indicator for Ohio	0.202	0.402	0.000	1.000
Indicator for Georgia	0.561	0.496	0.000	1.000

Table B.13. Summary Statistics for Table B.7

Variable	Mean	Std. Dev.	Min.	Max.
		Explained Variable		
Pct. absolute budget residual	34.255	147.448	0.000	3,096.092
		Explanatory Variables		
Budgetary uncertainty	8.237	2.460	1.609	16.022
Governor's party (1 is R)	0.360	0.480	0.000	1.000
Change in governor	0.167	0.373	0.000	1.000
Pct. Republican upper house	37.615	17.220	8.928	63.636
Pct. Republican lower house	36.712	15.434	13.333	60.606
Divided government	0.314	0.465	0.000	1.000
Pct. of overall state budget	0.261	0.713	0.000	7.190
Indicator for Ohio	0.239	0.427	0.000	1.000
Indicator for Georgia	0.527	0.500	0.000	1.000

Appendix C

A Note on the Sources

Interviews

This project would not have been completed without the exemplary assistance of forty interviewees who took the time to talk with a researcher far removed from their day-to-day tasks. Many of them continue to work in education as lobbyists, bureaucrats, and legislators—and as a result, most of them were hesitant to talk with me, except as confidential sources. I have honored that promise. The organizations employing my sources follow. One organization did not wish its name to be included even in this list, although its representative was very willing to talk with me. Any quotation not otherwise cited in the text came from one of my interviewees. I conducted interviews in 2002, 2003, 2004, and 2008.

Superintendents

Werner Rogers
Franklin Walter
John Goff
Herbert Grover
John Benson

Organizations

Georgia School Boards Association
Professional Association of Georgia Educators
Georgia Association of Educators
Georgia Association of Educational Leaders
Ohio Federation of Teachers
Ohio Education Association
Governor's Task Force on Financing Student Success
Ohio School Boards Association

Ohio Business Roundtable
Wisconsin Manufacturers and Commerce
Wisconsin Education Association Council
Wisconsin Association of School Administrators

Print Sources

I was able to get a glimpse of the day-to-day operations of both state departments of education and governor's offices using official state archives. They are cited to the extent possible. Archives are hit-or-miss affairs and are known to be incomplete—in Wisconsin, Governor James Doyle's office inadvertently sent dozens of boxes of Governor Tommy Thompson's papers to the recycling plant instead of the Historical Society during my research—but what does appear fills in the details where people's memories fade. Georgia Superintendent Linda Schrenko's papers had not yet appeared at the state's lovely new archive building south of Atlanta some two years after she had left office. One person there told me in hushed tones that there was considerable doubt that any material would be forthcoming for her at all. In the Wisconsin archives, the two boxes of Governor Tommy Thompson's papers that (I expect) dealt with his attempt to transfer the DPI to a cabinet department are missing.

Because few of my subjects are, or may ever be, well-known figures, and because some of the archive boxes had appeared in the state repository only months before my arrival, some material had no coherent indexing system. Material was not in numbered folders; folders were not in alphabetical or chronological order; and, in some cases, papers were not even in folders at all. Therefore, I give as full a citation as possible in the references. This citation always includes a full description of the material.

The primary archival sources I used were the following:

- Governor's Subject Files, Georgia Historical Society, Atlanta, Georgia (Governors Joe Frank Harris and Zell Miller)

- Superintendent's Subject Files, Georgia Historical Society, Atlanta, Georgia (Superintendents Jack Nix, Charles McDaniel, and Werner Rogers)

- George V. Voinovich papers, Ohio University, Athens, Ohio

- Richard F. Celeste papers, Ohio Historical Society Library, Columbus, Ohio

- Governor's Policy Staff Files, Wisconsin Historical Society, Madison, Wisconsin (Governors Lee Dreyfus, Tony Earl, and Tommy Thompson)
- Correspondence of the State Superintendent, Wisconsin Historical Society, Madison, Wisconsin (Superintendents Herbert Grover and James Benson)

I used the following newspapers extensively. Other papers are appropriately identified in the notes to the text.

- Atlanta *Journal, Constitution*, and *Journal-Constitution*
- Cleveland *Plain Dealer*
- Columbus (Ohio) *Dispatch*
- Cincinnati *Enquirer*
- Milwaukee *Journal, Sentinel,* and *Journal-Sentinel*
- Wisconsin *State Journal*
- Madison (Wisconsin) *Capital Times*
- *Education Week*

Notes

Chapter 1

1. Unless otherwise cited, all unattributed quotations are from interviews I conducted. See the appendix for a list of organizations my interviewees represented. Except for former state superintendents, all of my sources requested confidentiality.

2. Whitford (2005) shows how the federal Environmental Protection Agency is "whip lashed" between Congress and the president. An autonomous agency should be able to modulate these competing political demands.

3. This expectation is not unique to education. For example, as the federal Centers for Medicaid and Medicare Services rolled out the Medicare prescription drug benefit in 2005, it sent a "to-do" list to to state health agencies reminding them that they needed to rewrite state laws and regulations to comply with new federal law and regulation. Although several of the items were couched in terms such as "Have you talked to legislators about the need to pass new legislation?" CMS assumed that the health agency would have the ability to convince legislators of the need or be able to rewrite regulations in short order (Department of Health and Human Services, Centers for Medicare and Medicaid, "Medicare Modernization Act State Executive Branch Checklist," April 13, 2005).

4. Of course, agency leaders may not have wanted to do any of these things before No Child Left Behind. But that justifies the claim: If the department did not do any of them, the agency would be totally unprepared to implement NCLB changes.

5. Colorado, Department of Education, *Request Budget* (Denver, Colorado, 1998), p. ii. Excluding school foundation support, Colorado's Department of Education had a budget of about $205 million in fiscal year 1998–99, and Iowa's was about $302 million. In contrast, the Ohio Department of Education had a budget of $2.2 billion, excluding foundation support. Per student, Ohio's non-foundation-aid budget was double Iowa's and five times Colorado's (Ohio, Office of Budget and Management, *Executive Budget* [Columbus, Ohio, 1997], pp. E-103–E-119; Iowa, Department of Management, *Program & Budget Summary* [Des Moines, Iowa, 1997], pp. 105–107).

6. Indeed, New England meetinghouses, which were used for both town administration and church services, originally did not have religious iconography

to emphasize that the state and the church should cooperate in the same space (Marsden 2003, 189).

7. Still, the "victory" was not complete. Oregon went so far as to outlaw private schools (through a voter initiative), but the U.S. Supreme Court found that the state had infringed on parents' rights (*Society of Sisters v. Oregon* [1922]). Much later, Wisconsin later found itself in similar trouble in *Yoder v. Wisconsin* (1974), a court case about the rights of Amish families to educate their children.

8. See Kerchner and Mitchell (1988, chapter 3) and, for examples, Clark (1958, 13–14), Orr (1950, 196), and Ray (1943, 25–26). The relationship between education departments and teachers' associations was similar to that between the U.S.D.A. and county extensions, see Carpenter (2001a, chapter 7).

9. Hayes (1955) shows how Ohio interest groups were crucial to these finance reforms during the Great Depression.

10. Certainly the federal government had been active in education before, including the Morrill Act of 1862 (land-grant colleges) and the Smith-Hughes Act in 1937 (vocational education). The Elementary and Secondary Education Act (ESEA), however, was the most sustained, general-purpose education bill. The ESEA and the Education for All Handicapped Children Act (1974) have become the primary means through which the federal government influences local education policy. Both are examples of fiscal federalism.

11. Title V funds did far less than the original proponents hoped. One proponent of Title V called it the "biggest failure" of the 1965 ESEA in the early '00s (quoted in Manna 2006, 107). They did, however, spawn a number of cooperative, interstate studies on improving state administration and finance (Morphet and Jesser 1970, 33).

12. Gerring (2004) notes that case studies are excellent for understanding causal mechanisms even as they may be weak on representativeness. He argues, however, that "case" studies are often composed of far more distinct observations than is usually assumed. In this work, each case is observed at multiple points of time, increasing the number of "cases," even as the number of units under investigation remains at three. Here I observe each unit over approximately twenty years.

13. U.S. Congress, "An Ordinance for the Government of the Territory of the United States, North-West of the River Ohio," Article 3, July 13, 1787.

14. Previous works usually use only aggregate measures of the budget. Works along these lines include Krause et al. (2006), Bowling and Ferguson (2001), Alt and Lowry (2000), and Clarke (1998). It would be an understatement to say that state budgeting had undergone anything less than a complete transformation between 1980 and 2000. At the beginning of the period, documents are cumbersome, numbers often approximate, and predictions simplistic. At the end, computer technology had transformed both the format and detail of state budgets.

15. Groseclose and Stewart (1998) document the relative desirability of House seats (as does Munger 1988), but they view the committee preferences of members of Congress as driven by a desire for electoral success, campaign

contributions, or credit claiming. I make a corollary argument: committees that are more "important" to the public may also be more desirable (thereby presenting more opportunities for credit claiming).

Chapter 2

1. There are exceptions, such as Carpenter (2001b), which is a response to Kernell (2001) and Kernell and McDonald (1999). Kernell and McDonald attempt to show that rural free delivery resulted from constituent pressure on Congress rather than from an innovation by the Post Office Department, Carpenter's contention.

2. This is the assumption underlying the famous "fire alarms" of McCubbins and Schwartz (1984). Balla and Wright (2001) also take this stance when they show how Congress delegated oversight responsibility to a balanced panel of interest groups.

3. Lipsky (1980). Brehm and Gates (1997) introduce "sabotage" into the familiar work-or-shirk menu of options. They differentiate sabotage from shirking by defining sabotage as a "politically motivated act of attempting to wreck a policy or to prevent policy reform" (31). Shirking may either be an expression of dissent (without deliberate destruction) or an attempt at increasing leisure time.

4. This is especially the case when agents are assumed to be strategic, as they usually are. For one example, Ting (2003) writes, "[Agents] receive payoffs from outcomes and choose effort levels" (277). The major contribution of Brehm and Gates (1997) is to show that bureaucrats work without *needing* a payoff. They work because their preferences are aligned with that of the principal.

5. Following on this topic, some wonder whether principal-agent theories developed at the federal level hold in the states. Given that all fifty states are either patterned after the federal government or were patterns *for* it, there is no reason to suppose that states would work in a fundamentally different way. Said another way, states differ in degree. They have smaller budgets, smaller legislatures, and smaller populations, but they all address roughly the same policy issues and political pressures that the federal government does. And, as noted in this paragraph, states must respond to the federal government. Regardless, scholars have applied some federal principal-agent literature directly to the states. See, for example, Nicholson-Crotty, Theobald, and Wood (2006).

6. Nevertheless, most responsibilities are delegated (in Congress's case) to existing agencies. See Epstein and O'Halloran (1999).

7. To put it another way, the transaction costs of obtaining the information from some other source are usually prohibitively high. See Williamson (1983).

8. The Georgia case also shows how strong autonomy can be. Although the testing contracts were eventually withdrawn, they were withdrawn only when a *federal* probe uncovered the state superintendent funneling the money to herself (Salzer, Warren, and Torpy 2006).

9. A magazine advertisement that ran in *Governing* magazine in July 2005 by the American Federation of Teachers claimed that this is a major flaw of the law.

10. Davis, Dempster, and Wildavsky (1966) argue that agencies play a game by which they ask just a bit too much in the expectation that some will be cut. I am interested in when agencies *do* ask too much. Wildavsky (1992) explores incremental budgeting.

11. On funding sources, Thompson (1987) finds that agencies with significant federal funds are less likely to receive their requests for state money, while Chubb (1985) shows how federal money can shape the activity of agencies. Clarke (1997) and Thompson and Felts (1992) explore the influence of agency chiefs in securing a budget: although budgets tend to reflect the governor's priorities, in many cases agency chiefs who share a partisan tie are more successful. Although Sharkansky (1968) found that legislatures tended to defer to agency requests due to their own technical and time limitations, more professional legislatures have become more independent from both agency requests and gubernatorial desires, as shown by Thompson (1987) and Clarke (1997). Brudney and Hebert (1987) each show how the governor, legislature, and interest groups interact with agency funding.

12. Although NCLB contains provisions for school reconstitution (replacing a school's entire faculty), both of these examples predate NCLB. Georgia Department of Education threatened to take over the Quitman County Schools for poor student performance in the late 1980s, and the Ohio Department of Education took over the Cleveland School District for poor bookkeeping in the 1990s.

13. Ting (2003) suggests that multiple agencies might have similar responsibilities when "entrepreneurial agents can move unilaterally into new policy areas" (276). How entrepreneurial agents do that is the question here.

14. These factors are all causal in that they precede the growth or decay of autonomy and scope, but one could easily make the argument that many of these factors are recursive. The causal arrow may appear somewhat extended at times, but I believe that I have erred on the side of causality rather than correlation. That is, an agency with narrow scope and little autonomy may attract a weak leader, precisely because the agency is in this predicament. The more ambitious will seek better pastures. Nevertheless, with this example, a weak leader is unlikely to pull down new powers from the legislature in the same way a stronger one might.

15. Kotter is a well-known leadership guru. He received much adulation from one of my interviewees who had studied his state agency's internal structure. So much was Kotter idolized that my source had a life-size cutout of him in the corner of his office.

16. The difficulties of politically appointed leaders were noted in an earlier section. The effectiveness of the leader will be constrained by her method of selection and by her partisanship, if any. I discuss divided government later.

17. Both the president and an agency leader have to direct and respond to a legislature; both have multiple, competing constituencies; and if an agency chief is elected, both have electoral promises to fulfill.

18. The weakness of groups due to "density" appears in Gray and Lowery (2004) and Salisbury (1984). Business groups are covered in Rigdon (1995).

19. Carpenter (2004) argues that bureaucratic regulators learn from experience with firms. Large firms (or, by extension, interest groups) may *appear* to have an advantage over smaller firms when the outcome is actually a function of the firm's prior reputation for quality or effort. Therefore, the policy output of an agency may appear to be the result of capture when it is, rather, a reflection of the regulator's (untainted) conception of the public good.

20. The chiefs of state departments of education have a unique situation among agency leaders because many of them are (technically) independent of the governor. Therefore, *both* the agency leader and the governor may compete in setting the public's and the legislature's agenda using the same tactics.

21. Barrilleaux and Berkman (2003) find that governors can successfully corner legislatures into increased redistributive spending, despite a legislative propensity toward pork barrel. Both Thompson (1987) and Sharkansky (1968) found that legislators largely deferred to governors.

22. In addition, many governors have variations on the line-item veto (Rosenthal 1990). This gives the governor detailed bargaining power not available to the U.S. president. As a related note, the extensive federal scholarship on "veto bargaining" and signaling need not—and perhaps cannot—apply at the state level the way it does at the federal level (e.g., Cameron 2000).

23. Mayhew (1991) argues that it makes no difference, but Edwards, Barrett, and Peake (1997) and Binder (1999) show that major legislation is, in fact, more successful. For a thorough review of the divided government literature, see Coleman (1999).

24. Alt and Lowry (2000) do not consider differences among policy areas or whether a large majority affects outcomes, but Bowling and Ferguson (2001) do, and they find that "high-conflict" areas, such as welfare, energy and the environment, and education, are adversely affected by divided government (meaning fewer laws are passed). They also show that the greater diversity of interest groups, as opposed to the number of groups, hampers the passage of legislation across all policy areas, with the exception of environmental policy.

25. Assuming two parties and two legislative houses, the combinations are as follows: the governor and chief oppose the legislature; the governor and the senate oppose the chief and house; the governor and the house oppose the chief and senate; the governor and the legislature oppose the chief; and the governor opposes the chief and legislature.

26. Cameron (2000) makes the argument that the executive is advantaged over either house of Congress. Clarke (1998) argues that the governor's party has an advantage in a conference committee (perhaps, but the number of legislators on the committee who share the governor's party might also be important, especially if there is a separate budget-writing committee).

27. This contrasts somewhat with Whitford (2005), who argues that multiple principles will compete with each other to control the agency, "whiplash[ing]" the agency's output (45). Although he analyzes the ideology of members of Congress and the president, he does not study partisan effects. On the other

hand, Clarke (1997) finds that divided government prompts agencies to request budgets about 4 percent larger than under unified government (309).

28. Ringquist, Worsham, and Eisner (2003) note that salience may be less important if an agency is politically powerful or has a powerful leader.

29. There is some evidence that permit-granting agencies do respond to potential lawsuits (Canes-Wrone 2003).

Chapter 3

1. Truth be told, many state chief races are sleepy campaigns. As I will discuss in a later chapter, one exception, Georgia in 1994, proves the rule.

2. The classic national statement of gubernatorial interest is the National Governors' Association (1986). See also Manna (2006, chapter 5).

3. The Internet has further weakened information gatekeeping, but not to the extent that one might think. A veteran lobbyist in Ohio complained mightily that the Department of Education's Web site was a counterintuitive maze, and that she could not find any useful data on it. She still had to call ODE to find the information she needed. Having perused the site as well, the author empathizes with her.

4. Scholars of Congress and the federal bureaucracy have long noted that Congress often uses its oversight powers only in response to "fire alarms," which is analogous to the spikes in legislative interest noted here; see McCubbins (1985).

Chapter 4

1. For some interesting examples of "plagiarism" in state constitutional development, see Bridges (2003).

2. This and following sections on Georgia rely on Orr (1950).

3. This arrangement became the template for all new territories. Curiously, not all of the sixteenth sections have been sold as of this writing—for example, the City of Colorado Springs, Colorado, still holds title to its section 16. It is a park.

4. This and following sections regarding Ohio rely on Ray (1943) and Shreve (1989).

5. This and other sections on Wisconsin rely heavily on Jorgenson (1956).

6. In 1838, the legislature allowed Milwaukee a ten-mill property tax, although Milwaukee schools still charged quarterly tuition.

7. While the funding statistic is unreliable, it does show that local districts were willing to tax at some level above the legislature's limits (Clark 1958, 4).

8. Werner Rogers, of this chapter's epigraph, was reelected—with competition—in 1990. Since Collins, each superintendent had been appointed on the death or resignation of his predecessor and faced no opposition for reelection.

9. Kathy Cox has not had the same trouble, partly because she has a very supportive governor, and partly because she has gone out of her way to be amenable, engaging, and efficient after the department's experience with Schrenko, according to every Georgia interviewee of mine.

10. It should be noted that in 1986 British Prime Minister Margaret Thatcher did, in fact, take the mayor's job after tiring of longtime London Mayor "Red Ken" Livingston's jabs at her government. See http//www.london. gov.uk/mayor/.

11. The reverse has probably been true in Ohio—superintendents have outlasted many board members.

12. Two particularly vociferous proponents of anti-elitism were from Grant County. At the time, Grant County was full of rough-and-tumble lead miners who were especially suspicious of any nondemocratic means of governance, and these counties often spent the most on local schools.

13. The inflation approximation was calculated from Economic History Services (2002).

14. It is important to remember that parents were responsible for paying for textbooks. State law empowered district boards to purchase textbooks for students only when parents were unable to do so (Patzer 1924, 33).

15. State law also provided that the state superintendent was also required "to collect . . . such schoolbooks, apparatus, maps and charts as can be obtained without expense to the state, and also to purchase at an expense not exceeding fifty dollars a year, rare and valuable works on education, for the benefit of teachers, authors and others, who may wish to consult them" (Patzer 1924, 211).

16. Considering that as late as 1945, 4,622 one-room schools enrolled 18 percent of public school students, this was a major loophole (Callahan 1946, 38).

Chapter 5

1. Georgia's largest teacher's association, the Professional Association of Georgia Educators, split off from the Georgia Education Association (GEA) in 1974 because its leaders felt the National Education Association (NEA) was successfully pushing the GEA to be too political and too liberal.

2. Hansen (1991) explores the potential weaknesses of an interest group aligning with a particular political party.

3. Nevertheless, some of the ideas were circulating at the DPI in the late 1980s. An *Education Forward* article in January 1987 detailed a teacher career ladder developed by the Waunakee Teachers Association and the school board, complete with the three-part career ladder that became integral to PI34 (Hetzel 1987).

4. Only four interest groups were directly involved with setting the standards: WEAC, WASB, the Wisconsin Association of Non-Public Schools, and the Wisconsin Association of Middle Level Educators.

5. The full breakdown was the Department of Public Instruction, nine; the Wisconsin Education Association Council, eight; the Association of

Wisconsin School Administrators, seven; the University of Wisconsin System, six; the Wisconsin Association of School District Administrators, five; the Wisconsin Independent Colleges of Teacher Education, five; the Wisconsin Association of School Boards, three; the Wisconsin Federation of Teachers, two; the Cooperative Educational Service Agencies (government), one; the Metropolitan Milwaukee Alliance of Black School Educators, one; the Menominee Tribal School, one; the Wisconsin Association for Middle Level Education, one; the Wisconsin Association of School Personnel Administrators, one; and one person was a representative for the Advisory Council as a whole.

6. Benson already had the union label attached to him. The WEAC ran a series of commercials supporting his candidacy in 1993, although he denied being in the "pocket of the union" (Veteran administrator wins chief's race in Wisconsin 1993).

7. See chapter 7 and Wohlstetter (1994) for more details on QBE.

8. The state board's role was and is one of policy direction, according to the board members I interviewed, so that they should know little about the specifics is not surprising. Still, the state board was very sensitive to criticism, so it needed to be kept abreast of controversial actions, according to one long-time GADOE employee.

9. IOX Assessment Associates may still be found at http://www.ioxassessment.com.

10. IOX charged $199,667 to design the exam, $93,483 for its implementation, and $19,435 for each videotape to instruct teachers on how to give the test.

11. These cases are all *DeRolph v. State*: 78 Ohio St.3d 193, 677 N.E. 2d 733; 89 Ohio St.3d 1, 728 N.E.2d 993; 93 Ohio St.3d 309, 754 N.E.2d 1184; and 97 Ohio St.3d 434, 780 N.E.2d 529.

12. There was actually a fifth *DeRolph* decision, in 2003, that reiterated that the state supreme court had permanently removed itself from the case. On school finance generally, I found Odden and Picus (2003) and Underwood and Verstege (1990) helpful in understanding the relevant details, and I believe I am still of sound mind. Also, the pruning argument is similar to the "backlash" use of prerogative power for the president found in Pious (1996). The department used its autonomy, and other actors tried to squelch it and temporarily succeeded, but the department kept and even built its reputation and laid a base for a future expansion of scope.

13. For helpful summaries of the *DeRolph* cases, see Hogan (1998), Drummon (2000), and O'Brien (2003). A quick overview may be had from the League of Women Voters of the Cincinnati Area (2005). The governor had passed over William Phillis to replace Franklin Walter in 1991 and John Goff in 1995. One governor's aide pegged him as a "loose cannon" (Droste 1991a).

14. There was also a side argument as to whether the Supreme Court should maintain jurisdiction of the case. The ODE and the state wanted it to, believing the Perry County Court was a biased observer. The Supreme Court did not agree at this stage.

15. This is not to demean the politicians. Their range of interest, of necessity, had to be much wider, thus they had to rely on the budget director and superintendent for advice.

16. Interestingly, while this self-promotional pamphlet (for the state superintendent's job that Ted Sanders got) foreshadows many of the coalition's demands in 1997, school finance is the lowest ranked. Some of the coalition's ideas—particularly the ones for a revised state aid formula—also appeared in testimony that Phillis gave to the General Assembly in February 1990, while still an assistant superintendent (Ohio General Assembly 1990).

17. These provisions are in 1998 House Bill 650 and House Bill 770 (technical corrections).

18. These were H.B. 412, H.B. 697, S.B. 55, S.B. 103, and S.B. 230.

19. Note that even though ODE's proposals had to compete with others, it was still successful in *raising* the proficiency standards even farther than it had after *DeRolph I*, despite the court rebuke in *DeRolph II*—demonstrating considerable political autonomy (Welsh-Huggins 2000).

20. In part because of this suspicion, the court ordered ODE to turn over documents detailing how it calculated school funding numbers as part of fulfilling *DeRolph III* (School funding chronology 2003).

21. Part of the coalition's campaign included sending "informational" videotapes to libraries. In one, "The Time Is Now," the words of the original *DeRolph* case are read over a photograph of the capitol being hit by a lightning bolt.

Chapter 6

1. Although the literature on educational leadership is plentiful, it exclusively reports on leadership by principals and *district* superintendents (see, e.g., Crow and Grogan 2005) as far as this author can determine.

2. See Grover (1983c). Grover's relationship with the *Capital Times* has continued. In February 2005, he wrote a letter (that his friend and paper editor David Zweifel turned into an editorial) decrying the partisan nature of that year's state superintendent's race (Zweifel 2005). (Grover, however, is himself definitely partisan. He has served as an advisor for many Democratic candidates and has repeatedly boasted to me that he was the only Democrat ever to win his state legislative district.)

3. See, for example, Grover (1985b) and Volk (1985).

4. On mid-level agencies, see Grover (1981c) and State education issues (1983).

5. This section would be much richer if I had been able to contact Linda Schrenko. Unfortunately, despite repeated messages left on her home answering machine and cellular telephone throughout the summer and fall of 2004, she returned only one message—the first—to tell me to call back later. Toward the end of the year, she became involved in a legal action against her for actions as superintendent, and I suspect that she had been told by her lawyer not to

talk to people any more than necessary. She was eventually convicted of fraud (Salzer, Warren, and Torpy 2006).

6. Insider leadership was also a hallmark of Georgia education politics through Superintendent Charles McDaniel, who died in 1985. Although a few Georgia superintendents had explored public leadership, particularly Superintendent M. D. Collins in the 1950s and 1960s, the dominance of the Democratic Party and a strong race and class system rarely made anything more than a handshake deal necessary. I do not cover Superintendent McDaniel because my interviewees' memories were extremely foggy about him.

7. Emphases are in the original. One longtime observer with whom I spoke thought the complaint was likewise absurd: appointed or not, "all but one or two members of the State Board of Education are Republicans."

8. Rogers was very careful to avoid the outward show of partisanship, however, unlike his predecessor. Minutes from his staff meetings show him repeatedly exhorting his staff not to "get involved in the upcoming election" (Superintendent's minutes 1988a, 1988b). Some legislators felt comfortable asking McDaniel, a member of the state Democratic Party Committee, for campaign assistance, which apparently at least one received (Greer 1982; Newsome 1982).

9. Harris also helped Rogers campaign in 1986, when he was up for election.

10. Rogers answered legislators in detail, even when the request came from someone other than an education chair. A critical request for information about minority teachers received a four-page reply detailing every aspect of GADOE's minority teacher recruitment program (Rogers 1989).

11. Senator Terrell Star, a powerful, longtime legislator, claimed that "if [QBE] don't serve the purpose it intended, there's an awful lot of people to blame, an awful lot of organizations. It was a collection of the best minds and best efforts that could ever be put into anything" (Rice 1988).

12. A journalist from the Appleton *Post-Crescent* ended a note to Grover, asking, "When you decide to run for governor, give me the info first?" (Walter 1982). Representative Wayne W. Wood told people at a school area meeting in January 1985, that Grover was using the DPI's budget request to pave his way to the governor's mansion (Williams 1985). One of my interviewees who had worked with Grover in his later terms also said, "I wasn't certain that Bert wasn't using it [his office] as a stepping stone to the governor's office."

13. Although he apologized for the delay, Grover (uncharacteristically) did not reply to this letter for two months.

14. On property taxes in Wisconsin, see Mathis (1989a) and Blair (1999).

15. This report was filed in Thompson's staff files on school finance at the state archives.

Chapter 7

1. Miller (1998, 186). The Georgia Department of Education's total budget in FY1995 was $3.5 billion in state funds.

2. The classic national statement of gubernatorial interest is the National Governors' Association (1986). See also Manna (2006, chapter 5). After leaving office, Governor Roy Romer even became the superintendent of the Los Angeles Unified School District.

3. Between 1933 and 1994, every state superintendent was appointed by the governor to fill a vacancy in the post created by death or resignation. Many of the superintendents were also long-serving. Terms exceeding a decade were common. See chapter 4.

4. After Rogers lost his post, the governor promised another reorganization with the same goal in 1995 (Miller 1998, 8, 186).

5. Rogers also made an easy target for other reasons. He used state resources freely and extensively while campaigning. He did in 1994, and he had in 1986 (White 1994a; Today's lesson is how not to run for Georgia school superintendent 1986). In her 2002 campaign, Schrenko was targeted for the same reasons (Salzer 2002).

6. The GADOE received funds in excess of its requests in fiscal years 1997, 1998, and 1999. In fiscal year 2000, Roy Barnes's first budget, the GADOE received just $3.8 million less than requested. In the 1980s, the GADOE had routinely asked for $300 million more than it received in actual appropriations. See chapter 10 for more details on the state budget.

7. Barnes served in the state Senate prior to 1990. He ran against Miller for governor in 1990 and lost. He was elected to the House in 1992.

8. The Brickner case appears in many newspaper articles. See, in particular, Voinovich set to replace Brickner in "near future" (1991); State school board member replaced (1991); Brickner loses case; fails to regain state board seat (1991).

9. The governor wrote to Walter: "Everywhere I go, I let people know *you* invited in the Operations Improvement Task Force. The logic is well expressed in your letter to me" (Voinovich 1991c, emphasis in original). Walter did provide suggestions for areas to examine especially those the governor apparently took (Van Auken 1991).

10. The Buckeye Association of School Administrators and the Ohio School Boards Association were represented by ex-officio members.

11. Sanders (1993b) contains a diagram that describes "Project PASS" (for the ninth-grade exam) and explicitly routes authority through the ODE parallel to "state organizations."

12. Thompson's addresses were all roughly the same length, generally between 6,000 and 7,000 words. The same pattern appears if the data are shown relative to speech length. Reporting the raw numbers helps show how much detail Governor Thompson spent on education. Education did not play as great a role in budget addresses, because most governors balanced that speech among many departments, many of which were never mentioned in State of the State addresses.

13. Benson opposed Thompson's plans to control rising property taxes during his campaign for the superintendent's office but not the concept of controlling taxes in particular. Thompson's Secretary of Administration, James Klauser, was "encouraged," by Benson: "This is the first elected superintendent

to advocate cost controls" (Srb 1993). In an interesting sidelight, a news item from the Associated Press reporting Benson's comments on the governor's tax plan was titled "Benson Likes Senate School Plan" in Madison's moderate newspaper and "New School Chief: Senate Plan Flawed" in Madison's left-liberal newspaper; see *Wisconsin State Journal,* p. 3B, and *The* (Madison) *Capital Times,* p. 3A, both July 6, 1993.

14. See, for example, http://www.weac.org/BARGAIN/2004-05/qeoflu. htm.

15. The DPI was also the target of incessant attacks by Milwaukee Mayor John Norquist, who repeatedly called for the DPI to be dissolved because of its lack of attention (in his view) to the problems in Milwaukee schools. In one statement, Norquist said, "They're just shuffling the deck chairs on a sinking ship—and the DPI is a ship that ought to sink" (Milwaukee mayor rips DPI's plans 1994). On another occasion, Norquist said Benson "sort of specializes in standing in the schoolhouse door" and implied that he was racially insensitive by noting that "Milwaukee is much more racially diverse and integrated than Marshall," the village where Benson lived (Borsuk 1999). Late in his second term, Benson replied by issuing a terse memo claiming, "Mayor Norquist is contributing to the cycle of poverty not only with his attitude about education but by his failure to make the streets safe, to make quality housing available, to ensure children's health and well-being, and to secure employment opportunities that offer living wages for city residents" (Borsuk 1999). See also Mayor suggests scrapping DPI (1993).

Chapter 8

1. This difficulty is recognized and better elaborated on by Kingdon (2003). The "easy" cases are the occurrence of discrete and symbolic events such as bankruptcies, accidents, or other disasters.

2. There are exceptions. As Ringquist, Worsham, and Eisner (2003) note, complex policy issues are less attractive for elected politicians to address, even if salient. One example is monetary policy—if people "vote their pocketbooks," then the issue is salient—but the issue is also highly complex, so the Federal Reserve Board has a great deal of autonomy. See Kettl (1986) for a thorough study of the board's autonomy.

3. There could be more direct ways of measuring salience, such as newspaper coverage or public opinion polling. Unfortunately, state newspaper indexing is very limited before the mid-1990s, even in printed catalogs. Public opinion polling is also of limited value at the state level. I have included the number of substantive federal laws from the Policy Agendas Project (Jones, Wilkerson, and Baumgartner 2008) under the assumption that when education is salient at the national level, especially as this issue has long been a state and local issue, it is likely also legislatively salient in the states.

4. Groseclose and Stewart (1998) find an analogous effect for long-tenured members.

5. Some of these bills were vetoed, although the data are incomplete for Georgia. Its legislative journals run only during the legislative year, and the governor can act after the journals are closed. These activities sometimes made it into the next year's journals, but not always.

6. Time to passage is a poor measure because most bills are passed very close to the end of the session, regardless of their length or content.

7. The data are constructed so that legislators who leave the legislature entirely are not counted as "exits." I would postulate that their reasons for leaving a committee are different—an election loss, for example. That is, legislators only exit when they serve in the next term but do not serve on the education committee.

8. Data were compiled from state legislative journals. Online bill histories were available after 1995 in all three of these states, and I availed myself to them. Prior to 1995, I cross-checked bill indices with state legislative journals. I used the index terms "education," "education–department," "education–state," "education–state board," and "public instruction." I eliminated all bills pertaining to higher education, teacher retirement, school buses, drivers' licensing, and budget bills. While compiling histories from the journals, I also eliminated bills whose detailed summaries did not appear to directly reference education or the department of education. (For example, Georgia had a number of bills relating to the appropriate membership of county grand juries. They were indexed under education, because county or local superintendents were mentioned as participants by virtue of being a local official. These I excluded.)

9. The median is used because the previous analysis was done for individual legislators; this analysis is for the aggregate number of bills in a session.

10. This does not mean that I would expect them to support *federal* intrusion into state policy, as indeed they have not, as I noted in the first chapter.

11. Only somewhat at odds, however, because this analysis considers only education bills and does not consider bill passage, only their introduction.

12. I only use the first introduction of a bill. Although bills are referred to a committee in both houses, empirically, most bills in the second house were either reported immediately or never reported.

13. Georgia's legislative session is held between January and April every year. Both Ohio's and Wisconsin's sessions are essentially year-round. To ease cross-state comparisons, I expanded Georgia's calendar to be year-round by multiplying the number of days of each session to fill a calendar year.

14. Legislators who are not on the education committee in the session are coded as having zero tenure.

15. I accounted for the shorter schedule in the analysis, but legislators may still spend less relative time on bills in general. But it may also be that Georgia's situation is explained by a reversal of my argument: Georgia's department is highly autonomous and has great scope. Therefore, it is more able to dictate the terms of bills in the first place.

Chapter 9

1. School foundation support is excluded because it is formula driven. Although agencies may have a large say in changing that formula, it would be highly unusual that it would change in each budget.

2. Holtz-Eakin (1988) and Carter and Schap (1990) find no empirical budget changes in states with a line-item veto versus none, although Abney and Lauth (1997) report a survey of legislators who claim the line-item veto induces them to be fiscally responsible.

3. On biennial budgeting, see Fisher (1997). In Wisconsin, this situation reached an extreme. For example, the state's landmark and controversial school voucher program, charter school program, and inter-district open-enrollment programs were all created and later amended in the state budget, not in freestanding legislation. One measure of this tendency is the number of bills referred to the joint committee on finance. In the Wisconsin 1989 regular session, of the 67 education bills introduced, 16 were referred to the finance committee at some point. In 1991, 8 of 54 were; in 1993, 16 of 83 were. A cursory glance through the state budgets indicates that this tendency was not confined to education.

4. This measure is based on Krause (1996). Although both Wisconsin and Ohio agencies request monies for the off year, the state budget is only passed once, so there is little empirical justification for using anything other than the total biennial request and appropriations.

5. Wisconsin effectively only had one change of governor in this period rather than three (Ohio) or four (Georgia). The change was from Tony Earl to Tommy Thompson in 1986. Gov. Scott McCallum became governor after the 2001–2003 executive budget had been drafted under Thompson.

Chapter 10

1. Therefore, critics contend that national standards, such as the nationally administered National Assessment of Educational Progress, be imposed (Olson 2005).

2. Presciently because state officials had significant influence on the drafting of that act, although by no means were they the ultimate arbiters of its provisions. See Manna (2006).

3. Tennessee tried and abandoned the program—meant for the poor only—because it proved too expensive to operate.

4. On the Wisconsin Department of Natural Resources controversy, see Seely (2003) and Groups back bill on how DNR boss is picked (2003).

5. In some state legislatures, the problem is perhaps even worse. In Georgia, for example, most bills put upon passage in the last twenty-five years have passed by a unanimous vote, roll call or otherwise. Legislators opposed to a bill will not vote, making opposition to bills difficult to establish (is an abstention the same as opposition?) and providing cover for those supporting a

bill (because the vast majority of other legislators also supported the bill). This was true both of roll-call votes and voice votes; while there were exceptions, they were few in the House and even fewer in the Senate.

Appendix B

1. These data were compiled from Georgia's Official and Statistical Register and legislative journals; Ohio's Roster of the Members, Officers, Employees and List of Standing Committees of the Senate and House of Representatives; and Wisconsin's Blue Book. I used the data for the 1981 session to generate prior committee service, thus this session is not included in the observations.

2. A plot of Kaplan-Meier observed survival curves indicates that the predicted survival times from this estimation are good matches for the observed data.

3. This situation has irked some legislators for many years; in many sessions, a group of legislators has repeatedly introduced a bill to require zero-based budgeting to force agencies (and the governor) to justify every dollar spent.

4. See Gujarati (2003, chapter 22). Dickey-Fuller tests for individual state agency budget non-stationarity generally confirmed this choice at the 0.05 level.

References

Abney, Glenn, and Thomas P. Lauth. 1997. The item veto and fiscal responsibility. *Journal of Politics* 59 (August): 882–92.

Agranoff, Robert, and Michael McGuire. 2001. American federalism and the search for models of management. *Public Administration Review* 61 (November): 671–81.

Alt, James E., and Robert C. Lowry. 2000. A dynamic model of state budget outcomes under divided partisan government. *Journal of Politics* 62 (November): 1035–69.

Anton, Thomas J. 1989. *American federalism and public policy: How the system works.* New York: Random House.

Archer, Jeff. 2002. Governor's race tests power of merged teachers' union. *Education Week*, October 30.

Arnold, R. Douglas. 1990. *The logic of congressional action.* New Haven, CT: Yale University Press.

Ashford, Susan J., Nancy P. Rothbard, Sandy Kristin Piderit, and Jane E. Dutton. 1998. Out on a limb: The role of context and impression management in selling gender equity issues. *Administrative Science Quarterly* 43 (March): 23–57.

Augenblick, John. 1997. Letter to the Task Force on School Funding. June 10. Loose-leaf photocopy. Columbus, OH: Governor's Task Force on School Funding.

Axelrod, Robert. 1984. *The evolution of cooperation.* New York: Basic Books.

Bailyn, Bernard. 1960. *Education in the forming of American society.* New York: Vintage Books.

Bainbridge, William L., and Steven M. Sundre. 1997. School aid: Where's the logic? Columbus *Dispatch*, July 13, sec. B.

Balla, Steven J., and John R. Wright. 2001. Interest groups, advisory committees, and congressional control of the bureaucracy. *American Journal of Political Science* 45 (October): 799–812.

Barnes, teachers must mend their rift. 2000. Editorial. *Atlanta Journal-Constitution*, October 13, sec. A.

Barrilleaux, Charles, and Michael Berkman. 2003. Do governors matter? Budgeting rules and the politics of state policymaking. *Political Research Quarterly* 56 (December): 409–17.

Bawn, Kathleen. 1997. Choosing strategies to control the bureaucracy: Statutory constraints, oversight, and the committee system. *Journal of Law, Economics, and Organization* 131 (April): 101–26.

Beadie, Nancy. 2000. The limits of standardization and the importance of constituencies: Historical tensions in the relationship between state authority and local control. In *Balancing local control and state responsibility for K–12 education*, ed. Neil D. Theobald and Betty Malen, 47–91. Larchmont, NY: Eye on Education.

Beilke, Dustin. 2001. *Wisconsin Education Association Council: A History.* Madison: Wisconsin Education Association Council.

Bennett, Nigel, Christine Wise, Philip Woods, and Janet A. Harvey. 2003. *Distributed leadership.* Oxford, UK: National College for School Leadership.

Benson apologizes; vows no layoffs. 1993. *Wisconsin State Journal*, December 23, sec. B.

Benson, John. 1993. Memorandum to Tom Fonfara, July 14. Tommy G. Thompson Policy Staff Files, series 2836, box 2002/136, folder 15. Madison: Wisconsin Historical Society Archives.

Berman, Paul, and Milbrey W. McLaughlin. 1978. *Federal programs supporting educational change, vol. 8: Implementing and sustaining innovations.* Santa Monica, CA: Rand.

Bernknopf, Stan, and Joy Blount. 1989. An overview of GKAP. Memorandum to Paul Vail, Peyton Williams, and Billy Johnson, December 12. Associate State Superintendent Subject Files, series 12-09-089, box 31, folder 7. Atlanta: Georgia State Archives.

Berry, William D. 1990. The confusing case of budgetary incrementalism: Too many meanings for a single concept. *Journal of Politics* 52 (February): 167–96.

Binder, Sarah A. 1999. The dynamics of legislative gridlock, 1947–96. *American Political Science Review* 93 (September): 519–34.

Blackwell, J. Kenneth. 1997. Base state's funding on the individual child. Columbus *Dispatch*, August 20.

Blair, Julie. 1999. Wis. districts chafe under state's revenue limits. *Education Week*, January 27.

Blais, André, and Stéphane Dion. 1991. *Are bureaucrats budget maximizers?* Pittsburgh, PA: University of Pittsburgh Press.

Borsuk, Alan J. 1999. Benson, Norquist wage war of words. *Milwaukee Journal-Sentinel*, May 26, sec. A.

Bowling, C. J., and D. S. Wright. 1998. Change and continuity in state administration: Administration leadership across four decades. *Public Administration Review* 58 (September): 429–44.

Bowling, Cynthia J., Chung-Lae Cho, and Deil S. Wright. 2004. Establishing a continuum from minimizing to maximizing bureaucrats: State agency head preferences for governmental expansion—a typology of administrator growth postures, 1964–98. *Public Administration Review* 64 (July): 489–99.

Bowling, Cynthia J., and Margaret R. Ferguson. 2001. Divided government, interest representation, and policy differences: Competing explanations of gridlock in the fifty states. *Journal of Politics* 63 (February): 182–206.

Box-Steffensmeier, Janet M., Laura M. Arnold, and Christopher J. W. Zorn. 1997. The strategic timing of position taking in Congress: A study of the North American Free Trade Agreement. *American Political Science Review* 91 (June): 324–38.

Brace, Paul, and Daniel S. Ward. 1999. The institutionalized legislature and the rise of the antipolitics era. In *American state and local politics: Directions for the 21st century*, ed. Ronald E. Weber and Paul Brace, 71–96. New York: Chatham House.

Bradshaw, R. Scott. 1983. Letter to James W. Mullins, March 7. Associate State Superintendent Subject Files, series 12-09-089, box 25/1. Atlanta: Georgia State Archives.

Brehm, John, and Scott Gates. 1997. *Working, shirking, and sabotage: Bureaucratic response to a democratic public.* Ann Arbor: University of Michigan Press.

Bressers, H. T. A., and W. A. Rosenbaum. 2000. Innovation, learning, and environmental policy: Overcoming "a plague of uncertainties." *Policy Studies Journal* 28 (August): 523–69.

The Brickner affair. 1991. Ashtabula (Ohio) *Star Beacon*, June 4, sec. A.

Brickner loses case; fails to regain state board seat. 1991. Cleveland *Plain Dealer*, November 16, sec. A.

Brickner, Paul. 1991. Letter to George V. Voinovich, March 19, series 1.2, box 50, folder 11. George V. Voinovich Papers. Athens: Ohio University.

Bridges, Amy. 2003. Creating a place for themselves: Writing constitutions in Colorado, Arizona, and New Mexico. Presented at the American Political Development Brownbag, Department of Political Science, University of Wisconsin–Madison, October 16.

Brudney, Jeffrey L., and F. Ted Hebert. 1987. State agencies and their environments: Examining the influence of important external actors. *Journal of Politics* 49 (January): 186–206.

Budget fight with Celeste. 1987. Columbus *Dispatch*, February 25, sec. E.

Burden, Barry. 2007. *The personal roots of representation.* Princeton, NJ: Princeton University Press.

Büthe, Tim. 2002. Taking temporality seriously: Modeling history and the use of narratives as evidence. *American Political Science Review* 96 (September): 481–94.

Callahan, John P. 1946. *Education in Wisconsin.* Madison, WI: Department of Public Instruction.

Calvert, Randal, Mathew McCubbins, and Barry Weingast. 1989. A theory of political control and agency discretion. *American Journal of Political Science* 33 (September): 588–611.

Cameron, Charles. 2000. *Veto bargaining: Presidents and the politics of negative power.* New York: Cambridge University Press.

Candisky, Catherine, and Lee Leonard. 2003. School-funding suit laid to rest. Columbus *Dispatch*, May 17, sec. A.

Canes-Wrone, Brandice. 2003. Bureaucratic decisions and the composition of the lower courts. *American Journal of Political Science* 47 (April): 205–14.

Canon, David T. 1999. *Race, redistricting, and representation*. Chicago, IL: University of Chicago Press.

Canon, David T., and Charles Stewart, III. 2001. The evolution of the committee system in Congress. In *Congress reconsidered*, 7th ed., ed. Lawrence C. Dodd and Bruce I. Oppenheimer, 163–90. Washington, DC: Congressional Quarterly Press.

Carpenter, Daniel P. 2001a. *The forging of bureaucratic autonomy: Reputations, networks, and policy innovation in executive agencies, 1862–1928*. Princeton, NJ: Princeton University Press.

Carpenter, Daniel P. 2001b. The political foundations of bureaucratic autonomy: A response to Kernell. *Studies in American Political Development* 15 (Spring): 113–23.

Carpenter, Daniel P. 2004. Protection without capture: Product approval by a politically responsive, learning regulator. *American Political Science Review* 94 (November): 613–31.

Carter, John R., and David Schap. 1990. Line-item veto: Where is thy sting? *Journal of Economic Perspectives* 4 (Spring): 103–18.

Celeste says Walter turning districts against him. 1989. Columbus *Dispatch*, February 9, sec. A.

Celeste "slaps" State Board of Education. 1989. Columbus *Dispatch*, May 19, sec. D.

Chalfant, John. 1995. Senator, governor differ over State School Board. Associated Press, May 2.

Chubb, John E. 1985. The political economy of federalism. *American Political Science Review* 80 (December): 1003.

Cibulka, James G. 1996. Reforming public education in Wisconsin: Moving from bureaucracy to accountability. Report 7. Thiensville: Wisconsin Policy Research Institute.

Clark, James Ira. 1958. *Education in Wisconsin*. Madison: State Historical Society of Wisconsin.

Clarke, Wes. 1997. Budget requests and agency head selection methods. *Political Research Quarterly* 50 (June): 301–16.

Clarke, Wes. 1998. Divided government and budget conflict in the US states. *Legislative Studies Quarterly* 23 (February): 5–22.

Clinton, Bill. 1997. State of the Union address. January 31. http://www.cnn.com/2005/ALLPOLITICS/01/31/sotu.clinton1997.2/. Accessed October 10, 2006.

Cohen, Deborah L. 1989. Georgia to drop paper-and-pencil test for kindergarteners. *Education Week*, March 15.

Cohen, Jeffrey E. 1995. Presidential rhetoric and the public agenda. *American Journal of Political Science* 39 (February): 87–107.

Coleman, John. 1999. Unified government, divided government, and party responsiveness. *American Political Science Review* 93 (December): 821–36.

Colorado Department of Education. 1998. *Request budget.* Denver: Colorado
Department of Education.

Connecticut Attorney General. 2005. State sues federal government over illegal
unfunded mandates under No Child Left Behind Act, August 22. Press
release. Hartford: Connecticut Attorney General.

Cook, James F. 1987. Interview of Joe Frank Harris, August 5. Transcript.
Georgia Government Documentation Project, box A-1, folder 6. Atlanta:
Georgia State University.

Cooperative Educational Service Agency #7. 2002. School improvement meeting minutes, November 4. http://www.cesa7.k12.wi.us/schoolimprove/.
Accessed June 23, 2003.

Copland, Michael A. 2003. Leadership of inquiry: Building and sustaining capacity for school improvement. *Educational Evaluation and Policy Analysis*
25 (Winter): 375–95.

Cosgrove, Tim. 1991. Memorandum to Jean [Droste], March 25, series 1.2, box
50, folder 1, George V. Voinovich Papers. Athens: Ohio University.

Cox, Jerome C. 1967. *A history of school-system supervision in Georgia.* PhD diss.
Tallahassee: Florida State University.

Cremin, Lawrence A. 1980. *American education: The national experience,
1783–1876.* New York: Harper & Row.

Crow, Gary M., and Margaret Grogan. 2005. The development of leadership
thought and practice in the United States. In *The Sage handbook of educational leadership,* ed. Fenwick W. English, 362–79. Thousand Oaks,
CA: Sage.

Cumming, Doug. 1998a. Pasts enter school chief race. *Atlanta Journal-Constitution,* October 12, sec. B.

Cumming, Doug. 1998b. Read her lips: It's time for more phonics lessons.
Atlanta Journal-Constitution, May 16, sec. D.

Cumming, Doug. 1998c. Superintendent calls for rating Georgia schools. *Atlanta
Journal-Constitution,* December 9, sec. B.

Cumming, Doug. 1999a. Education panel likes Barnes' initiatives. *Atlanta
Journal-Constitution,* December 17, sec. A.

Cumming, Doug. 1999b. Schrenko cuts contact with AJC. *Atlanta Journal-
Constitution,* June 5, sec. F.

Cumming, Doug. 1999c. State School Board has Barnes majority. *Atlanta
Journal-Constitution,* May 8, sec. E.

Dantley, Michael E. 2005. Moral leadership. In *The Sage handbook of educational
leadership,* ed. Fenwick W. English, 34–46. Thousand Oaks, CA: Sage.

Davis, Otto A., M. A. H. Dempster, and Aaron Wildavsky. 1966. A theory of
the budgetary process. *American Political Science Review* 60 (September):
529–47.

Dehli, Joyce. 1993. Voters to decide education agenda. *Wisconsin State Journal,*
April 4, sec. C.

Dezhbakhsh, Hashem, Soumaya M. Tohamy, and Peter H. Aranson. 2003. A new approach for testing budgetary incrementalism. *Journal of Politics* 65 (May): 532–58.

Diegmueller, Karen. 2002. Unions labor to shape education policy. *Education Week*, October 30.

Dillon, Sam. 2005. Facing state protests, U.S. offers more flexibility on school rules. *New York Times*, April 8, sec. A.

Dometrius, Nelson C. 1999. Governors: Their heritage and their future. In *American state and local politics: Directions for the 21st century*, ed. Ronald E. Weber and Paul Brace, 38–70. New York: Chatham House.

Dorsher, Mike. 1993a. Benson requests DPI audit. *Wisconsin State Journal*, April 17, sec. D.

Dorsher, Mike. 1993b. DPI audit finds supervisory staff up 45%. *Wisconsin State Journal*, October 27, sec. D.

Dorsher, Mike. 1993c. DPI chief conducts retreat. *Wisconsin State Journal*, July 10, sec. D.

Dorsher, Mike. 1993d. DPI reorganization uses team approach. *Wisconsin State Journal*, December 18, sec. B.

Drezner, Daniel W. 2000. Ideas, bureaucratic politics, and the crafting of foreign policy. *American Journal of Political Science* 44 (October): 733–49.

Driscoll, Bill, and Howard Fleeter. 2000. Reforming education funding in Ohio: Analysis of proposed responses to *DeRolph*. Columbus, OH: Education Tax Policy Institute.

Droste, Jean. 1991a. Handwritten notes on potential state superintendent hires for Ohio Governor George Voinovich [April], series 1.2, box 50, folder 1. George V. Voinovich Papers. Athens: Ohio University.

Droste, Jean. 1991b. Letter to Judi Miller, Kansas State Board of Education, September 6, series 1.2, box 49, folder 7. George V. Voinovich Papers. Athens: Ohio University.

Drummond, Suzanne Ernst. 2000. Deja vu: The status of school funding in Ohio after *DeRolph II. University of Cincinnati Law Review* 68: 435–61.

Durfee-Hidalgo, Janet. 1990. Memorandum to governor's staff, November 30, series 5.1, box 1R, folder 12. George V. Voinovich Papers. Athens: Ohio University.

Economic History Services. 2002. What was the GDP then? EH.net. Accessed February 2, 2002.

Education battlefield: School Board's targeting of State Superintendent and browbeating of her subordinates show that the Board's power needs to be redefined. 2000. Editorial. *Atlanta Journal-Constitution*, October 16, sec. A.

Edwards, George C., III. 1989. *At the margins: Presidential leadership of Congress.* New Haven, CT: Yale University Press.

Edwards, George C., III, Andrew Barrett, and Jeffrey Peake. 1997. The legislative impact of divided government. *American Journal of Political Science* 41 (April): 545–63.

Edwards, George C., III, and B. Dan Wood. 1999. Who influences whom? The president and the public agenda. *American Political Science Review* 93 (June): 327–44.

Elmore, Richard F. 1996. Getting to scale with good educational practice. *Harvard Educational Review* 66 (Spring): 1–25.

Elmore, Richard F. 2000. *Building a new structure for school leadership.* Washington, DC: The Albert Shanker Institute.

Epstein, David, and Sharyn O'Halloran. 1999. *Delegating powers: A transaction cost politics approach to policy making under separate powers.* New York: Cambridge University Press.

Farney, Dennis. 2004. Insufficient funds. *Governing* 18 (December): 26–29.

Fessler, Diana M. 1996. Letter to George V. Voinovich, August 8, series 1.2, box 48, folder 15. George V. Voinovich Papers. Athens: Ohio University.

Fiorina, Morris P. 1994. Divided government in the American states: A byproduct of legislative professionalism? *American Political Science Review* 88 (June): 304–16.

Fiorina, Morris P. 1997. Professionalism, realignment, and representation. *American Political Science Review* 91 (June): 156–62.

Firm with Grover tie loses state contract. 1993. Madison (Wisconsin) *Capital Times*, August 27, sec. B.

Fisher, Louis. 1997. Biennial budgeting in the federal government. *Public Budgeting and Finance* 17 (September): 87–97.

Fonfara, Tom. 1993. Handwritten meeting notes for meeting with John Benson, April 13, series 2836, box 2002/136, folder 15. Tommy G. Thompson Personal Staff Files. Madison: Wisconsin Historical Society Archives.

Foster, John C., and William C. Magnum Jr. 1989. Letter to Governor Joe Frank Harris, Comments on the proposed policy and guidelines for the first grade readiness assessment, February 8, series 012-02-027, box 100, folder 3. Georgia Superintendent's Subject Files. Atlanta: Georgia State Archives.

Frederickson, H. George, and Kevin B. Smith. 2003. *The public administration primer.* Boulder, CO: Westview Press.

Gallagher, Karen. 1990. Voinovich education agenda, Memorandum to Jean Droste, November 30, series 1.2, box 48, folder 5. George V. Voinovich Papers. Athens: Ohio University.

General Assembly of Ohio. 1876. *A history of education in the state of Ohio: A centennial volume.* Columbus, OH: General Assembly.

Georgia Department of Education. 1970. *100 years of public education.* Atlanta: Georgia Department of Education.

Georgia Department of Education. 1987. Staff meeting minutes, October 2, series 012-09-089, box 29, folder 32. Georgia Assistant Superintendent's Subject Files. Atlanta: Georgia State Archives.

Georgia Department of Education. 1988. Internal memorandum from Dr. Dixon to staff [winter 1988 or spring 1989], series 12-09-089, box 31, folder 7. Georgia Assistant Superintendent's Subject Files. Atlanta: Georgia State Archives.

Georgia Department of Education. 2005. Georgia kindergarten assessment program-revised (GKAP-R), October 7. Brochure. Atlanta: Georgia Department of Education.

Georgia Family Connection Partnership. 2005. Family Connection Partnership. http://www.gafcp.org. Accessed July 15, 2005.

Georgia House of Representatives. 1982. *Report of the subcommittee on educational accountability of the House Education Committee.* December. Atlanta: Georgia House of Representatives.

Georgia Office of Planning and Budget. 2000. *Budget report, fiscal 2001.* Atlanta: Georgia Office of Planning and Budget.

Georgia Office of Planning and Budget. 2001. *Budget report, fiscal 2002.* Atlanta: Georgia Office of Planning and Budget.

Gerring, John. 2004. What is a case study, and what is it good for? *American Political Science Review* 98 (May): 341–54.

Gerschenkron, Alexander. 1962. *Economic backwardness in historical perspective.* Cambridge, MA: Harvard University Press.

Glasser, William. 1990. *The quality school.* New York: HarperCollins.

Goff, John. 1995a. Letter to the Superintendent Search Committee, June 23, series 5.1, box 1U. George V. Voinovich Papers. Athens: Ohio University.

Goff, John. 1995b. Memorandum to George V. Voinovich, July 17, series 5.1, box 1U. George V. Voinovich Papers. Athens: Ohio University.

Goff, John. 1997. Letter to Jo Ann Davidson, June 4. http://www.fessler.com/SBE/goff.htm. Accessed April 10, 2004.

Goff steps up. 1995. Editorial. Akron (Ohio) *Beacon Journal,* August 17, sec. A.

Goff, John, and Jennifer L. Sheets. 1997. Letter to Rep. Ben Espy, August 29, series 5.1, box 1U, folder 7. George V. Voinovich Papers. Athens: Ohio University.

Gold, Deborah L. 1988. Georgia to test kindergarteners for promotion. *Education Week,* March 2.

Gormley, William T. 2006. Money and mandates: The politics of intergovernmental conflict. *Publius* 36 (Fall): 523–40.

Governor's Task Force on Education. 1991. Model for the future: An organization study of the Ohio Department of Education. August. Columbus, OH: Governor's Task Force on Education.

Gray, Virginia, and David Lowery. 2004. Bias in the heavenly chorus: Interests in society and before government. *Journal of Theoretical Politics* 16 (January): 5–30.

Greenleaf, Robert K. 2002. *Servant leadership.* Mahwah, NJ: Paulist Press.

Greer, John W. 1982. Letter to Charles McDaniel, n.d. [received May 19], series 012-02-027, box 72, folder 6. Georgia Superintendent Subject Files. Atlanta: Georgia State Archives.

Groseclose, Tim, and Charles Stewart, III. 1998. The value of committee seats in the house, 1947–91. *American Journal of Political Science* 42 (April): 453–74.

Groups back bill on how DNR boss is picked. 2003. *Wisconsin State Journal*, April 23.

Grover denies influence peddling. 1993. *Capital Times* (Madison, WI), April 16, sec. A.

Grover, Herbert J. 1981a. Letter to all assembly members and senate education committee, June 8, series 651, box 2001/111, folder 3/1. Correspondence of the State Superintendent. Madison: Wisconsin Historical Society Archives.

Grover, Herbert J. 1981b. Letter to all senators and the assembly education committee members, October 1, series 651, box 2001/111, folder 3/2. Correspondence of the State Superintendent. Madison: Wisconsin Historical Society Archives.

Grover, Herbert J. 1981c. Letter to Ed Jackamonis, September 28, series 651, box 2001/111, folder 3/1. Correspondence of the State Superintendent. Madison: Wisconsin Historical Society Archives.

Grover, Herbert J. 1982a. Letter to G. W. Ison, [early 1982], series 651, box 2001/111, folder 2/16. Correspondence of the State Superintendent. Madison: Wisconsin Historical Society Archives.

Grover, Herbert J. 1982b. Letter to Milton G. Kier, July 29, series 651, box 2001/111, folder 2/14. Correspondence of the State Superintendent. Madison: Wisconsin Historical Society Archives.

Grover, Herbert J. 1983a. Letter to Calvin Potter, September 19, series 651, box 2001/111, folder 3/52/B6, F5. Correspondence of the State Superintendent. Madison: Wisconsin Historical Society Archives.

Grover, Herbert J. 1983b. Letter to C. E. Hierlmeier, November 30, series 651, box 2001/111, folder 1/2. Correspondence of the State Superintendent. Madison: Wisconsin Historical Society Archives.

Grover, Herbert J. 1983c. Letter to David Zweifel, September 14, series 651, box 2001/111, folder 3/12. Correspondence of the State Superintendent. Madison: Wisconsin Historical Society Archives.

Grover, Herbert J. 1983d. Letter to Senator Rodney C. Moen, March 1, series 651, box 2001/111, folder 3/1. Correspondence of the State Superintendent. Madison: Wisconsin Historical Society Archives.

Grover, Herbert J. 1984a. Letter to Barbara Ulichny, December 26, series 651, box 2001/111, folder 3/9. Correspondence of the State Superintendent. Madison: Wisconsin Historical Society Archives.

Grover, Herbert J. 1984b. Letter to John D. Kammerud, January 9, series 651, box 2001/111, folder 1/1. Correspondence of the State Superintendent. Madison: Wisconsin Historical Society Archives.

Grover, Herbert J. 1984c. Letter to Joseph Czarnezki, November 5, series 651, box 2001/111, folder 3/9. Correspondence of the State Superintendent. Madison: Wisconsin Historical Society Archives.

Grover, Herbert J. 1984d. Letter to Linda K. Jatzo, January 9, series 651, box 2001/111, folder 1/1. Correspondence of the State Superintendent. Madison: Wisconsin Historical Society Archives.

Grover, Herbert J. 1984e. Letter to Tom Loftus, February 10, series 651, box 2001/111, folder 3/7. Correspondence of the State Superintendent. Madison: Wisconsin Historical Society Archives.

Grover, Herbert J. 1985a. Letter to Bill Heath, February 1, series 651, box 2001/111, folder 3/12. Correspondence of the State Superintendent. Madison: Wisconsin Historical Society Archives.

Grover, Herbert J. 1985b. Letter to Richard A. Shoemaker, January 9, series 651, box 2001/111, folder 3/10. Correspondence of the State Superintendent. Madison: Wisconsin Historical Society Archives.

Grover, Herbert J. 1985c. Teacher preparation standards exemplify hearing process. *Education Forward* (December): 2.

Gujarati, Damodar N. 2003. *Basic econometrics.* Boston, MA: McGraw-Hill.

Haass, Joanne M. 2003. Education students gain broader vision of their roles, November 10. http://www.weac.org/Resource/2003-04/nov03/teachered2.htm. Accessed October 18, 2005.

Hall, Andy. 1997. School standards get fine-tuning; McCallum says out-of-state experts will edit the standards. *Wisconsin State Journal,* August 3, sec. C.

Hall, Peter A. 1986. *Governing the economy: The politics of state intervention in Britain and France.* New York: Oxford University Press.

Halperin, Samuel. 1975. *Essays on federal education policy.* Washington, DC: Institute for Educational Leadership, George Washington University.

Hansen, John Mark. 1991. *Gaining access: Congress and the farm lobby, 1919–1981.* Chicago, IL: University of Chicago Press.

Harris, Joe Frank. 1985. Letter to Franklin Shumake, July 18, series 001-01-005, box 110, folder 6. Governor's Subject Files. Atlanta: Georgia State Archives.

Harris, Joe Frank. 1988. Form letter to respond to QBE paperwork complaints, February 28, series 001-01-005, box 200, folder 40. Governor's Subject Files. Atlanta: Georgia State Archives.

Harp, Lonnie. 1995. Wis. court to decide balance of policy power. *Education Week,* December 13.

Haass, Richard N. 1999. *The bureaucratic entrepreneur.* Washington, DC: Brookings Institution Press.

Hayes, Paul C. 1955. *The influence of the Ohio Education Association upon the Public School Foundation Program in the state of Ohio from its inception until 1955.* PhD diss. Ottawa, Ontario, Canada: University of Ottawa.

Head, John. 1998. Education needs another Isakson. *Atlanta Journal-Constitution,* November 17, sec. A.

Heclo, Hugh. 1977. Political executives and the Washington bureaucracy. *Political Science Quarterly* 92 (Fall): 395–424.

Heinz, John P., Edward O. Laumann, Robert L. Nelson, and Robert H. Salisbury. 1993. *The hollow core: Private interests in national policy making.* Cambridge, MA: Harvard University Press.

Hetzel, Mark. 1987. Career ladder highlights teacher incentive program in Waunakee. *Education Forward* (January): 13.

Hills Jr., Roderick M. 1999. Dissecting the state: The use of federal law to free state and local officials from state legislatures' control. *Michigan Law Review* 97 (March): 1201–86.

Hoff, David J. 2002. States revise the meaning of "proficient." *Education Week,* October 9.

Hogan, James. 1998. School funding . . . not so elementary: Determining the constitutionality of Ohio school funding legislation after *DeRolph v. State,* 77 N.E.2d 733 (Ohio 1997). *University of Cincinnati Law Review* 67: 323–62.

Holtz-Eakin, Douglas. 1988. The line-item veto and public sector budgets: Evidence from the states. *Journal of Public Economics* 36: 269–92.

Honig, Meredith I. 2006. Street-level bureaucracy revisited: Frontline district central-office administrators as boundary spanners in education policy implementation. *Educational Evaluation and Policy Analysis* 28 (Winter): 357–83.

Howie, Stephen. 1994. DPI changes attitude on charter idea. Madison (Wisconsin) *Capital Times,* May 9, sec. A.

Ingraham, Patricia W., Jessica E. Sowa, and Donald P. Moynihan. 2004. Linking dimensions of public sector leadership to performance. In *The art of governance,* ed. Patricia Ingraham and Laurence Lynn, 152–70. Washington, DC: Georgetown University Press.

IOX Assessment Associates. 1989. Development of a kindergarten assessment program for the Georgia Department of Education, April 10, memorandum, series 12-09-089, box 31, folder 7. Assistant Superintendent's Subject Files. Atlanta: Georgia State Archives.

Jacobson, Linda. 1999. Outspoken state chief in Georgia still an "outsider" in second term. *Education Week,* June 16.

Jacobson, Linda. 2002. Parting words. *Education Week,* October 23.

Jennings, John F. 1998. *Why national standards and tests? Politics and the quest for better schools.* Thousand Oaks, CA: Sage.

Johnson, Ronald N., and Gary D. Libecap. 1994. *The federal civil service system and the problem of bureaucracy.* Chicago, IL: University of Chicago Press.

Jones, Bryan D., James L. True, and Frank R. Baumgartner. 1997. Does incrementalism stem from political consensus or from institutional gridlock? *American Journal of Political Science* 41 (October): 1319–39.

Jones, Bryan D., John Wilkerson, and Frank R. Baumgartner. 2008. Policy agendas project. http://www.policyagendas.org. Accessed January 9, 2008.

Jones, Louann. 1988. Letter to Gov. Joe Frank Harris, February 7, series 001-01-005, box 200, folder 40. Governor's Subject Files. Atlanta: Georgia State Archives.

Jorgenson, Lloyd P. 1956. *The founding of public education in Wisconsin.* Madison: State Historical Society of Wisconsin.

Judicial lawmaking high court wreaks havoc on Ohio schools. 1997. Editorial. Columbus *Dispatch,* March 25, sec. A.

Keesecker, Ward W. 1951. *State boards of education and chief state school officers: Their status and legal powers.* Bulletin 1950, no. 12. Washington, DC: Federal Security Agency, Office of Education.

Keller, Bess. 2005. NEA files "No Child Left Behind" lawsuit. *Education Week,* April 20.

Kellett, William R. 1970. Preliminary report of the governor's commission on education. Madison, WI: Governor's Commission on Education.

Kelley, Tim. 1993. School choice fails on grades. *Wisconsin State Journal,* December 23, sec. B.

Kerchner, Charles Taylor, and Douglas E. Mitchell. 1988. *The changing idea of a teachers' union.* London: The Falmer Press.

Kernell, Samuel. 2001. Rural free delivery as a critical test of alternative models of American political development. *Studies in American Political Development* 15 (Spring): 103–12.

Kernell, Samuel. 2006. *Going public.* Washington, DC: CQ Press.

Kernell, Samuel, and Michael P. McDonald. 1999. Congress and America's political development: The transformation of the Post Office from patronage to service. *American Journal of Political Science* 43 (July): 792–811.

Kessler, Daniel, and Keith Krehbiel. 1996. Dynamics of cosponsorship. *American Political Science Review* 90 (September): 555–66.

Kettl, Donald F. 1986. *Leadership at the fed.* New Haven, CT: Yale University Press.

Kettl, Donald F. 2007. *System under stress.* 2d ed. Washington, DC: CQ Press.

Kiel, Joyce L. 2002. Teacher licenses and teacher education program approval. LCA 02-2. Madison: Wisconsin Legislative Council.

Kiewiet, D. Roderick, and Mathew D. McCubbins. 1991. *The logic of delegation: Congressional parties and the appropriations process.* Chicago, IL: University of Chicago Press.

Kingdon, John W. 2003. *Agendas, alternatives, and public policies.* 2d ed. New York: Longman.

Kotter, John P. 1990. What leaders really do. *Harvard Business Review* 68 (May): 103–11.

Krause, George A. 1994. Federal reserve policy decision making: Political and bureaucratic influences. *American Journal of Political Science* 38 (February): 123–44.

Krause, George A. 1996. The institutional dynamics of policy administration: Bureaucratic influence over securities regulation. *American Journal of Political Science* 40 (November): 1083–1121.

Krause, George A., David E. Lewis, and James W. Douglas. 2006. Political appointments, civil service systems, and bureaucratic competence: Organizational balancing and executive branch revenue forecasts in the American states. *American Journal of Political Science* 50 (July): 770–87.

Krause, George A., and J. W. Douglas. 2005. Institutional design versus reputational effects on bureaucratic performance: Evidence from U.S. government macroeconomic and fiscal projections. *Journal of Public Administration Research and Theory* 15 (April): 281–306.

Krehbiel, Keith. 1998. *Pivotal politics: A unified theory of U.S. lawmaking.* Chicago, IL: University of Chicago Press.

Kreuger, Clifford W. 1981. Letter to Robert P. Moser, July 3, series 651, box 2001/111, folder 3/1. Correspondence of the State Superintendent. Madison: Wisconsin Historical Society Archives.

LaMorte, Michael W., and Robert B. Meadows. 1978. *Financing the public schools in Georgia: 1777–1978.* Athens: University of Georgia College of Education.

League of Women Voters of the Cincinnati Area. 2005. Funding public education in Ohio: Where are we in the new century? January 31. http://www.lwvcincinnati.org/publications/FundingPublicEduInOhio.html. Accessed March 8, 2006.

Leech, Beth L. 2002. Asking questions: Techniques for semi-structured interviews. *PS* 35 (October): 665–68.

Leithwood, Kenneth. 1992. The move toward transformational leadership. *Educational Leadership* 49 (February): 8–12.

Let George do it. 1995. Cincinnati *Enquirer*, April 21, sec. A.

Lewis, David E. 2002. The politics of agency termination: Confronting the myth of agency immortality. *Journal of Politics* 64 (February): 89–107.

Light, Paul C. 1995. *Thickening government: Federal hierarchy and the diffusion of accountability.* Washington, DC: Brookings Institution.

Lindsay, Drew. 1994. Chief's race puts history to test in Ga. *Education Week,* October 19.

Lindsay, Drew. 1995. Citing politics, 2 states pull out of chiefs' group. *Education Week*, September 13.

Lipsky, Michael. 1980. *Street-level bureaucracy: Dilemmas of the individual in public services.* New York: Russell Sage Foundation.

Lohmann, Susanne. 1998. An information rationale for the power of special interests. *American Political Science Review* 92 (December): 809–28.

Lost in paperwork, teachers lack time to help children. 1989. *Atlanta Journal-Constitution,* January 22, sec. E.

Loupe, Diane. 1997. Schrenko's PTA remark prompts outcry. *Atlanta Journal-Constitution,* September 19, sec C.

Loupe, Diane, and Lucy Soto. 1997. Senate passes weaker version of Schrenko school safety bill. *Atlanta Journal-Constitution*, March 15, sec. C.

Lowery, David, and Virginia Gray. 1995. The population ecology of Gucci Gulch, or the natural regulation of interest group numbers in the American states. *American Journal of Political Science* 39 (February): 1–29.

Lowry, Robert C., James E. Alt, and Karen E. Ferree. 1998. Fiscal policy outcomes and electoral accountability in American states. *American Political Science Review* 92 (December): 759–74.

Lusi, Susan. 1997. *The role of state departments of education in complex school reform.* New York: Teachers College Press.

Magnum, William C., and John C. Foster. 1989. Letter to Superintendent Werner Rogers, September 21, series 012-02-027, box 100, folder 3. Georgia Superintendent's Subject Files. Atlanta: Georgia State Archives.

Maher, Marianne. 1991. Education should be Ohio's top priority. *OSBA Journal* (May): 13, 22.

Majone, Giandomenico. 1989. *Evidence, argument, and persuasion in the policy process.* New Haven, CT: Yale University Press.

Malen, Betty. 2001. Generating interest in interest groups. *Educational Policy* 15 (January): 168–86.

Manna, Paul. 2003. *Federalism, agenda setting, and the development of federal education policy, 1965–2001.* PhD diss. University of Wisconsin, Madison.

Manna, Paul. 2006. *School's in: Federalism and the national education agenda.* Washington, DC: Georgetown University Press.

Manna, Paul, and Amanda Guthrie. 2008. Leadership continuity and educational performance in the American states. Paper presented at the annual meeting of the Midwest Political Science Association, Chicago, April 3–6.

March, James G. 1999. *The pursuit of organizational intelligence.* Malden, MA: Blackwell.

Marsden, George E. 2003. *Jonathan Edwards: A life.* New Haven, CT: Yale University Press.

Mathis, Nancy. 1989a. Battle lines are drawn in Wisconsin over proposed property-tax change. *Education Week,* January 11.

Mathis, Nancy. 1989b. Escalating "brick-and-mortar" cost: The problem nobody wants. *Education Week,* March 1.

Mayers, Jeff. 1994. Benson defends GED drop. *Wisconsin State Journal,* August 24, sec. D.

Mayhew, David B. 1974. *Congress: The electoral connection.* New Haven, CT: Yale University Press.

Mayhew, David B. 1991. *Divided we govern: Party control, lawmaking, and investigations, 1946–1990.* New Haven, CT: Yale University Press.

Mayor suggests scrapping DPI. 1993. *Wisconsin State Journal,* September 21, sec. D.

Mazzoni, Tim. 2000. State politics and school reform: The first decade of the "educational excellence" movement. In *Balancing local control and state responsibility in K–12 education,* ed. N. D. Theobald and B. Malen, 147–96. Larchmont, NY: Eye on Education.

McAtee, Andres, Susan Webb Yackee, and David Lowery. 2003. Reexamining the dynamic model of dynamic partisan government. *Journal of Politics* 65 (May): 477–90.

McCarty, Nolan, and Lawrence S. Rothenberg. 1996. Commitment and the campaign contribution contract. *American Journal of Political Science* 40 (August): 872–904.

McCubbins, Mathew, Roger Noll, and Barry Weingast. 1989. Structure and process, politics and policy: Administrative arrangements and the political control of agencies. *Virginia Law Review* 3: 243–77.

McCubbins, Mathew, and Thomas Schwartz. 1984. Police patrols vs. fire alarms. *American Journal of Political Science* 28 (March): 165–79.

McCubbins, Mathew D. 1985. The legislative design of regulatory structure. *American Journal of Political Science* 29 (November): 721–48.

McDade, Phil. 1993. ACT's controversial reign ends over statewide student testing. *Wisconsin State Journal,* August 27, sec. C.

McDaniel, Charles. 1980. Letter to George Busbee, November 24, series 12-09-089, box 25, folder 1. Assistant State Superintendent Subject Files. Atlanta: Georgia State Archives.

McDaniel, Charles. 1982. Letter to all senators and representatives, December 16, series 012-02-027, box 72, folder 6. Georgia Superintendent's Subject Files. Atlanta: Georgia State Archives.

McDaniel, Charles. 1983. Memorandum to members of Education Review Commission [for QBE], June 23, series 012-02-027, box 81, folder 19. Superintendent's Subject Files. Atlanta: Georgia State Archives.

McDaniel, Charles. 1985. Letter to Commissioner Larry L. Clark, September 30, series 012-02-027, box 87, folder 9. Superintendent's Subject Files. Atlanta: Georgia State Archives.

McDermott, Kathryn A. 1999. *Controlling public education*. Lawrence: University Press of Kansas.

Measure accountability with state examinations. 1999. Editorial. *Atlanta Journal-Constitution*, July 30, sec. A.

Miller, Zell. 1998. *Listen to this voice: Selected speeches of governor Zell Miller.* Macon, GA: Mercer University Press.

Mills, C. Wright. 1958. The structure of power in American society. *British Journal of Sociology* 9 (March): 29–41.

Milwaukee mayor rips DPI's plans. 1994. Madison (Wisconsin) *Capital Times*, April 6, sec. B.

Mintrom, Michael. 2000. *Policy entrepreneurs and school choice*. Washington, DC: Georgetown University Press.

Moe, Terry M. 1989. The politics of bureaucratic structure. In *Can the government govern?*, ed. John E. Chubb and Paul E. Peterson, 267–329. Washington, DC: Brookings Institution Press.

Moen, Rodney C. 1983. Letter to Herbert J. Grover, February 27, series 651, box 2001/111, folder 3/1. Correspondence of the State Superintendent. Madison: Wisconsin Historical Society Archives.

Mooney, Christopher. 1994. Measuring U.S. state legislative professionalism: An evaluation of five indices. *State and Local Government Review* 26 (Spring): 70–71.

Morphet, Edgar L., and David L. Jesser. 1970. *Emerging state responsibilities for education*. Denver, CO: Improving State Leadership in Education.

Munger, Michael. 1988. Allocation of desirable committee assignments: Extended queues versus committee expansion. *American Journal of Political Science* 32 (March): 317–44.

Murphy, Jerome T. 1974. *State education agencies and discretionary funds*. Lexington, MA: Lexington Books.

Murphy, Jerome T. 1976. Title V of ESEA: The impact of discretionary funds on state educational bureaucracies. In *Social program implementation*, ed. W. Williams and Robert F. Elmore, 77–100. New York: Academic Press.

Nathan, Joe. 1996. *Charter schools: Creating hope and opportunity for American education*. San Francisco, CA: Jossey-Bass.

National Association of State Boards of Education. 2007. *State education governance at-a-glance*. Alexandria, VA: National Association of State Boards of Education.

National Governors' Association. 1986. Time for results: The governors' 1991 report on education. Washington, DC: National Governors' Association.

Neustadt, Richard E. 1991. *Presidential power and the modern presidents: The politics of leadership*. New York: Free Press.

Nicholson, Stephen P., Gary M. Segura, and Nathan D. Woods. 2002. Presidential approval and the mixed blessing of divided government. *Journal of Politics* 64 (August): 701–20.

Nicholson-Crotty, Sean, Nick A. Theobald, and B. Dan Wood. 2006. Fiscal federalism and budgetary tradeoffs in the American states. *Political Research Quarterly* 59 (June): 313–21.

Niskanen, William A. 1971. *Bureaucracy and representative government*. New York: Aldine-Atherton.

Niskanen, William A. 1975. Bureaucrats and politicians. *Journal of Law and Economics* 18: 617–43.

News updates. 1991. *Education Week*, November 6.

Newsome, Glenn. 1982. Letter to Charles McDaniel, March 30, series 012-02-027, box 72, folder 6. Superintendent's Subject Files. Atlanta: Georgia State Archives.

O'Brien, Molly Townes. 2003. At the intersection of public policy and private process: Court-ordered mediation and the remedial process in school funding litigation. *Ohio State Journal on Dispute Resolution* 18: 391–438.

O'Brien, Thomas V. 1999. *The politics of race and schooling: Public education in Georgia, 1900–1961*. Lanham, MA: Lexington Books.

Odden, Allan R., and Lawrence O. Picus. 2003. *School finance: A policy perspective*. New York: McGraw-Hill.

Ogawa, Rodney T., and Steven T. Bossert. 1995. Leadership as an organizational quality. *Educational Administration Quarterly* 31 (May): 224–43.

Ohio Coalition for Equity and Adequacy of School Funding. 1997. Components of school funding reform. April. Brochure. Columbus: Ohio Coalition for Equity and Adequacy.

Ohio Department of Education. 1995. Derivation of the cost of an adequate basic education. November. Columbus: Ohio Department of Education.

Ohio Department of Education. 1997. State education leaders respond to supreme court's decision in school-funding case. March 24. Press release. Columbus: Ohio Department of Education.

Ohio General Assembly. 1876. *A history of education in the state of Ohio*. Columbus: Ohio General Assembly.

Ohio General Assembly. 1990. Testimony to the Select Committee to Study Ohio's School Foundation Program and the Senate School Finance Task Force by William L. Phillis, February 1, Columbus, OH.

Ohio Office of Budget and Management. 1979. *Executive budget*. Columbus: Ohio Office of Budget and Management.

Ohio Office of Budget and Management. 1997. *Executive budget.* Columbus: Ohio Office of Budget and Management.

Ohio State Board of Education. 1989. *Milestones: A history of the state board of education of Ohio, 1956–1989.* Columbus: Ohio State Board of Education.

Olson, Lynn. 1997. Veterans of state takeover battles tell a cautionary tale. *Education Week,* February 12.

Olson, Lynn. 2005. Nationwide standards eyed anew. *Education Week,* December 7.

Orr, Dorothy. 1950. *A history of education in Georgia.* Chapel Hill: University of North Carolina Press.

Outcomes: Ousted. 1994. Editorial. *Akron Beacon Journal,* January 17.

Palagyi, Paul. 1995. Memorandum to Tom Needles, June 8, series 5.1, box 1U. George V. Voinovich Papers. Athens: Ohio University.

Patzer, Conrad E. 1924. *Public education in Wisconsin.* Madison, WI: Department of Public Instruction.

Peters, B. Guy. 2001. *The future of governing: Four emerging models.* 2d ed. Lawrence: University Press of Kansas.

Pfeffer, Jeffrey. 1977. The ambiguity of leadership. *Academy of Management Review* 2 (January): 104–12.

Pfeffer, Jeffrey, and Gerald Salancik. 1978. *The design and management of externally controlled organizations.* New York: Harper & Row.

Phillis, William L. 1991. William L. Phillis: Education leader for the '90's. (April?). Pamphlet published by author.

Pierson, Paul. 1994. *Dismantling the welfare state?* New York: Cambridge University Press.

Pious, Richard M. 1996. *The presidency.* Needham Heights, MA: Allyn & Bacon.

Polsby, Nelson. 1968. The institutionalization of the U.S. House of Representatives. *American Political Science Review* 62 (March): 145–53.

Porter, Foster B., N. E. Masterson, W. W. Clark, et al. 1948. Report of the commission on improvement of the educational system. Madison, WI: Commission on Improvement of the Educational System.

Posner, Paul L. 1998. *The politics of unfunded mandates: Whither federalism?* Washington, DC: Georgetown University Press.

Potter, Calvin. 1983. Letter to Herbert J. Grover, August 22, series 651, box 2001/111, folder 3/52/B6, F5. Correspondence of the State Superintendent. Madison: Wisconsin Historical Society Archives.

Price, Rita. 1998. The great debate. Columbus *Dispatch,* April 26, sec. A.

Puckett, Patti. 1999. School board fears plague of suits over Bible classes. *Atlanta Journal-Constitution,* August 6, sec. A.

Ramage, Stephanie. 1997. School of hard knocks: Linda Schrenko battles with school board. (Atlanta) *Creative Loafing,* January 4.

Ravitch, Diane. 1974. *The great school wars.* New York: Basic Books.

Ravitch, Diane. 1983. *The troubled crusade: American education, 1945–1980.* New York: Basic Books.

Ravitch, Diane. 2000. *Left back: A century of failed school reforms.* New York: Simon & Schuster.

Ray, Kenneth Clark. 1943. *The evolution and the reorganization of the Ohio State Department of Education.* PhD diss., Ohio State University, Columbus.

Redmond-Jones, Donna, and Betty Malen. 2002. Sources of victory, seeds of defeat: Linking enactment politics and implementation developments. In *Theory and research in educational administration,* vol. 1, ed. Wayne K. Hoy and Cecil Miskel, 41–76. Greenwich, CT: Information Age Publishing.

Rice, Bradley. 1988. Interview of Terrell Star, August 1, box B-8, folder 6. Georgia Government Documentation Project. Atlanta: Georgia State University Archives.

Rigdon, Mark E. 1995. *The business of education reform.* PhD diss., University of Wisconsin, Madison.

Ringquist, Evan J. 1995. Political control and policy impact in EPA's Office of Water Quality. *American Journal of Political Science* 39 (May): 336–63.

Ringquist, Evan J., Jeff Worsham, and Marc Allen Eisner. 2003. Salience, complexity, and the legislative direction of regulatory bureaucracies. *Journal of Public Administration Research and Theory* 13 (April): 141–64.

Rogers, Werner B. 1989. Letter to Representative Bob Holmes, November 20, series 012-02-027, box 100, folder 3. Georgia Superintendent's Subject Files. Atlanta: Georgia State Archives.

Rogers to miss first debate in school chief's race. 1986. *Atlanta Constitution,* July 23, sec. A.

Rosenthal, Alan. 1990. *Governors and legislatures: Contending powers.* Washington, DC: Congressional Quarterly Press.

Ross, Randy. 1995. Ohio state proficiency tests, memorandum to Ted Sanders, March 7, series 5.1, box 1T. George V. Voinovich Papers. Athens: Ohio University.

Rossmiller, Richard A. 1990. *As nearly uniform as practicable?: An historical review of Wisconsin's equalized aid formula.* Madison: Wisconsin Association of School District Administrators.

Rubin, Herbert J., and Irene S. Rubin. 1995. *Qualitative interviewing: The art of hearing data.* Thousand Oaks, CA: Sage.

Ruling threatens legality of Ga. school regulations. 1988. *Education Week,* September 7.

Salisbury, Robert H. 1984. Interest representation: The dominance of institutions. *American Political Science Review* 78 (March): 64–76.

Salzer, James. 1999a. GOP to fight Barnes on education oversight. *Atlanta Journal-Constitution,* December 15, sec. C.

Salzer, James. 1999b. Leaders split over reform of schools. *Atlanta Journal-Constitution,* December 12, sec. H.

Salzer, James. 1999c. Schrenko defends her accountability. *Atlanta Journal-Constitution,* November 18, sec. E.

Salzer, James. 2000a. Barnes' letter to teachers spurs anger. *Atlanta Journal-Constitution*, November 26, sec. C.

Salzer, James. 2000b. Many students don't made grade on new state tests. *Atlanta Journal-Constitution*, August 30, sec. A.

Salzer, James. 2000c. Schrenko draws GOP fire. *Atlanta Journal-Constitution*, February 1, sec. D.

Salzer, James. 2000d. Schrenko, school board go to war. *Atlanta Journal-Constitution*, October 13, sec. F.

Salzer, James. 2002. Schrenko travel tab is state's highest. *Atlanta Journal-Constitution*, February 28, sec. D.

Salzer, James. 2006. Reporter's notebook: Schrenko swam in different stream. *Atlanta Journal-Constitution*, May 10, sec. A.

Salzer, James, Beth Warren, and Bill Torpy. 2006. Schrenko pleads guilty to fraud. *Atlanta Journal-Constitution*, May 11, sec. A.

Sanders, Ted. 1993a. Letter to Wayne Jones, September 20, series 5.1, box 1R. George V. Voinovich Papers. Athens: Ohio University.

Sanders, Ted. 1993b. Project PASS, memorandum to George V. Voinovich, February 1, series 1.2, box 50. George V. Voinovich Papers. Athens: Ohio University.

Sanders, Ted. 1993c. Weekly communications, memorandum to George V. Voinovich, October 7, series 5.1, box 1R. George V. Voinovich Papers. Athens: Ohio University.

Sanders, Ted. 1994. Development of elementary and secondary education standards, memorandum to the Learner Outcomes Panel, January 11, series 5.1, box 1T. George V. Voinovich Papers. Athens: Ohio University.

Sanders, Ted. 1995a. Letter to George V. Voinovich, October 31, series 5.1, box 1U. George V. Voinovich Papers. Athens: Ohio University.

Sanders, Ted. 1995b. Letter to Sue Ann Norton, July 7, series 5.1, box 1U. George V. Voinovich Papers. Athens: Ohio University.

Schattschneider, E. E. 1960. *The semi-sovereign people*. New York: Holt, Rinehart and Winston.

Schiller, Wendy J. 1995. Senators as political entrepreneurs: Using bill sponsorship to shape legislative agendas. *American Journal of Political Science* 39 (February): 186–203.

Schmidt, Peter. 1992. Cleveland seeks new superintendent, end to court case. *Education Week*, March 25.

Scholz, J. T., J. Twombly, and B. Headrick. 1991. Street-level political controls over federal bureaucracy. *American Political Science Review* 85 (September): 829–50.

School funding chronology. 2001. *Associated Press*, June 5.

School funding chronology. 2003. *Associated Press*, May 16.

School superintendent contest set cost record. 1993. *Wisconsin State Journal*, July 24, sec. D.

Schrenko blind to own failings. 1999. Editorial. *Atlanta Journal-Constitution*, December 16, sec. A.

Schrenko, Linda. 1995. Values, sex ed., tests—Schrenko speaks out on issues. *Atlanta Journal-Constitution*, February 1, sec. A.

Scott, W. Richard. 1992. *Organizations: Rational, natural, and open systems.* 3rd. ed. Englewood Cliffs, NJ: Prentice Hall.

Seely, Ron. 2003. Black is hopeful on bill to shift DNR chief. *Wisconsin State Journal*, January 24, sec. B.

Selznick, Philip. 1948. Foundations of the theory of organizations. *American Sociological Review* 13: 25–35.

Sensky, Jacqui. 1993a. Briefing for Ted Sanders 9/17/93 meeting, memorandum to George V. Voinovich, September 10, series 5.1, box 1R. George V. Voinovich Papers. Athens: Ohio University.

Sensky, Jacqui. 1993b. Weekly communication, memorandum to George V. Voinovich, March 5, series 5.1, box 1R. George V. Voinovich Papers. Athens: Ohio University.

Sergiovanni, Thomas J. 1984. Leadership as cultural expression. In *Leadership and organizational culture*, ed. Thomas J. Sergiovanni and J. E. Corbally, 105–14 . Urbana: University of Illinois Press.

Sharkansky, Ira. 1968. Agency requests, gubernatorial support, and budget success in state legislatures. *American Political Science Review* 62 (December): 1220–31.

Sheridan, Chris. 2001. Justices drop their dignity and run. Cleveland *Plain Dealer*, September 22, sec. A.

Shipan, Charles R., and Megan L. Shannon. 2003. Delaying justice(s): A duration analysis of Supreme Court confirmations. *American Journal of Political Science* 47 (October): 654–68.

Shober, Arnold F., Paul Manna, and John F. Witte. 2006. Flexibility meets accountability: State charter school laws and their influence on the formation of charter schools in the United States. *Policy Studies Journal* 34 (November): 563–87.

Shreve, Robert B. 1989. *History of Ohio's county boards of education, 1914–1989.* Columbus: Ohio Department of Education.

Simms, Patricia. 1993. Thompson gives old foe Grover a new job. *Wisconsin State Journal*, April 9, sec. A.

Simms, Patricia. 1995. DPI taking on voucher plan. *Wisconsin State Journal*, January 29, sec. C.

Sinclair, Barbara. 1989. *The transformation of the U.S. Senate.* Baltimore, MD: Johns Hopkins University Press.

Smith, Marshall S., and Jennifer O'Day. 1991. Systemic school reform. In *The politics of curriculum and testing: The 1990 yearbook of the politics of education association*, ed. Susan H. Fuhrman and Betty Malen, 233–68. London: The Falmer Press.

Snyder, Cooper. 1995. Education governance structure, letter to George V. Voinovich, May 8, series 5.1, box 1T. George V. Voinovich Papers. Athens: Ohio University.

Spady, William G. 1994. *Outcome-based education: Critical issues and answers.* Arlington, VA: American Association of School Administrators.

Squire, Peverill. 1997. Another look at legislative professionalization and divided government in the states. *Legislative Studies Quarterly* 22 (August): 417–32.

Srb, Arthur L. 1993. Benson likes caps without tax freeze. *Wisconsin State Journal*, July 7, sec. A.

Starratt, Robert J. 1996. *Transforming educational administration: Meaning, community, and excellence*. New York: McGraw-Hill.

State education issues. 1983. *Education Week*, March 9.

State journal: Demanding answers; counterattack. 1991. *Education Week*, March 27.

State legislatures pass education reforms as 1984 sessions end. 1984. *Education Week*, April 11.

State school board member replaced. 1991. Cleveland *Plain Dealer*, August 22.

State school chief to cut jobs. 1993. Madison (Wisconsin) *Capital Times*, December 2, sec. A.

Steiner, Curt. 1997. Memorandum to George V. Voinovich, March 30, series 5.1, box 1U. George V. Voinovich Papers. Athens: Ohio University.

Still, Thomas W. 1995. Thompson holds trump cards on DPI's Benson. *Wisconsin State Journal*, January 29, sec. B.

Stockinger, Jacob. 1981. Grover puts firm imprint on DPI office. Madison (Wisconsin) *Capital Times*, August 25, sec. A.

Superfine, Benjamin Michael. 2005. The politics of accountability: The rise and fall of Goals 2000. *American Journal of Education* 112: 10–43.

Superintendent's minutes. 1988a. January 1, series 012-09-089, box 29, folder 32. Georgia Associate State Superintendent Subject Files. Atlanta: Georgia State Archives.

Superintendent's minutes. 1988b. June 10, series 012-09-089, box 29, folder 32. Georgia Associate State Superintendent Subject Files. Atlanta: Georgia State Archives.

Taking charge of school reform, Harris in-law Bill Gambill is hard worker. 1985. *Atlanta Constitution*, May 20, sec. E.

Talbert, Jeffrey C., and Matthew Potoski. 2002. Setting the legislative agenda: The dimensional structure of bill cosponsorship and floor voting. *Journal of Politics* 64 (August): 864–91.

Teacher task force prepares recs for state supt. 1983. *Education Forward* (August): 4.

Thompson, James D. 1967. *Organizations in action*. New York: McGraw-Hill.

Thompson, Joel A. 1987. Agency requests, gubernatorial support, and budget success in state legislatures revisited. *Journal of Politics* 49 (August): 756–79.

Thompson, Joel A., and Arthur A. Felts. 1992. Politicians and professionals: The influence of state agency heads in budgetary success. *Western Political Quarterly* 45 (March): 153–68.

Thompson, Tommy. 1981. Letter to Herbert J. Grover, August 27, series 651, box 2001/111, folder 3/1. Correspondence of the State Superintendent. Madison: Wisconsin Historical Society Archives.

Thompson, Tommy. 1989. Budget address. Journal of the Wisconsin Senate (January 31): 47.

Thompson, Tommy. 1995. Budget address. Journal of the Wisconsin Senate (February 14): 77.

Timar, Thomas B. 1997. The institutional role of state education departments: A historical perspective. *American Journal of Education* 105 (May): 231–60.

Ting, Michael M. 2003. A strategic theory of bureaucratic redundancy. *American Journal of Political Science* 47 (April): 274–92.

Tobin, R. J. 1992. Environmental protection and the new federalism—a longitudinal analysis of state perceptions. *Publius* 22 (Winter): 93–107.

Today's lesson is how not to run for Georgia school superintendent. 1986. *Atlanta Constitution,* July 11, sec. A.

Truman, David B. 1951. *The governmental process: Political interests and public opinion.* New York: Alfred A. Knopf.

Tyack, David. 1974. *The one best system.* Cambridge, MA: Harvard University Press.

Tyack, David, and Larry Cuban. 1995. *Tinkering toward utopia.* Cambridge, MA: Harvard University Press.

Underwood, Julie K., and Deborah A. Verstege, eds. 1990. *The impacts of litigation and legislation on public school finance: Adequacy, equity, and excellence.* San Francisco, CA: Harper & Row.

U.S. Government Accountability Office. 2008. Nuclear security: NRC and DHS need to take additional steps to better track and detect radioactive materials. June. Report GAO-08-598. Washington, DC: Government Printing Office.

Vail, Paul. 1990. Memorandum to Georgia district superintendents, January 11, series 12-09-089, box 31, folder 7. Georgia Assistant Superintendent's Subject Files. Atlanta: Georgia State Archives.

Van Auken, Bob. 1991. Letter to Jean Droste, March 1, series 1.2, box 50, folder 1. George V. Voinovich Papers. Athens: Ohio University.

Veteran administrator wins chief's race in Wisconsin. 1993. *Education Week,* April 14.

Vinovskis, Maris A. 1999. *The road to Charlottesville: The 1989 education summit.* Washington, DC: National Education Goals Panel.

Voinovich set to replace Brickner in "near future." 1991. Ashtabula (Ohio) *Star Beacon,* June 6, sec. A.

Voinovich, George V. 1991a. Letter to Chester A. Roush, April 1, series 1.2, box 50, folder 1. George V. Voinovich Papers. Athens: Ohio University.

Voinovich, George V. 1991b. Memorandum to Franklin B. Walter, April 10, series 1.2, box 49, folder 7. George V. Voinovich Papers. Athens: Ohio University.

Voinovich, George V. 1991c. Memorandum to Franklin B. Walter, July 2, series 1.2, box 50, folder 11. George V. Voinovich Papers. Athens: Ohio University.

Voinovich, George V. 1992a. Letter to Ted Sanders, April 16, series 1.2, box 49, folder 4. George V. Voinovich Papers. Athens: Ohio University.

Voinovich, George V. 1992b. Letter to Ted Sanders, May 11, series 1.2, box 50, folder 1. George V. Voinovich Papers. Athens: Ohio University.

Voinovich, George V. 1993a. Letter to Ted Sanders, January 28, series 1.2, box 50, folder 1. George V. Voinovich Papers. Athens: Ohio University.

Voinovich, George V. 1993b. Memorandum to Ted Sanders, March 9, series 5.1, box 1R, folder 9. George V. Voinovich Papers. Athens: Ohio University.

Voinovich, George V. 1995a. Letter to Virginia Purdy, president, State Board of Education, April 13, series 5.1, box 1U, folder 7. George V. Voinovich Papers. Athens: Ohio University.

Voinovich, George V. 1995b. Press release, March 31, series 5.1, box 1U. George V. Voinovich Papers. Athens: Ohio University.

Volk, John. 1985. Letter to Herbert J. Grover, n.d., series 651, box 2001/111, folder 3/11. Correspondence of the State Superintendent. Madison: Wisconsin Historical Society Archives.

Walter, Franklin B. 1986. Letter to Richard F. Celeste, November 14, series 4142, folder 2453. Richard F. Celeste Papers. Columbus: Ohio Historical Society.

Walter, Franklin B. 1987a. Letter to Richard F. Celeste, January 14, series 4142, folder 2453. Richard F. Celeste Papers. Columbus: Ohio Historical Society.

Walter, Franklin B. 1987b. Letter to Richard F. Celeste, June 15, series 4142, folder 2453. Richard F. Celeste Papers. Columbus: Ohio Historical Society.

Walter, Franklin B. 1987c. Letter to Richard F. Celeste, October 16, series 4142, folder 2453. Richard F. Celeste Papers. Columbus: Ohio Historical Society.

Walter, Mary. 1982. Letter to Herbert J. Grover, February 23, series 651, box 2001/111, folder 3/12. Correspondence of the State Superintendent. Madison: Wisconsin Historical Society Archives.

Walters, Steven, and Tom Heinen. 1996. DPI education goals called fuzzy, feel good. *Milwaukee Journal-Sentinel,* October 21, sec. A.

Walton, Charlie. 1990. Script for GKAP promotional piece, January 10, series 12-09-089, box 31, folder 7. Georgia Assistant Superintendent's Subject Files. Atlanta: Georgia State Archives.

Watchke, Gary. 1998. Qualified economic offer. Budget Brief 98–5. Madison: Wisconsin Legislative Reference Bureau.

Wawro, Gregory. 2000. *Legislative entrepreneurship in the U.S. House of Representatives.* Ann Arbor: University of Michigan Press.

Weatherly, Richard, and Michael Lipsky. 1977. Street-level bureaucrats and institutional innovation: Special education reform. *Harvard Educational Review* 47 (May): 171–97.

Weber, Max. 1946. *From Max Weber: Essays in sociology.* New York: Oxford University Press.

Wehling, R. L. 1995. Letter to George V. Voinovich, March 31, series 5.1, box 1U, folder 7. George V. Voinovich Papers. Athens: Ohio University.

Welsh-Huggins, Andrew. 2000. State education board proposes school funding increase. *Associated Press,* October 2.

West, Allan M. 1980. *The National Education Association: The power base for education.* New York: The Free Press.

White, Betsy. 1994a. Charges fly over status of students. *Atlanta Journal-Constitution*, November 3, sec. B.

White, Betsy. 1994b. Schrenko: Ga. schools should be run locally. *Atlanta Journal-Constitution*, December 8, sec. G.

White, Betsy. 1994c. Schrenko wants to redirect school funds. *Atlanta Journal-Constitution*, November 10, sec. D.

White, Betsy. 1995a. Education chief tries to soothe superintendents. *Atlanta Journal-Constitution*, October 19, sec. D.

White, Betsy. 1995b. Schrenko's cuts to save $3 million. *Atlanta Journal-Constitution*, May 12, sec. H.

Whitford, Andrew B. 2005. The pursuit of political control by multiple principals. *Journal of Politics* 67 (February): 29–49.

Wildavsky, Aaron. 1992. *The new politics of the budgetary process.* 2d ed. New York: HarperCollins.

Williams, Kenneth F. 1985. Letter to Wayne W. Wood, January 18, series 651, box 2001/111, folder 3/10. Correspondence of the State Superintendent. Madison: Wisconsin Historical Society Archives.

Williamson, Oliver. 1983. *Markets and hierarchies: Analysis and antitrust implications.* New York: The Free Press.

Wisconsin Association of School Boards. 2000. *PI 34: New teacher license rules.* Madison, WI: Author.

Wisconsin Department of Public Instruction. 1983. *Disequalizing factors in Wisconsin's school aid formula.* Madison: Wisconsin Department of Public Instruction.

Wisconsin Department of Public Instruction. 1990. *1991–1993 biennial budget request.* Madison: Wisconsin Department of Public Instruction.

Wisconsin Department of Public Instruction. 1992. *1993–1995 biennial budget request.* Madison: Wisconsin Department of Public Instruction.

Wisconsin Department of Public Instruction. 1994. *1995–1997 biennial budget request.* Madison: Wisconsin Department of Public Instruction.

Wisconsin Department of Public Instruction. 1995. *Restructuring teacher education and licensure in Wisconsin.* Madison: Wisconsin Department of Public Instruction.

Wisconsin Department of Public Instruction. 1996. *1997–1999 biennial budget request.* Madison: Wisconsin Department of Public Instruction.

Wisconsin Department of Public Instruction. 1997. *Restructuring teacher education and licensure in Wisconsin: Final report on teacher assessment, license stages, and license categories.* Madison: Wisconsin Department of Public Instruction.

Wisconsin Department of Public Instruction. 2003. *Wisconsin standards: Teacher development and licensure.* http://www.dpi.state.wi.us/dpi/dlsis/tel/stand 10.html. Accessed June 23, 2003.

Wisconsin School Counselors' Association. 1999. Board minutes, November 13. Madison, WI.

Wohlstetter, Priscilla. 1994. Georgia: Reform at the crossroads. In *Ten years of state education reforms*, ed. D. Massell and Susan Fuhrman, 137–52. New Brunswick, NJ: Center for Policy Research in Education.

Wong, Kenneth K. 1999. *Funding public schools: Politics and policies.* Lawrence: University Press of Kansas.

Wood, B. Dan, and Richard W. Waterman. 1991. The dynamics of political control of the bureaucracy. *American Political Science Review* 85 (September): 801–28.

Wood, B. Dan, and Richard W. Waterman. 1993. The dynamics of political–bureaucratic adaption. *American Journal of Political Science* 37 (May): 497–528.

Zald, Mayer N., and Roberta A. Garner. 1987. Social movement organizations: Growth, decay, and change. In *Social movements in an organizational society*, ed. Mayer N. Zald and John D. McCarthy, 121–41. New Brunswick, NJ: Transaction Books.

Zweifel, David. 2005. Something's got to give on school chief. Madison (Wisconsin) *Capital Times*, February 4, sec. A.

Index

Tables are indicated with boldface type. *Figures* are indicated with italics. Years of service follow state superintendents' names.